CORRECTION CHAR

D0162881

lev Write at a level appropriate to 59

mm Misplaced modifier: place it el modifies the intended word. **25**

mo Use the mood required by your sentence. **57**

ms Follow conventional manuscript form. **77, 78**

p Correct the punctuation

[ ]	brackets **40**	( )	parentheses **39**
:	colon **37**	.	period **33**
,	comma **29–32**	?	question mark **34**
—	dash **38**	" "	quotation marks **40**
...	ellipsis **40**	;	semicolon **36**
!	exclamation point **35**		

pred Make the subject and predicate of this sentence relate to each other logically. **26**

ps Know the parts of speech and their uses. **83**

ref Make this pronoun refer clearly to its antecedent. **52**

rep Eliminate the obvious repetition. **70**

shift Correct the shift in verb or pronoun use. **58**

sp Proofread for proper spelling, and work on your spelling weaknesses. **47**

sub Use subordination to relate secondary details to main ideas. **20**

t Use the correct verb tense. **55**

trite Replace this trite expression with fresher language. **67**

ts Use a topic sentence to focus each paragraph on one point. **16**

u Unify this paragraph by making all sentences relate to the topic sentence. **17**

vague Use specific and concrete words. **62**

vb Use the correct form of this verb. **56**

wdy Tighten this wordy expression. **70**

ww Wrong word: choose a more exact word. **63, 64**

THE **SHORT HANDBOOK** FOR
Writers

SECOND EDITION

Gerald J. Schiffhorst
University of Central Florida

Donald Pharr
Valencia Community College

The McGraw-Hill Companies, Inc.
New York · St. Louis · San Francisco · Auckland
Bogotá · Caracas · Lisbon · London · Madrid
Mexico City · Milan · Montreal · New Delhi
San Juan · Singapore · Sydney
Tokyo · Toronto

McGraw-Hill

A Division of The McGraw·Hill Companies

THE SHORT HANDBOOK FOR WRITERS

Copyright © 1997, 1991 by The McGraw-Hill Companies, Inc. All rights reserved. Previously published under the title of *Short English Handbook*. Copyright © 1986, 1982, 1979 by Scott, Foresman and Company. All rights reserved. Printed in the United States of America. Except as permitted under the United States Copyright Act of 1976, no part of this publication may be reproduced or distributed in any form or by any means, or stored in a data base or retrieval system, without the prior written permission of the publisher.

The Acknowledgments appear on pp. 399–400, and on this page by reference.

This book is printed on acid-free paper.

2 3 4 5 6 7 8 9 0 DOC DOC 9 0 9 8 7

ISBN 0-07-092096-6

This book was set in Versailles Roman by York Graphic Services, Inc.
The editors were Tim Julet and Larry Goldberg;
the designer was Wanda Lubelska;
the production supervisor was Elizabeth J. Strange.
R.R. Donnelley and Sons Company was printer and binder.

Library of Congress Cataloging-in-Publication Data

Schiffhorst, Gerald J.
    The short handbook for writers / Gerald J. Schiffhorst, Donald
Pharr.—2nd ed.
        p.   cm.
    Includes index.
    ISBN 0-07-092096-6 (acid-free paper)
    1. English language—Rhetoric—Handbooks, manuals, etc.
2. English language—Grammar—Handbooks, manuals, etc.   I. Pharr,
Donald.   II. Title.
PE1408.F38   1997
808′ .042—dc20   96-32739

http://www.mhcollege.com

GERALD J. SCHIFFHORST is Professor of English at the University of Central Florida, where he has taught since 1970. He received his Ph.D. from Washington University in St. Louis and has taught at the University of Missouri–St. Louis. He is the author of several works on John Milton and has edited two volumes of Renaissance studies, the most recent being *The Witness of Times* (Duquesne University Press, 1993).

DONALD PHARR is Professor of English at Valencia Community College and adjunct instructor at the University of Central Florida, both in Orlando. He received his Ph.D. in 1994 from the University of Georgia. In addition to teaching writing and literature since 1981, he has for ten years been a consultant and copy editor for several publishing companies. He has edited two books and is the author of *Indexing and Filing Workbook,* 4th ed. (H. M. Rowe, 1991).

C O N T E N T S

PART II **EDITING YOUR WRITING**

Chapter 7
Editing for Punctuation and Mechanics 111

Chapter 8
Editing for Grammar 167

Chapter 9
Using Appropriate Diction 215

PART III A PRACTICAL GUIDE TO WRITING

Chapter 10
Writing a Research Paper 249

Chapter 11
Other Types of Writing 327

Chapter 12
Grammatical Definitions and ESL Concerns 355

P R E F A C E

Our purpose in this book is to provide students with a handy source of reference as they write as well as essential information on the composing process. As such, *The Short Handbook for Writers* can function both as a classroom text and as an independent tool for students responding to questions posed by their instructors.

The second edition of *The Short Handbook for Writers* is a substantial revision of the first edition. Our goal is to concentrate on the *practical* needs of the composition student, and to this end we have written a text with a sharpened focus. Changes to the first edition involve the following areas:

• **The Writing Process:** Part I now includes six chapters on planning and writing an essay, beginning with topic selection and continuing through rhetorical context, drafting, revising, and writing effective paragraphs and sentences. Our emphasis in this section is on careful planning of the essay and careful revision of the preliminary draft. Chapter 6, "Writing Effective Sentences," includes many numbered exercise sections to test the areas covered in each section of the chapter.

• **Editing Your Writing:** Part II emphasizes mechanical problems and how to fix them. The three chapters concentrate on editing for grammar, mechanics, and diction. We have included an abundance of example sentences, usually set up as "not acceptable" and then followed by "acceptable" or "preferred" versions in the same context. Part II also has an extensive series of numbered exercises to challenge the student.

• **A Practical Guide to Writing:** Part III has been completely revised. Chapter 10, "Writing a Research Paper," begins with a discussion of the various issues that affect the planning, writing, and documenting of the research paper, and then the chapter offers separate sections on MLA and APA documentation, with annotated student research papers included. We also emphasize, in both the MLA and APA sections, documentation of electronic sources. Chapter 11,

"Other Types of Writing," examines the types of applied writing most likely to be valuable to composition students: the literary analysis, the business letter, the memo, and the résumé. Chapter 12, "Grammatical Definitions and ESL Concerns," provides a useful guide to grammatical terms and to issues that concern the student whose first language is not English.

• **Glossaries:** The first glossary defines the terms used in the text. The second glossary draws distinctions between accepted usage and usage not appropriate for modern college-level writing.

• **Ancillaries:** Four ancillaries are available with this text: *The McGraw-Hill Guide to Electronic Research and Documentation, A Brief Guide to Persuasion and Critical Thinking, A Brief Guide to Avoiding Bias,* and *ESL Workbook.* These titles address areas of immediate concern to today's composition student.

Our book thus provides a useful source of clear, brief answers to the major questions that arise for composition students. We rely as little as possible on formal terminology, explaining essential terms both in the text and in Chapter 12 or the Glossary of Terms.

We are pleased to acknowledge the invaluable assistance of many students and colleagues. At the University of Central Florida, Catherine Schutz and John F. Schell have been generous with their advice. The following reviewers provided helpful suggestions during the revision: Joy W. Bashore, Central Virginia Community College; Christopher Belcher, Community College of Allegheny County; Elizabeth Jo Dallas, Community College of Allegheny County; Woodrow L. Holbein, The Citadel; Jill Karle, Piedmont Virginia Community College; Tom Kmetzo, Naugatuck Valley Community Technical College; Judith L. Merrell, Community College of Allegheny County; and Michael Robertson, Trenton State College. We are especially grateful to Donna French for word processing and a keen eye, to Kerime Toksu for skillful and conscientious copy editing, to Wanda Lubelska for creating an attractive and user-friendly text design, and to our editors, Phillip A. Butcher, Tim Julet, and Larry Goldberg, for making the book possible.

Gerald J. Schiffhorst
Donald Pharr

The Writing Process

Finding Something to Say

Overview

Instead of reading this book straight through, you will probably refer to various chapters and parts of chapters as you need them. Even so, to put things in perspective and to help you get the most from your time, we will begin with an overview of the whole subject of writing.

We are not going to present a simple, foolproof formula guaranteed to make you a competent writer. Unfortunately, there is no such formula. Writing is like playing tennis: you learn and improve by doing—by practicing, by listening to criticism, and by practicing some more. Good writing does more than just avoid blunders. It holds the reader's interest. When you write well, you begin by thinking through what you want to say. Then you say it, in clear, logical sentences and carefully chosen words, expressing your thoughts and feelings so that your audience will understand them just as you want them to be understood.

Most writing—certainly all the writing we will be concerned with here—has a purpose and a method suited to it. Writers tell stories: they say what happens (narration). Or they argue: they speak for or against something (argument). Or they describe: they tell how something looks, sounds, or moves (description). Or they explain: they tell how something works (exposition) or why something happens (analysis). As you plan what you want to say in a paper, you will also be deciding which of these five approaches you will use. This does not mean that you will choose one approach and ignore the rest. You may be called on to explain, argue, describe, analyze, or narrate, or explain and argue, or describe and narrate, or do all of these in one paper. Nevertheless, the assignment, your own purpose, or a combination of your assignment and your purpose will usually make one approach predominant. For example, you may start out by describing ways in which consumers are deceived by television commercials and then end up arguing that there should be stricter regulation of such advertising. Since the emphasis in this case should fall on the argument, your purpose in describing commercials is to prepare your reader to believe as you do about regulation.

In an essay on Al-A-Teen, your main purpose might be to explain what this support group does and how it functions. You might compare it with Alcoholics Anonymous, or you might classify various programs for substance abusers and their families in relation to in-patient or out-patient treatment centers. You might also analyze different theories of teenage alcoholism and drug abuse, using quotations from magazine and newspaper articles dealing with the causes of these problems. Perhaps you could attend an Al-A-Teen meeting and then describe the range of people you met or provide a narrative account of your visit. Finally, you might conclude an essay with your opinion of the issues involved: Is Al-A-Teen helping to solve the problems of adolescents faced with substance abuse? Still, your essay would remain mostly expository: to explain the role of Al-A-Teen, based on your experience and reading.

To a certain degree, all writing must be persuasive. It must persuade readers that it is worth their time and attention. What you have to say will get a fair hearing only if you make sure it deserves one. Writing that deserves to be read is the kind we will be concerned with throughout this book.

Writing is a process of generating ideas, and the first four chapters divide this ongoing process, for convenience, into prewriting, considering the reader, drafting, and revising. At each stage, focus on a few things at a time. Allow yourself time to plan and develop ideas by learning to think on paper, and do not worry about editing or correcting what you write until the composing process has run its course. Since writing is a complex activity, the stages often overlap or double back: you will simultaneously generate and react while considering your purpose and reader. But you must first find something to say.

 Explore what you want to say.

Most writers have experienced the frustration of being un-able to think of a fresh idea—or of discovering one too late. Thinking through some of the many possible subjects for writ-ing and exploring what we already know about those subjects can keep us from becoming "stuck." Anything can be turned into material for writing; how to do so through invention, the first stage in the writing process, is the topic of this chapter.

If you are new to college or university life, for instance, you might jot down whatever comes to mind as you think about your experiences as a freshman. Here are one student's notes:

big campus	a lot of reading
dorm living	major—in what?
freedom—on my own	pledge a fraternity?
working—how many hours?	football team
large lectures	spending money

You could then underline some of the more promising points on such a list, ones that could easily be developed with exam-ples. If living away from home sounds like a good topic, you could write about the need to budget your time so that daily chores do not consume too much of it. Or you could compare high school with college, perhaps with a younger sister or brother in mind. Or you could consider the pros and cons of Greek life or the problems of working while pursuing a degree. Listing ideas in the order they occur to you is an easy way to

1

get started. Such invention strategies are helpful both in locating subjects and in exploring them before you write your essay.

Sometimes, however, a subject is readily available or assigned. For example, you are upset by a newspaper editorial about the state legislature and write a letter to the editor. Or your employer asks for a report on computer safety devices. Or your instructor suggests five topics for an essay. Yet even when the subject is provided or limited for you, you will have to determine your own approach and decide what to say about it. In any case, careful planning is essential; successful writers seldom produce effective work without it.

In exploring what to say about a subject, try out some of the following invention strategies to determine which works best for you:

1. *Brainstorming* is one of the simplest ways to begin the writing process. You can generate ideas by talking about possible topics with a friend or group of friends. The result will be uneven, but ideas will emerge. If you don't have a friend willing to brainstorm with you, try using a tape recorder, talking freely about your subject for fifteen minutes. Then play the tape back, noting any important ideas. To explore a point you have discovered, try another fifteen minutes on the tape recorder.

2. *Freewriting* is like tape recording on paper. Jot down your thoughts about your topic, writing continuously for fifteen minutes without stopping. Try to record your thoughts as fast as they occur. Ignore correctness or neatness. If you get stuck, write "I'm stuck" and keep going. After fifteen minutes, select anything from your notes that looks worthwhile. When you discover something promising, you can use the freewriting exercise again on this new idea. Here is an example of a student's freewriting exercise:

Raise the minimum driving age to 18? There'd be chaos! You spend half your life waiting to get a driver's license, and then they tell you to wait two more years? Kids would start hitchhiking too – they've got jobs, and school, and their parents don't have time to take them everywhere. But there would be less accidents, I have to admit. And insurance would surely go down (?). All in all it's an interesting idea – I'm just glad that I'm already 18.

Even in this short excerpt, several possible points emerge for further exploration: fair treatment under the law, the dangers of hitchhiking, the high rate of traffic accidents involving young drivers, how insurance companies determine premiums.

Freewriting is most successful if you try to capture your mind in action without planning, structuring, or editing.

3. *Clustering* can also help you generate ideas and see the relations between them. Instead of sentences, clustering uses single terms, which are easier to jot down quickly. And instead of moving down the page, you begin clustering by writing down a possible subject in the middle of the page inside a circle (or balloon). From there you can take off in any direction with another term. Each new balloon may give rise to additional ideas, which get attached to the balloon that sparks them.

CLUSTERING

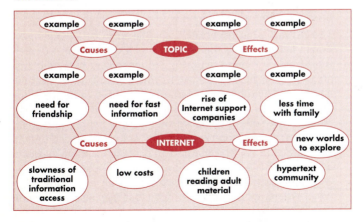

Again, work freely and quickly for fifteen minutes; then look at the clusters to see which ones look most promising. Using this technique, you could explore the causes and effects of the growth in popularity of the Internet.

4. *Asking questions* can help you recall specific experiences or attitudes. If, for example, the subject of tattoos arises, you could ask yourself these questions:

Do I like tattoos? Why?
Do I like only certain types of tattoos? Which ones?
Is it a good idea to alter your skin permanently when you may change as a person as you grow older?

Such exploratory questions involve classifying, analyzing, and persuading as you determine your own feelings about the subject. Various possible ideas can emerge:

Tattoos can be visually appealing.
Some tattoos seem tasteful enough, but others are disgusting.
Permanently altering your skin might seem a good idea when you are young, but twenty years from now you may well curse the day you thought of it.

Asking questions about the meaning of a word, the design of an object, or your reactions to a book or a movie can produce numerous topics for writing.

5. The *pentad* is an especially valuable form of asking questions. According to this technique, developed by Kenneth Burke, every human action is influenced by five elements: act (what), scene (where, when), agent (who), agency (how), and purpose (why). *Act* refers to anything that happens (or could happen) or anything that is the result of an activity. *Scene* is the setting or background of the action. The *agent* is the person (or force) responsible for (or influenced by) the action. *Agency* is the method that makes a thing happen, and *purpose* is the reason or motive for an action. These five elements parallel the journalist's familiar questions *who, what, where, when, how,* and *why,* but they also go further.

You can use these five terms to analyze current, histori-cal, or fictional events; to explore characters in novels or films; to learn more about the people involved in a narrative; or to analyze your audience in an argument. However, the pentad is not applicable to objects (computers, for example).

Imagine, for a moment, that your college or university has announced a new policy to test incoming students for drugs. Those who test positive must undergo counseling while their admission is delayed. As a student senator, you are asked to write a column in the campus newspaper op-posing this ruling. You think through the topic in terms of the penta

What was done? (act)	new ruling? unconstitu-tional act? bold initiative?
When/where was it done? (scene)	after long consultation? in private? on campus?
Who did it? (agent)	governor? legislature? president of college? outsiders?
How was it done? (agency)	by open vote? secret agree-ment? outside pressure?
Why was it done? (purpose)	to protect young people? to keep out undesirables? to earn votes? to appear strong? to appear innova-tive? to take a stance against drug dealing?

When we compare and relate the five terms, here is what happens when we think about the act (mandatory testing) in terms of the scene (university):

How does the campus setting influence this act?
Is the university being "used"?
Are students being singled out because they are unsympathetic victims?
Do officials hope the students will protest, hence turning public opinion against the students?

This example shows some of the many questions that can be generated when each of the five terms is considered in relation to the other four.

6. *Cubing* means examining a subject from six perspectives (a cube has six sides):

1. Describe the subject. (What is its content?)
2. Compare it. (What is it similar to or different from?)
3. Associate it. (What does it remind you of?)
4. Analyze it. (Explain how it was made.)
5. Apply it. (Explain how it can be used.)
6. Argue for or against it. (Take a stand.)

Write briefly (for three to five minutes) about the subject from *each* of the six points of view, beginning with what you know. Unlike the pentad, this exercise can be used for objects (a car, building, sculpture) as well as for persons, events, and ideas.

7. Writing informally in a *journal* can provide valuable ideas for assigned essays. Unlike a diary or class notebook, a journal is a record of interesting impressions and experiences that you could share with others. It provides an opportunity for private writing and thinking. Some suggestions for writing in a journal:

a. Find a quiet spot where you can write for about fifteen minutes a day, freely recalling what you have observed and read. Do not worry about correct form. You can include the people you met, the ideas you discussed, the movies or lectures you attended, the food you ate—but note your reactions, explaining why you liked or disliked what you experienced.
b. Write about your progress in your writing and in other classes. What are you learning? What are your feelings about your work?
c. Keep a record of a major local or national event (such as a political scandal) as it unfolds over several weeks.

Since writing is a way of learning, journal entries will help you observe and reflect on your experience. And they will often be of use in other, more formal writing.

Considering Your Context, Reader, and Role

In collecting information for an essay, you initially focus on your observations, memories, and thought processes. But your aim as a writer is not just to get facts and ideas on paper but to communicate them to a reader for a purpose. This chapter discusses the ways in which your writing is shaped by the need to communicate to others. People are involved in all aspects of the writing act: the human occasion for the writing, the real or presumed audience, and the human agent, the writer. Each of these—the occasion of the writing, the audience, and the writer—influences both the content and the form of a specific piece of writing.

 Consider the writing context.

Every writing act responds to a specific occasion or context. A technician takes notes while reading an article to understand and retain important information. A police detective writes up the facts of an unsolved case to find a key to its solution. Writing is not spontaneous, like breathing; it is a deliberate act in response to a given situation.

2

What you write

Your reason for writing greatly influences what you write, too. For instance, feeling guilty after a fight with your date, you sit down and write an apology. This situation calls for a personal expression of your feelings. But if a shirt you bought from a mail-order house has a flaw, the letter you write should be factual, providing the information necessary to correct the error. And if you decide to write a notice in your campus newspaper's "Personals" section to solicit a date, your writing will be persuasive, making yourself appealing to another person.

Why you write

We often begin to write without first identifying what it is we want to accomplish. For example, a simple letter home may seem to be purely informational. But on further reflection, we may discover that the letter is really an attempt to explain a failing grade. Or a sarcastic letter to your college paper, after more careful thought, may prove to be defeating your intention of getting the editor to change her point of view.

As a writer, always be sure of your purpose. Is your aim to persuade? To inform? To scold? To disclose your feelings? To investigate? Different purposes call for different strategies, so know your aim before you begin.

How you write

Context also helps to determine *how* you write; many situations have conventions that are often taken for granted. For instance, you would not type an apology to your date on business stationery, using formal style; but a letter to your insurance company should be formal.

College writing

College writing is also determined by context. The written report of a biology experiment must conform to the conventions of lab reports, and a review of a book for a history course must meet the standards of book reviews. Before beginning any kind of writing assignment in any of your classes, be sure you know the context and follow the expected conventions.

3

Consider your readers.

The greatest influence on the content and form of a piece of writing may well be the audience. Children's fiction, for instance, tells stories that are appropriate for young minds, using a simple, direct style. On the other hand, novels written for an adult audience often treat mature subjects, using irony, ambiguity, and symbolism. The sophistication of the audience determines the difference.

Because we usually write to communicate some idea or feeling to another person, that person becomes central to the writing act. Nearly every piece of writing is aimed at a specific audience. Whenever we write, we should be actively imagining our readers, not writing *at* them but creating a dialogue *with* them that meets their expectations and needs.

You should think of these readers as intelligent people who want to be informed and pleased. You are addressing people who want to solve a problem, make a decision, or learn something new. They do not want you to repeat what they already know. They expect original approaches to ideas, clearly organized essays that are easy to follow, and writing that is free of errors in grammar and mechanics. They are sure to think less of you if they find any lack of care in the form and content of your writing.

Nonacademic writing

When you are writing outside the classroom, the issue of audience is important but relatively easy to address because you have a clear idea of your readers. If you are writing a memo to the person across the hall at work, you can be friendly; you can assume that the two of you share interests and information. If the same information is included in a report for a customer outside your office, your tone becomes less relaxed and you assume less knowledge and interest on the reader's part. If exactly the same information is written for a professional journal, there is again a change. Now you use a more formal style and include more background information, references to other articles, and significant attempts at keeping your audience's interest.

Academic writing

When you respond to an assignment from your instructor, your audience may be imaginary. In such cases you create a fictional and sympathetic person and write to him or her. Your instructor, of course, will have a significant interest in the information you provide.

Having a sense that your work is directed to specific readers—your instructor, your classmates, your fellow employees, other citizens, or club members, for example—will help you establish your purpose.

Identify your audience

The one constant audience for academic writing is the person who assigns it. This is an easy audience to identify. Whether you are writing a physics exam, a marketing report, or even a teacher evaluation, the product of your efforts will be aimed at your instructor.

When you are assigned writing that addresses readers in addition to your instructor, take time to identify the multiple audiences. To do this, think of yourself as the starting point of the activity and follow your writing as it leaves you and passes through other hands.

For instance, your instructor assigns you the task of writing an editorial for your school newspaper. Before you

3

begin to write, imaginatively trace the journey of your writing after it leaves your hand. First, your boyfriend or girlfriend may volunteer to type the essay for you: Audience Number One. Then, of course, your essay will find its way into the hands of the newspaper editorial board, which will consider it for publication: Audience Number Two. If your editorial is published, the obvious audience comes into play, your fellow students: Audience Number Three. However, faculty, staff, alumni, and parents also have access to the school newspaper: Audience Numbers Four, Five, Six, and Seven. And should you be unlucky enough to libel someone, your writing may go to court: Audience Number Eight.

Identify as many of the types of readers as you can who may read the following pieces of writing:

- a letter to the regional Exxon office complaining about a local manager
- a complaint to the college president about your sociology instructor
- a short autobiography to accompany your application to law school
- a letter to the local newspaper complaining about unsafe intersections

Define your audience

Have you ever written a nasty letter to a company that cheated you or to a public personality who angered you? That sort of writing is intended to make you feel good and make your reader feel bad. But most writing tries to create a common ground between the reader and writer. Writers—in order to persuade, entertain, or teach readers—try to convince the audience that they have mutual backgrounds, interests, beliefs, aspirations, and needs. Successful writing reflects a feeling of concern for the reader and tries to gain the reader's trust; it wants to generate a dialogue. To do this, writers must not just identify their readers; they must also learn what their readers are like. In short, a good writer defines the personalities of his or her readers. For example, are your readers

3

> young or old?
> male or female?
> Southern, Northern, Eastern, or Western?
> of average intelligence or above average?

In addition to these traits over which your readers have no control, consider those characteristics that they have chosen. Are they

> single or married?
> urban or rural?
> liberal or conservative?
> people who prefer to work with their hands or with their minds?
> religious or nonreligious?

Most important, think about how your readers relate to your subject matter. What is their level of knowledge about your subject? Must you provide extensive background information? Must you define terms, identify aspects, and explain concepts, or will you insult your readers by explaining things that they already know?

Think about the level of knowledge each of these audiences has about the following subjects, considering what would and would not be appropriate in an essay:

Audience	Subject
college students	the World Wide Web
senior citizens	skateboards
coal miners	United Mine Workers of America
college students	United Mine Workers of America
senior citizens	the World Wide Web

In addition to your readers' knowledge, their interest in your subject is also important. For example, if your subject is important to them, you will immediately have their attention. If not, then you will have to work harder to get them involved.

3

Finally, is your subject one toward which your audience is favorably inclined, or is there a likelihood they will disagree with you? If they favor what you say, you can approach your topic more aggressively than you would if you knew you had a hostile audience.

Asking yourself these questions can help you create a vivid picture of your audience and can aid you in writing to "real" people in convincing prose. Try to think of readers as partners in the writing process, people who ask questions, require information, and need to be satisfied.

If you imagine your readers as people seriously interested in what you have to say, and if you imagine that they see you as a competent, self-assured friend, your tone will be friendly, relaxed, and conversational. This is the case in most informal essays. If you see yourself as the expert and your readers as learners, as in a research report, your tone will be more formal (see **59**).

Your instructor

Although you may be writing for a variety of audiences, your composition instructor will still evaluate your writing. Because your instructor *must* read what you write (you have a captive audience), you might unconsciously assume that you need not excite, interest, or persuade your instructor. But every reader wants to be delighted with fresh insights and with original or amusing approaches to familiar subjects. This is especially true of busy, critical readers—and of teachers who have evaluated thousands of student essays.

To avoid putting both you and your instructor to sleep, try to see your instructor simply as another human being. As you get to know this person, what idea of his or hers would you like to change? What important issue would you like to disclose to this person? What fascinating point would you like to explain? What would you like to think through, consider, or test with this person? Analyze your audience—your

4

instructor—to discover those subjects that you might argue or investigate with her or him.

At the same time, this human being is still your instructor, an audience to whom you must demonstrate your competence in the handling of your material, the structuring of your thought, and the quality of your style.

4 ▸ Consider your role as writer.

Each of us assumes various roles in life—as someone's child, grandchild, or parent and as a member of some civic, social, or religious group. Similarly, as a writer you may assume one of many different roles. You may be an adult writing to children, or you may be a child (no matter how old) writing to your parents. You may be an expert writing to amateurs or an angry person trying to communicate that anger. The role you assume in a piece of writing has a major influence on what you write.

Be aware of your role

Are you addressing your readers as a college student, part-time waiter, rock musician, tennis player, or family member? Selecting one of the roles you play in everyday life means drawing on specific experiences and interests, and these roles affect the way you "talk" to your readers. Here, for example, is one student's list of roles:

college freshman	keyboard player
consumer	amateur auto mechanic
taxpayer	fraternity member
U.S. citizen	Campus Escort
Catholic	computer programmer
son	swimmer
brother	soccer player

Each of these roles could suggest possible topics and readers:

4

Topic:	Safety Tips for Beginning Divers
Readers:	People interested in learning to dive
Topic:	Majoring in Computer Science
Readers:	Many college students
Topic:	The Problem of Date Rape
Readers:	Parents, all college students, general readers

Be consistent throughout a composition in the role you choose to assume. If you write as a clarinet player, stick with that role rather than—in the same essay—also trying to be a streetwise teenager. If you write as a student researcher on cognitive psychology, keep in mind that you are not an expert on your topic and that you are reporting the results of your reading. When writing an exam, remember that you are a student trying to reveal your mastery of the subject matter. Be consistent in displaying your knowledge and understanding.

Whether you write as a credit-card holder seeking an increase in your limit, as an outraged citizen, or as a well-prepared student, be aware of the identity you take on. If you are an authority, act like one. If you are committed to your subject, don't be afraid to show it. If you lack information, locate the necessary facts or data before you proceed. If you are not enthusiastic about your subject, don't pretend you are; you will probably sound insincere. If you are not an expert, don't pose as one; the chances of being found out are almost certain.

Know how your audience perceives you

It is important that you anticipate how your audience will respond to you and your subject. The way an audience perceives you as a writer influences how you approach your topic, what level of detail you need, and what tone you should use.

4

If your readers respect you as an authority, you will not have to establish your expertise as much as you would if they thought of you as a beginner. Of the following student topics, determine which ones reflect a student's experience. Ask yourself this question: How does the reader's perception of my expertise affect what I will write about each topic?

The Benefits of Joining the Business Fraternity
The Personal Gains of Ethical Behavior
Increasing Sales by Using the "Fear" Appeal
Malcolm X, Martin Luther King, Jr., and the U.S. Civil Rights Movement

Also work toward creating a sense of trust between you and your readers. Is your writing objective? Do you show some personal bias toward your subject? Is your tone reasonable and mature?

Finally, does your audience like you? If your readers don't like you, they won't feel any commitment to what you write, no matter how expert or how credible you may be as an author. Since readers are usually busy people, they respond favorably to a writer who can

- present information clearly
- structure ideas so readers can easily follow them
- avoid obnoxious or insulting language
- provide all the details an audience needs
- be generous, understanding, and modest
- hold the reader's interest by freshness of thought

Being aware of who you are in each writing act and anticipating how your audience sees and reacts to you is an important step in the writing process.

Drafting Your Essay

This chapter will help you compose the first draft of an essay. Having collected information and considered your purpose and audience, you now come to the point when you must focus and arrange this information. Begin by reading over your prewriting material to see what interesting insights or connections you can explore. Look for points to be developed, subdivided, or deleted. Next, make the subject your own by turning it into a manageable topic, one that you know and have an opinion on. Before you write, you will probably ask yourself these basic questions, which are covered in the following pages:

How can I limit my subject?
What is my main idea?
How will I plan the essay?
How will I begin?

5   Limit your topic.

Before you write the first draft, examine your subject for a topic that will interest your reader and that will be possible for you to handle. Consider whether you have enough information about your topic to develop it effectively. Do you have sources available? Do you have enough time to make use of the library? Return to your prewriting strategy to narrow your subject. For example, if you had begun with a broad subject such as physical fitness, your prewriting might have helped you limit your focus to jogging. Now, with further thought, you find that this topic is also too broad. Continue to narrow your focus:

Jogging
↓
Benefits of Jogging
↓
Benefits of Jogging for Cardiovascular Improvement

Many beginning writers choose the broadest possible topic because they fear that they have too little to say. However, a more limited topic will actually be easier to develop and will provide more opportunities for specific details. For instance, if you were to write about the meaning of love or the value of moral behavior, the result would likely be a series of general statements that would be both boring and unconvincing. Choose instead your experience in caring for a terminally ill relative or the benefits of a difficult moral choice you once made. For an essay on the latter subject, you realize that you cannot discuss everything that led up to your moral dilemma, so you select one revealing or unusual episode:

Not: Life Isn't Always Easy *or*
Some Choices Can Tear You Apart

But: Why I Can't Be Friends with a Shoplifter *or*
Vandalism Isn't Funny When the Police Arrive

There are several ways to narrow a subject. You might ask yourself these questions: What aspect of the subject do I know the most about? What aspect most interests me? What aspect would most interest a reader? Your prewriting might also have helped you narrow the subject. For instance, in addressing the issue of football safety, you might have subdivided this subject into specific areas, such as head injuries, improved helmets, artificial turf, and the role of coaches. Any one of these points can become a limited topic for a short essay:

Broad subject:	Football Safety
Still too broad:	Reasons for Football Injuries
Limited topic:	The Role of Artificial Turf in Football Injuries
Broad subject:	Cable Television
Still too broad:	How Cable Television Differs from Broadcast Television
Limited topic:	Creative Freedom and "Adult" Topics on Cable Television
Broad subject:	Modern Technology and the Environment
Still too broad:	Industrial Chemicals and Global Warming
Limited topic:	Long-term Possible Effects of Global Warming

To convince others that what you write is worth reading, make sure that *you* find the topic interesting. Picking a topic that you feel something about will make planning and developing the paper easier and more pleasant. It will also give the finished paper an authenticity, authority, and enthusiasm that will capture and hold your reader's interest. (If a topic is assigned to you, make sure that you are comfortable with it before you start to write.) You must understand just what is being asked of you, and you must know—or find out—enough about the subject so that you can handle it with sufficient confidence.

If you are given a general topic, begin by studying the broad assignment ("For your classmates, write an explanation of a process or a technique that you have found useful") and the specific suggestions ("Possibilities range from planting tomatoes to programming a VCR to housebreaking a puppy").

Here are examples of topics that students chose for papers addressed to an audience of classmates:

Inappropriate: A Simple Method of Determining Chi-Square with a Pocket Calculator

Appropriate: A Foolproof Method of Balancing a Checkbook with a Pocket Calculator

Inappropriate: U.S. Policy in Central Europe

Appropriate: Reasons for U.S. Involvement in Bosnia

The first inappropriate example assumes a stronger background in statistics than most readers have. It would be appropriate for a group of students who use chi-square in interpreting research data, but not for students in the average writing class. The second inappropriate topic deals with a broad subject that most students could treat successfully only through extensive research. A thorough paper on that topic would require more time and space than the typical college essay permits.

The first appropriate topic has a broad appeal. Many of us know nothing about chi-square, but almost all of us know about unbalanced checkbooks. The second appropriate topic is more sensible in scope than the overly ambitious topic on Central Europe as a whole, and it gives the writer more opportunity to present personal judgments.

6 Clarify your purpose with a thesis statement.

Stating your main idea—your thesis—will help you define your purpose in writing: to inform, analyze, describe, or argue, among others. What, you ask yourself, will I say about my topic? What main point do I hope to make in my essay? Although your prewriting exercises will probably have focused on such questions, it is important to solidify your central idea as you begin to write.

Sometimes it is helpful to complete this open-ended sentence: "In this paper I hope to _____." (Note that such a statement would *not* be included in your paper.) This technique allows you to clarify your goal as well as some plan for achieving this goal. Rather than stating, "My purpose is to write an essay on animal research," define more explicitly your goal, plan, and audience: "My purpose is to persuade my classmates of the need for stronger government regulations on the use of animals in scientific research." This more clearly focused statement includes a basic writing strategy: to persuade.

In organizing your material, determine your basic aim in presenting the topic: to explain how a thing works, to analyze its parts, to define what it means, to describe what it looks like, to tell what happened to it, or to argue for or against it. Often in an essay you will use several of these rhetorical strategies. When you decide on your principal rhetorical aim, you can often identify a method of organization, such as listing events in chronological order or presenting the causes of a problem in the order of their importance. Often the topic itself will suggest a method of organization: an essay on how to prepare for a job interview would follow a step-by-step order; an essay analyzing the differences between a novel and a film would employ comparison and contrast.

Having decided what you want to do, next construct a sentence that expresses the main idea you intend to present to your audience. This thesis statement should reflect a clear, definite expression of your stand on the topic. Your statement of purpose will help you formulate a tentative thesis statement: "Better government regulations are needed to reduce the suffering of animals used in laboratory research." Such a statement, subject to change, will guide you as you compose, helping you to make sure that the essay will make one main

6

point. Also, including the thesis in the introduction of your paper will clearly identify your most important point for your audience.

A thesis statement does not announce the subject you are going to write about. (Never include a thesis statement like this one: "This paper will discuss teacher strikes.") It specifies the point you will make about the topic. For example, you may want to use one of the following sentences:

Tax increases tend to favor the rich at the expense of the poor.

Or: Tax increases are not justified unless there is a clearly defined, limited need for more revenue.

Or: Tax increases should not be used to fund "corporate socialism."

Each of these thesis statements serves three functions:

1. It identifies the limited subject and thus provides a test for what material should go into your essay.
2. It makes clear your attitude toward the subject.
3. It focuses the reader's attention on the specific features of the subject that you will discuss.

The inadequate thesis statements that follow perform only one or two of the three functions:

Inadequate: The health professions are very promising today.

Improved: Many new, well-paying, challenging positions are opening up in medical technology.

Inadequate: Police officers today are different from the way they used to be.

Improved: As increasing numbers of college-educated men and women join police forces, the old stereotype of the stupid cop is rarely valid.

The inadequate thesis statements do not provide a limited focus or indicate the writer's feelings or stance: Why are health professions promising? How are police officers different—and what does the writer think of this change? The revised statements answer such questions by revealing a more specific approach to the topics. The improved thesis statements point to the kind of material that should be presented in the paper and indicate the writer's attitude. Such thesis statements make it much easier to locate information. For instance, if you were developing the essay on jobs in medical technology, you would know that you need data on recent developments in the field, on salaries, and on jobs that call for more than routine performance; you would also know that you should ignore information with no bearing on these matters.

Despite the importance of a thesis statement, you need not feel bound to the first one you write. If you come upon contradictory information or if your attitude changes as you think about the topic, you can always revise your thesis. For example, you might decide to change your thesis statement on the new breed of police officers to something like this one:

> The change in big-city police forces today results not so much from college graduates entering police work as from policemen and policewomen taking advantage of in-service opportunities for advanced education and specialized training.

A good thesis statement, one that is complete and specific, will guide you in developing and supporting it. It will help you know what to emphasize and what to exclude. An effective thesis clarifies your aim: you know why you are writing on the topic and what it means to you. Since nearly all our writing tries to persuade the reader to accept our opinion, try to think of your topic in arguable terms, as one side in a debate. Sharpening your topic so that it has an argumentative edge will help you clarify your stance and purpose.

7   Plan your draft with a rough outline.

As you begin to write, you need to consider a plan to help you group the various points you have developed. Your first (rough) draft allows you to think through the topic fully, concentrating on the larger issues of content and organization, not style. Sometimes you may begin writing at once, referring to your prewriting notes, and sketch out the body of the essay before returning to the introduction. More often you will start with a rough outline to give you a clear sense of direction and to make sure that your essay has a logical sequence that the reader can follow.

Most writers make rough outlines before they compose and then continue to organize as they write. They use outlines to guide the development of their ideas and do not feel restricted by them. Outlines are meant to be changed, not followed as though they represented a contract. Rough outlines, consisting of phrases arranged to show some relationship, can emerge from your prewriting material, as in this example:

Thesis: Modern cars are much more sophisticated than older ones.

1. Electronic fuel injection

2. Enhanced safety features: air bags, antilock brakes

3. Expert mechanical attention a must

Conclusion: A 1997 automobile is an improvement over a 1977 version, but the day of the shade-tree mechanic may be over.

Such an outline suggests the overall plan of the typical essay with its beginning, middle, and end:

Introductory paragraph

Body paragraphs
1. First point
2. Second point
3. Third point, etc.

Concluding paragraph

With your thesis in mind, write out three or four major points in the order that seems most logical. As you write, you can place the supporting information (facts, examples, details) under the headings in your list. Again, these headings are flexible: if you discover considerable new material, you may need to adjust your outline or simply compose freely, with the rough outline as your initial guide.

Here is a sample thesis statement with two rough outlines—one unsuccessful, one more effective.

Thesis:	AIDS is a disease that is both lethal and cunning.
Ineffective outline:	1. AIDS must be taken seriously
	2. AIDS is a ghastly disease
	3. How do you get AIDS?
	4. Many people ashamed to go to a doctor
	5. Having blood drawn can be painful
Effective outline:	1. AIDS is always fatal
	2. Many people confused about how it is contracted
	3. Many people would rather be in the dark than undergo testing
	4. Blood tests not always accurate
	5. Possible ten-year gap between infection and symptoms

The second rough outline is superior because each point develops from, and clearly relates to, the thesis statement, whereas the first outline contains generalities and less relevant points (2, 4, 5).

A more formal topic outline can provide a complete point-by-point layout of your entire essay. To develop a good topic outline, start by using the points on your rough outline as the major divisions (labeling them with Roman numerals I, II, III, etc.). Then develop subdivisions (labeling them A, B, C, etc.) for each major point. Although two levels may be enough for a short paper, a third level (labeled 1, 2, 3, etc.) will help you organize details in longer projects. Sometimes even a fourth level is useful (labeled a, b, c, etc.).

Topic outline

THESIS: Businesses should not use polygraph tests to screen job applicants.

 I. Why businesses use polygraph tests
    A. To keep employees from stealing
    B. To determine the honesty of job applicants

 II. What kind of businesses use polygraph tests

III. How the polygraph test works
    A. Records one's physical response to questions
    B. The response pattern interpreted by an examiner
    C. Is not a "lie detector"

IV. Why businesses should not use polygraph tests
    A. Potentially good employees frightened away
    B. Lack of scientific evidence that tests are accurate
    C. Unreliability of examiners
    D. Unethical uses of confidential information
    E. Illegal invasion of privacy

A sentence outline can do even more. It can give topic sentences to organize your explanations for all of your points. Detailed topic or sentence outlines are excellent guides to organization and can be especially helpful in preparing a long paper. See Chapter 10 for an example.

8

8 Your introductory paragraph should focus the reader's interest on your thesis.

A good introduction serves two important functions: it attracts the reader's interest and focuses that interest on the thesis. Therefore, to write a good introduction, you need to know what your thesis is and why your reader might care about what you have to say. If you can be sure that your reader is already interested in your topic and if your essay is short, then you might not need an introduction. You could start with the thesis statement and move to the first point:

> Anyone who has been approached by telephone callers promising "giveaways" that sound too good to be true should be aware of three issues. The first and most obvious of these . . .

To treat the same subject in a longer paper, involving more than just a few paragraphs, you might need to mention all three issues in the introduction so that the reader would know what to expect. Then the next paragraph could begin discussing the first issue.

If your reader needs background information in order to understand why your topic is significant, provide that information in your introductory paragraph. For example, if you were going to report on new techniques for catching shoplifters at the store where you work, you could first discuss what shoplifting costs the average consumer and then lead your reader to the specific case of your store and finally to your thesis statement.

The pattern just discussed for the introductory paragraph on shoplifting is the most reliable way of introducing college papers:

General statement(s) related to topic and to reader's interests
↓
Any necessary background material
↓
Thesis statement

8

Sometimes you will start with your thesis and include an outline of your main points in the introductory paragraph:

> *Chinatown* is Roman Polanski's greatest movie. Released in 1974, this classic has multiple areas of appeal. One is the theme, a study of Noah Cross's addiction to power and the horrifying acts that he is drawn to. His foil is J. J. Gittes, an honest private investigator who is as much driven by his need to understand Noah Cross as he is to see justice done. The movie is very much in the *film noir* style, except at its most basic requirement: Polanski uses "natural" color to play off the darkness of Cross's deeds. Finally, the three principal actors, John Huston (as Cross), Jack Nicholson (as Gittes), and Faye Dunaway (as Cross's estranged daughter) give top-level performances.

The body paragraphs would analyze these issues in detail. One effective way to capture the reader's interest is to open with an interesting example, experience, or anecdote. Sometimes a quotation or proverb is effective:

> "It is better to be silent and thought a fool than to open your mouth and remove all doubt." I remember this old saying whenever I choose to listen in class rather than speak. . . .

Instead of stating his thesis—that football is unnecessarily brutal—this student begins with his own experience:

> I spent the Christmas of my senior year in the hospital with my neck in a brace, wondering if the cut nerves in my right arm would leave me permanently crippled. In the next room, a classmate was recovering from spinal surgery to correct a massive herniation that made him, a strong young man of 21, immobile. He took a year to recover; I spent three months in

traction. We still undergo therapy and face further hospitalization. Although we both survived, we paid a terrible price for playing football.

Sometimes you will find that the revision stage of the writing process provides the best opportunity to produce a good introduction. After you have completed a first draft and have clarified your ideas, you can then return to the opening and rework it. Consider these introductory paragraphs:

First draft: Elvis Presley, who died in 1977, lives in the minds of many of his fans and in the pages of tabloids, which proclaim his reincarnation. Books, too, recount psychic experiences involving the dead singer and stories of his reincarnation. Visitors pour into his home and buy memorabilia, making his estate much more valuable than it was when he was alive. To thousands of loyal worshippers, the King is not dead. He and the Elvis phenomenon have become larger than life.

Revised draft: Each year on August 16, the anniversary of Elvis Presley's death, the faithful converge on Memphis to hold a candlelight vigil at the "shrine" of the King. Many of them look forward to his return or recount psychic experiences in which Elvis appears to them. Books and tabloids proclaim "The King lives," thus adding fuel to the reports of his reincarnation. Millions of dollars are spent on statues, records, pictures, and other memorabilia because of a belief that if Elvis is not alive, he is a saint. Elvis worshippers have formed a religious cult unlike anything associated with other dead celebrities.

In revising, the writer has developed an introduction with specific examples that clarify the suggestion of a religious cult.

9 Your concluding paragraph should reemphasize your main points.

The conclusion should restate your thesis in different words and reemphasize its importance. Merely repeating your ideas is unnecessary and tedious, but a concluding paragraph can effectively summarize the main points of a long essay. Here is the conclusion of an essay on the importance of lifelong exercise:

> Although older people may well have reduced physical abilities and must be wary of broken bones, exercise programs can be tailored to meet the needs of every age group. Just as very young children can be taught to swim or jog for exercise and pleasure, the elderly can continue a tradition of fitness and good health by exercising in a safe and appropriate manner. Physical fitness is never "age-specific."

Sometimes you can recommend a course of action or solution to problems presented in the paper, as in this ending of an essay on low voter turnouts in U.S. elections:

> After all that our ancestors went through to secure political freedom and establish a democratic republic, it is shameful that so few Americans bother to vote. By adopting the Australian model and requiring adults to vote in national elections, we will inevitably have a better-informed populace, one more like the vision of our nation's founders. There will be problems at first, as I have illustrated, but the eventual result will be a vast improvement on our current state of voter apathy.

Whether you cover all of your main points or just your thesis, follow these guidelines in writing concluding paragraphs:

1. Do not introduce new topics; everything you present should emphasize points that you have already made.

2. Do not repeat the same words and examples you used earlier.

3. Make your writing forceful; do not overestimate the importance of what you have said, but do not hesitate or apologize, either.

Though it should be concise, a conclusion cannot be so vague and general that the reader feels let down, as in this ending of a literary analysis that compares two short stories:

First draft: These two stories, despite their many differences, have much in common. They show how two writers, using different subjects and styles, can say similar things.

To satisfy the reader with an appropriate conclusion, the writer should restate the reason for comparing the stories and then sum up what the analysis has revealed:

Revised draft: These two stories, though different in subject and tone, force us to think about what a successful life is. By presenting their readers with failures, both authors imply that success does not come from possessing material goods but from living according to the enduring values of love, self-sacrifice, and honesty.

Revising

Revision means to "look again," to rethink and clarify what you have written. You step back from your work to examine it from a new perspective. Revision does not mean recopying or correcting errors but recognizing that your draft is unfinished, that words and ideas can be added, deleted, or rearranged. A good writer is never satisfied with a first draft and never forgets that writing involves rewriting. Rarely would you want to hand in an essay without making changes in its content as well as in its structure and style. If you assume that nearly every piece of writing can be improved, you will not hesitate to drop entire paragraphs, to condense, shift, and rearrange. As you revise, you are examining your initial ideas, purpose, and audience to get a more objective perspective on your work; after you revise, you then edit, making changes and corrections to the altered text.

Revision occurs throughout the writing process. After you complete a sentence, for example, you read and react to it, considering whether to expand it or delete from it. But most rewriting occurs after you have written a first draft. You read that draft with your own intentions in mind, and you also read with your reader in mind. To satisfy the reader's needs, you consider what you have produced and what might be missing. Reading your own work objectively and considering the comments of other readers will help you discover if your meaning is clear and if your structure and style express your meaning effectively.

When you read your first draft, you may need to change your thesis, purpose, and writing strategy as you compare what you have written with your original intention. When you proceed from large overall concerns to specific sentence and word changes, your focus will shift from yourself to the reader. First, read what the draft says, then read from the reader's viewpoint, and finally read with an eye for problems to be solved. Here are some basic tips for revising:

1. As you write, leave plenty of space for changes.
2. When you revise, try to work from a typed or printed, not handwritten, draft so that you can approach your work more objectively.
3. Revise in stages, setting the draft aside for a "cooling off" period. When you return to it, you can then view it more critically.
4. Read each draft aloud. If a sentence sounds awkward, reword it until it sounds right. Listen also for omissions and repetitions.
5. Let someone else read your drafts, and ask this person to react honestly to your ideas and style. Collaborative work is especially useful as you revise. The comments of your fellow students and instructor can help you develop a more objective view of your work.
6. Be willing to discard anything that does not relate to your purpose and thesis. But revising does not involve changing *everything;* your prewriting will have produced some valuable material.
7. Save all your drafts, but do not waste time by recopying the whole paper after each stage of the revision process.

In making your work clearer for your reader, you make it clearer for yourself. This point has been made by Donald M.

Murray, who suggests a three-stage "clarification" process. With each reading, he says, the writer should focus on a different aspect of the writing:

1. meaning
2. structure
3. style

10

▼ **10 Revise for overall meaning.**

Consider the major areas of your essay before worrying about the minor ones. First, read your draft quickly for content and ideas. Try to be objective, ignoring word choice and other details as you ask yourself these questions about the content:

1. What is my main point?
2. Does everything in the draft relate to this point?
3. Do I have enough solid evidence to develop my point?
4. What else does the reader need to know?
5. Is the draft too short or too long?
6. Are there parts I could cut?
7. Does the draft follow through on what the title and introduction promise?

To make sure that your essay has unity, compare your thesis and introduction with the body of the paper. If they do not match, rewrite the introduction or revise paragraphs that stray from the main point. Use arrows to indicate any paragraphs that need to be altered.

11   Revise for structure.

Read the draft quickly again, this time with your method of organization in mind. Again, avoid questions of style and try to be as objective as you can. Focus on whether each part of the essay is developed well and is in the right order by asking yourself these questions:

1. Is my title effective?
2. Will my introduction capture the reader's interest? (see **8**)
3. Do I have a clear thesis statement? (see **6**)
4. Is every paragraph related to my thesis?
5. Does each paragraph make one point? Is each paragraph fully developed? (see **16, 19**)
6. Am I using facts and examples, not just general statements, to support my thesis?
7. Have I defined my major terms?
8. Am I bringing myself into the paper too much, distracting the reader from the subject?
9. Does the conclusion sum up the main points and return to the thesis? (see **9**)

At this stage in the revision, look for any irrelevant information that can be cut. Then examine your paragraphs. If they are skimpy, consider what examples or facts you can add from your prewriting. Remember that making changes is easier than starting from scratch.

To make sure that your essay is effectively organized, make a rough outline of your draft or, if you prefer, briefly summarize each paragraph. This will allow you to stand back from your work and see if your points flow naturally and proceed logically and if each point is properly developed.

Read this draft of a paragraph, then the revised version below. Notice how the writer has eliminated one irrelevant sentence and kept himself out of the piece while reducing wordiness and clarifying vague, impersonal subjects.

First draft: Although you can find many differences between rugby and football, I believe that the major difference is that rugby is unlike professional football since you get involved with it for the love of the sport. Participating in the game means that outside jobs are necessary to support the players and their hobby. And expenses on the road must be paid by the players. This is not so much the case in England, where the game was first played and where it is much more popular than American football. In this country, the problem with attracting large crowds to support rugby is no doubt due to the fact that it is an amateur sport that is less well promoted and so less popular than football.

Revised draft: The major difference between rugby and football is that rugby players play the sport not for pay but for love. To participate in the sport, players must have outside jobs to support themselves, and they must pay their expenses on the road. Rugby in this country does not attract large crowds because it is an amateur sport that is not as well promoted as football or as popular.

12

12   Revise for style.

After a short break, read the draft a third time for style. Now that the content is well established and the structure is firm, slowly read your essay out loud, line by line. Examine your sentence patterns and word choice. Ask yourself these questions:

1. Are my sentences all starting the same way? If so, could I use subordination and variety (combining)? (see **20**)
2. If any of my sentences contain series or lists, are the items grammatically parallel? (see **28a**)
3. Are there any unnecessary repetitions, wordy phrases, clichés, or jargon? (see **24, 67, 69**)
4. Are there any words whose meanings I am unsure of? Is my diction appropriate for my audience and purpose? (see **59, 63**)
5. Have I avoided unnecessary passive verbs? (see **23e**)
6. Are my tenses consistent? (see **58a**)
7. Have I deleted all unnecessary words and phrases? (see **70**)
8. Do I lead the reader smoothly from one point to another and from start to finish?
9. Does the paper sound like me speaking to the reader?

12a   Check the point of view.

As you polish your essay, make sure that you have selected the proper person and that you have not shifted person: first person *(I, we),* second person *(you),* third person *(he, she, it, one,* or *they).* Most academic and professional writing uses third person because it emphasizes the subject, not the writer.

> **Weak:**   I found as I read the novel that the plot was implausible.

> **Revised:**   The novel's plot was implausible.

In this example, the use of *I* distracts the reader from the subject. However, some beginning writers mistakenly think that

I is never suitable in college writing and go out of their way to avoid it:

| Weak: | It is this writer's contention that watching the videocassette recording of a movie is nothing like seeing the same film at a theater. |

| Improved: | Watching the videocassette recording of a movie is nothing like seeing the same film at a theater. |

12

Or, if your audience is such that you can use a more informal tone:

> For me, watching a videotape is a pale imitation of going to the theater to see a "real" movie.

The *I* point of view is appropriate if you are writing from your own experience. In this example from a personal narrative, the writer is the subject:

> I remember a morning many years ago when I was backing out of the parking lot near the railroad station in Brewster, New York. There was a near collision. The driver of the other car jumped out and started to abuse me; he had his fists ready. Then he looked hard at me and said, "Why, you're an old man." He got back into his car, slammed the door, and drove away, while I stood there fuming. "I'm only 65," I thought. "He wasn't driving carefully. I can still take care of myself in a car, or in a fight, for that matter."
>
> —*Malcolm Cowley*

The *you* point of view, which emphasizes the reader, is used in instructional materials—such as this book, which talks directly to the student. The indefinite *you* (referring to anyone in general) is inappropriate (see **52b**).

| Inappropriate: | Being sent to prison makes you stop and take account of your life. |

12b Rely on topic sentences.

When revising for style, examine the topic sentence of each of your paragraphs to see if that sentence clearly defines the doer (subject) and the action (verb). By asking *who, what, where, when, how,* and *why,* you can give each paragraph a more specific focus and place the emphasis where it is needed.

12

Weak: There are numerous differences between the old U.S.S.R. and the fragmented republics that took its place.

Revised: The old U.S.S.R. and the fragmented republics that took its place offer different, but still significant, threats to world peace.

The first topic sentence above is weak because it fails to address *how* the two governments differ. The following paragraph is poorly developed because the writer did not ask any of the basic questions about the doer, the action, and the purpose:

> Beginning life on a college campus is exciting yet difficult and frustrating in many ways. For the first time there are new ideas, responsibilities, and attitudes that are challenged. Yet with these challenges come many problems for the new freshman.

The first sentence has no doer: Who is beginning life? The writer uses *there are* (in the second sentence) rather than a human subject, such as "the freshman for the first time encounters new . . . " The use of *many ways* and *many problems* gives the reader no mental picture. To revise this vague paragraph, the writer examines each sentence to see how it can become more specific and then draws on her experience to generate examples. Here is a later version of that paragraph with final revisions included:

A freshman's

~~One's~~ introduction to college life is often *less* exciting ~~as well as~~ *than* difficult and ~~very~~ frustrating. I spent most of my first day at the University standing in lines, ~~I waited~~ first at registration ~~and~~ then at the bookstore. *When* I returned exhausted to the dorm after getting none of the classes I *had* wanted, ~~and~~ *I* went to the cafeteria, hoping to ~~see~~ *find* my roommate, but ended up eating alone. That night I was ~~really~~ ready to ~~call it quits and~~ go home. But now, after two weeks here, I have learned to cope with dorm problems and *to* enjoy the independence. Having made new friends ~~in my classes and at several parties,~~ I find college challenging and fun. My experience shows that if ~~one~~ *freshmen* can handle *the hassles of* the first week, they can manage to enjoy ~~life in college.~~

12

Revising should also help you develop your own style. Your aim is to express your convictions clearly and honestly, not to try to impress readers with a formal, stilted style of borrowed phrases and unfamiliar words. Pay close attention to sentence structure (see Chapter 6) and word choice (see **63**), simplify wordy phrases (see **70**), reduce the passive voice (see **23e**), and reword for emphasis (see **23**). Note the following troublesome sentences and their revisions:

Not: There is no reason single mothers should not be allowed to stay in high school. *(confusing double negative)*

But: Single mothers should be allowed to finish their high school education.

Not: The house was purchased for $88,500, but Carlos sold it for $115,900. *(shifts from passive to active)*

But: Carlos purchased the house for $88,500 but sold it for $115,900.

Rather than worry about having an inadequate number of words, imagine that you will be rewarded for the words you can delete. Consider the advice of Strunk and White in *The Elements of Style:* "A sentence should contain no unnecessary words, a paragraph no unnecessary sentences, for the same reason that a drawing should have no unnecessary lines and a machine no unnecessary parts." Notice how each of these sentences can be more concise:

Weak: The reason why I was late was due to the fact that I overslept.

Improved: I was late because I overslept.

Weak: What that machine does is enable the blind to read without Braille.

Improved: The machine enables the blind to read without Braille.

13   Use collaboration in revising.

Writing need not be an entirely solitary activity. By having others respond to your work, you can receive valuable help, and you can see that your instructor is not your only reader. Moreover, by reading another student's paper, you can also become a better reader of your own writing.

Friends and family members can react to your work as outsiders. Fellow students, who know the assignment and the standards for evaluating it, can approach your work more objectively; they are insiders who know the problems involved with incomplete drafts. As partners, for example, they can help you reexamine your ideas.

Here are some suggestions for collaborative revising:

1. Make helpful, positive suggestions and comments. Your aim is not to "play teacher." Recognize also that the criticism you receive is directed at your work, not at you. Respect others' responses, but know that you must decide what to accept and what to reject.

2. Be prepared with a legible draft and with specific questions about your work.

3. Do not focus on errors, style, or word changes.

4. If your instructor divides the class into groups, you can focus on three or four specific aspects of your partners' work. For example, you can determine if there is a clear purpose and thesis, adequate development, and an introduction that captures the reader's attention and indicates how the paper will be structured.

5. Outside of class, you could exchange a draft with another student and agree to examine each other's work before it is due. Don't try to focus on everything; examine the introductory paragraph, the first sentence of each subsequent paragraph, and the conclusion to determine if the structure is clear and logical. Or work with your partner to develop some of your own criteria for evaluating each other's writing. Try writing a short summary of the student's thesis and purpose; then write a short comment, indicating your assessment of the paper's strengths and weaknesses.

14

14 Revising on a computer

Most writers are more objective and critical when reacting to computer-printed drafts than to handwritten ones. Writing undergoes an important transformation when you move from reading your own penmanship to seeing your words in type, and you become aware of problems not apparent before. Also, revising from a printed copy can help you spot smaller stylistic problems as well as larger problems of organization and development.

15

If you compose your first drafts on a PC, you are ahead of the game. Modern technology has greatly simplified the time-consuming retyping once required for revision. Computers allow you to make multiple changes: with the text on the computer screen, it is easy to add, delete, or rearrange elements. However, most writers think it best to edit on hard copy (paper), which they mark up before entering the changes into the computer. Similarly, proofreading is best done on hard copy before you print the final text. Remember that you should not rely exclusively on a spell-checking function, which cannot help you distinguish between easily confused words (*their* and *there,* for example). Writers must be responsible for editing their own errors and correcting their own spelling. Sophisticated grammar-checking software is also available, but remember that *you* will receive the grade on your essay—the software is merely a tool. Whether you revise by working on-screen or by marking up your printout, be sure to save and print copies of each stage of your essay. You may want to return to earlier drafts as you progress through the assignment.

15   Edit for errors.

The final stage in revising is editing the final draft for correctness. If your work is to make a good impression, a thorough word-by-word examination of your completed essay for errors and omissions is essential. No matter how interesting the topic, and no matter how imaginative your development, if the essay contains errors, the reader is sure to think less of your work.

The proofreading stage is the time not for major changes but for checking keyboarding errors or slips of the pen. Put the draft aside for a while; then read it carefully, looking at individual words, not at whole statements. To locate misspellings, read backwards, starting with the last word. Check for repeated words as well as for spelling, punctuation, and grammatical errors. Check the dictionary for the meanings of any words you are unsure of. To change a wrong or misspelled word, draw a line through it and write the correction directly above. If you have omitted a word, place a caret (^) below the line at the place where the omission occurs. Then write the word directly above the caret. The following passage includes most of the frequently used proofreading marks:

15

Most of us have difficulty	
proof reading our own work properly	close up
because of the way we read it: for	
content. Our eyes normally move	transpose
across a line of print in a series	transpose
of "jumps" that Allow us to focus	lowercase
one point of information, then	insert
another. in proofreading, we must	caps
interrupt this normal reading-for-	insert space
information method and read words	insert
as words, concentrating on form	
(spelling, grammar, etc.), on not	transpose
meaning.	

After you have proofread your essay, carefully make your final corrections in your PC file. A good way to ensure that you haven't missed anything is to make a small check mark beside each correction on the hard copy. When you have finished, run

your spell-checking function one last time, or print your finished work so that you can compare it to your marked-up draft.

As you read these drafts of a student's paragraph, notice
where changes were made and the overall effect of the revision.

First draft:

15

 There are many reasons why <u>Star Trek</u> has
been a huge success world wide, the main
reason being that it offers a hopeful view of
the future. Life in what we call present
reality is filled with violence and conflicts
of all types, but <u>Star Trek</u> and <u>The Next
Generation</u> give an optimistic view of life in
the future. It is a time when negotiation and
compromise are seen as possible in solving
social issues. It was the creator, Gene
Roddenberry's vision that the future will not
be overwhelming or complex but human. His
belief was in a logical, rational approach to
life, and this is the other major reason for
the success of these shows, which have moved
millions of people, who might otherwise not
identify with science fiction plots or
futuristic stories. The idea that the human
mind has the power to answer life's eternal
questions is a major reason why this adventure
series has become a popular classic and will
remain so.

Second draft:

Of the many reasons <u>Star Trek</u> has been a huge, worldwide success, perhaps the main reason is that it offers a hopeful view of the future. In contrast to the very violent, conflict-ridden world of present reality, <u>Star Trek</u> and <u>Star Trek: The Next Generation</u> picture life in the future optimistically. This is due to creator Gene Roddenberry's vision that future centuries will not be overwhelmingly complex but human. His belief in a rational approach to life is what has moved millions of viewers. The idea that the mind has the power to answer life's eternal questions is a major reason why this adventure series has become, and will remain, a popular classic.

Final draft:

<u>Star Trek</u> has been a huge, worldwide success mainly because it offers a hopeful vision of the future. In contrast to the present, with its cynicism, violence, and racial conflicts, <u>Star Trek</u> and <u>Star Trek: The Next Generation</u> picture the future optimistically. This hopeful view is due to

creator Gene Roddenberry's belief that life in the twenty-third century need not be overwhelmingly technical and complex. Rather, his future is one in which negotiation and compromise can solve national rivalries and racial bigotry. Millions of viewers have been moved by the emphasis in this adventure series on the mind's power to answer life's eternal questions. Because of this positive philosophy, <u>Star Trek</u> has become, and will remain, a popular classic.

Writing Paragraphs

Writers use paragraphs to build sentences into blocks of thought that can then join other paragraphs to develop the main idea of an essay or other piece of writing. A paragraph can introduce a thesis (the main idea of an essay), develop one of the points supporting the thesis, conclude the discussion, or supply a transition between parts of a fairly long paper. The paragraphs that support the thesis often correspond to the points in a rough outline—for example, you might begin an essay on ways of controlling pollution with a paragraph outlining three main solutions to the problem. Then, in three longer paragraphs, you would discuss each of these solutions in turn.

Paragraphs come in various sizes. The length of a paragraph depends on the difficulty of the subject, the size of related paragraphs, and the background of the intended audience. An essay consisting of very brief paragraphs (fewer than three sentences each) will suggest inadequate thought. If your paragraphs are frequently under one hundred words in length, you are probably not giving them the development they deserve. More important than paragraph length, however, is making sure that each paragraph develops essentially one point.

A good paragraph presents enough facts and examples to satisfy the reader that its topic has been properly developed, and it does so in sentences that fit together, or cohere, to form a single unit. The following sections examine the main qualities of effective paragraphs.

16 ▶ Use a topic sentence to focus each paragraph on one point.

16

The topic sentence of a paragraph states the central idea that the rest of the paragraph clarifies, exemplifies, or otherwise supports. It promises what is to come. Therefore, a good topic sentence is useful to both writer and reader. The writer can use it to guide the development of the rest of the paragraph; the reader uses it as a clue to what lies ahead. Although a topic sentence is often the first sentence in a paragraph, it sometimes follows a transitional opening sentence. It may even appear at the end of a paragraph, leading the reader to a climactic conclusion. Experienced writers often do not give every paragraph a topic sentence, but beginning writers are usually well advised to use topic sentences consistently and to make them easily recognizable.

A good topic sentence identifies the subject of the paragraph and the specific issue to be developed. When the focus is blurred, the topic sentence offers no direction to the reader, who may suspect that the writer was not sure where the paragraph was heading. In the following examples, note how the sharpened topic sentences point to the supporting sentences:

Not focused: A business plan does more than just indicate the initial direction of a new company.

Sharpened: *A business plan not only specifies the goals and procedures of a new company but also outlines how the lender will be repaid.*

A more specific topic sentence will help you find examples and details to develop the paragraph.

Not focused: The Thunderbird is a classic automobile.

Sharpened: *The appearance of the 1957 Thunderbird is both striking and simple.* The body is devoid of heavy amounts of chrome that tend to be ostentatious. The style, with its low-slung design and smooth curves, is very sleek and aerodynamic. The tail fins, which begin at the door handle and continue straight back to just over the taillights, are tasteful and not as outlandish as the fins of the 1960 Cadillac, for example. Even though many people refer to the Thunderbird as a sports car, its rear wheel skirts still retain the aura of a luxury automobile. The side porthole hardtop as well as the low-profile hood scoop are stylish additions to a classic car.

—*Scott Wilson (student)*

16

Not focused: Video games are useful for young people.

Sharpened: *Video games give many young people their first experience with computer technology.* In fact, despite the ongoing controversy over questionable content and the amount of time some children expend, these games play a large part in educating youth about our information-driven society. Students lacking formal instruction in computers usually find that a video game is the first computer they learn to control. And the skills involved in playing the game can help prepare them for more complex computer systems. Many middle-class children have computers at home, but less fortunate youngsters must learn about this technology in video game arcades, which have been criticized by parents as a waste of time and money. However, adults who object to video games should realize the educational value that they can provide.

Not Focused: Early morning classes are not always wise.

Sharpened: *Most young people don't function well enough in the early morning to benefit from 8 A.M. classes.* As my psychology professor told us, recent studies of sleep disorders show that teenagers naturally function poorly in the early morning. A hormone that regulates the body's cycles of sleep and waking has more impact on morning sleepiness than does staying up late. As a result, many students are deprived of the amount of sleep they need and can't be expected to get up early and perform well before 10 o'clock. So it seems better to blame biology, not late night hours, for students' morning yawns.

—Alison Smith (student)

In a first draft, begin every paragraph with a topic sentence. Doing so will help you make sure that the paragraph accomplishes its purpose. When you revise your early draft, you may want to move the topic sentence to another position or get rid of it entirely. Occasionally, you may choose to place the topic sentence at the end of the paragraph to give it special emphasis.

U

17 Make all other sentences in the paragraph relate to the topic sentence.

If a paragraph is to succeed, it must be unified (see also **18**). In a unified paragraph, each sentence contributes to the central idea. Every detail supports the topic sentence to produce a single, unfolding idea.

Examine your paragraphs to make certain that each sentence follows from and develops the topic sentence. Details not directly relevant to the central point do not belong in the paragraph. For instance, if your topic sentence is "I support our university's policy of recruiting student athletes because it benefits the students academically and the school economically," your supporting sentences should deal with the advantages to student athletes and to the university recruitment budget. Sentences about the problems raised by the policy of building winning teams would violate the unity of the paragraph. To write about such problems, you would need a new paragraph.

The first step in achieving paragraph unity is to construct a clear, specific topic sentence. The next step is to develop, throughout the rest of the paragraph, the idea that the topic sentence expresses. When you revise your rough draft, eliminate all irrelevant points, no matter how interesting or well stated they may be. The two underlined sentences in the following paragraph violate unity:

> Psychoanalysis, as developed by Sigmund Freud at the end of the last century, was originally a therapy, but it eventually evolved into a theoretical system. <u>As a therapy, psychoanalysis experienced its greatest popularity in this country during the 1950s and 1960s.</u> According to Freudian theorists, along with or underneath the conscious mind, we have an unconscious mind, a type of mental energy we are unaware of. Therefore, nothing that happens, consciously or unconsciously, is without some cause. Another basic part of psychoanalytic theory is that, in everyday life, we often use defense mechanisms to hide from unpleasant truths about ourselves. <u>In his celebrated break with Freud, C. G. Jung rejected the idea that major problems can be traced to sexual disturbances.</u>

Note that the last sentence in the preceding paragraph could well be the topic sentence of a new paragraph.

17

coh

18 Provide coherence within and between paragraphs.

For an essay to be effective, it must be coherent: its parts must fit together. The content of your paragraphs should lead the reader from the beginning of your essay to the end in a logical order. When you move from one paragraph to a new one, include signals that show the relationship between the two. These signals are transitional devices to indicate, for example, that you are moving from an introductory paragraph that states a problem to supporting paragraphs that explain causes and effects, offer solutions, or provide examples.

In a paragraph, coherence is the natural flow from one sentence to the next. The sentences interlock so that the first idea leads to the second, the second to the third, and so on. You can't write a succession of isolated sentences and expect your reader to supply the words and phrases that tie them together. You must make the reader feel that by the end of the paragraph you have made your point clearly and smoothly.

18a Achieve coherence by following a clear order.

The first step in achieving coherence is to follow a clear, logical order. That is, point *A* might precede point *B* because *A* happened before *B*, because *A* led to *B* or caused *B*, or because *B* illustrates *A*. Or your purpose might determine the order: you might put *A* first to give it special prominence; you might lead up all the way to point *G*, leaving it until last for emphasis. Always try to find a pattern that will seem sensible to your reader.

The main patterns involve the order of time, space, and climax as well as the general-to-specific and specific-to-general order. In all cases, the structure determines the coherence.

Time order.   Paragraphs that relate either a series of incidents or steps in a process often follow chronological order. The first example is a narrative; the second is a factual explanation of a process.

<table>
<tr><td>**First:**</td><td rowspan="1">The most terrifying day in my life came in July of 1946. I was washing lunchtime dishes in our farmhouse in middle Georgia when my husband unexpectedly appeared at the door. "Appeared" is the best word that I can think to use, because he</td></tr>
<tr><td>**Second:**</td><td>was not walking but crawling, dragging his left leg. I got out of him as quickly as possible that he had been bitten by a copperhead of some three feet, a snake large enough for its venom to be fatal. We lived thirty miles from the nearest hospital, I did not have a driver's license (and, in fact, had never driven</td></tr>
<tr><td>**Third:**</td><td>a car), but my husband was dying before my eyes. I pushed/pulled him into the back seat of our Chevrolet and pointed the car toward Atlanta.</td></tr>
</table>

18

Every angler knows that fishing can be a bewildering sport. Days that look perfect frequently turn into casting exercises, and awful, dreary days sometimes produce huge yields. So what is the "ideal" time to catch fish? Roughly, two elements are involved. **First**, a reasonable amount of food supply should be present—normally insects or minnows—so that fish are in the "habit" of eating. Weather is the **second** consideration. Fish are moved to eat not only by hunger but also by the lowering of barometric pressure in the atmosphere, a process that affects the sensory organ called the "lateral line," which runs along the body of most fish. Thus, when a storm is approaching, fish are sometimes moved to violent feeding activity, a phenomenon that produces the strange—and sometimes dangerous—sight of an angler hauling in fish after fish while a storm rages overhead.

Spatial order.   An arrangement in space (from top to bottom, left to right, and so on) is often possible in descriptive paragraphs, such as in the following excerpt:

Fred went into the kitchen and dropped a chop into a frying pan that was crackling with hot grease. He has a fairly new four-burner stove that uses bottled gas. He keeps water in a large bowl on the table in the kitchen and ladles some when he wants it. While he cooked the meat, he looked out a window through a stand of pitch pines and into the cranberry bog. "I saw a big buck out here last night with velvet on his horns," he said. "Them horns is soft when they're in velvet." On a nail high on one wall of the room that Bill and I were sitting in was a large meat cleaver. Next to it was a billy club. The wall itself was papered in a flower pattern, and the wallpaper continued out across the ceiling and down the three other walls, lending the room something of the appearance of the inside of a gift box. In some parts of the ceiling, the paper had come loose. "I didn't paper this year," Fred said. "For the last couple months, I've had sinus." The floor was covered with old rugs. They had been put down in random pieces, and in some places as many as six layers were stacked up. In winter, when the temperature approaches zero, the worst cold comes through the floor. The only source of heat in the house is a wood-burning stove in the main room. There were seven calendars on the walls, all current and none with pictures of nudes. Fading into pastel on one wall was a rotogravure photograph of President and Mrs. Eisenhower.

—*adapted from John McPhee, "The Pines"*

Climactic order. Some topics will suggest an order of increasing importance. In this example, the sentences lead up to the highest point of interest:

In the center of the grove an oak stood, tall and stately but bulging in the middle. On this venerable bulge a pair of ravens had taken up residence for so many years that the tree was known as the "raven tree." Children often tried without success to get at the nest, the difficulty of the task whetting their appetites. But when they climbed up to the swelling, it jutted out so far beyond their grasp that they found the undertaking too hazardous. And so the birds lived on, building nest after nest in perfect security until a February day when the grove was to be cleared. Men came with their saws, the woods echoed the clamor, but the mother raven remained on her nest, even when the tree began to tilt. At last, when it gave way, the bird was flung from her nest, whipped to the ground by twigs. She deserved a better fate.

—*adapted from Gilbert White*

General-specific. Paragraphs often begin with a general statement or topic sentence (see **16**), followed by supporting details and examples. However, many writers start with specifics and end with a general comment that summarizes the point of the paragraph, as in this example:

18

When the baby is born, he's given a little bag with a garlic, a bit of lime, salt, and tobacco in it to hang round his neck. Tobacco is important because it is a sacred plant for Indians. This all means that the child can ward off all the evil things in life. For us, bad things are like spirits, which exist only in our imagination. Something bad, for instance, would be if the child were to turn out to be a gossip—not sincere, truthful, and respectful, as a child should be. It also helps him collect together and preserve all our ancestors' things. That's more or less the idea of the bag—to keep him pure. The bag is put inside the four candles as well, and this represents the promise of the child when he grows up.

—*Rigoberta Menchú*

In contrast, the following paragraph offers a good example of the general-to-specific pattern:

Pleasure is a notion (a sensation) absent from traditional Yankee cuisine. Not pleasure but health, not correspondence between savors but the satisfaction of a need—these are its two values. One is physical and the other moral; both are associated with the idea of the body as work. Work in turn is a concept at once economic and spiritual: production and redemption. We are condemned to labor, and food restores the body after the pain and punishment of work. It is a real *reparation,* in both the physical and the moral sense. Through work the body pays its debt; by earning its physical sustenance, it also earns its spiritual recompense. Work redeems us and the sign of this redemption is food. An active sign in the spiritual economy of humanity, food restores the health of body and soul. If what we eat gives us physical and spiritual health, the exclusion of spices for moral and hygienic reasons is justified: They are the signs of desire, and they are difficult to digest.

—*Octavio Paz*

18b Use transitional devices to improve coherence.

18

On reading over your rough draft, you may find that, logical as your pattern is, the sentences do not flow from one to the next. Sentence A ends with a thump. Then sentence B starts up. And so on. Transitional devices can bridge the gaps. These devices connect the sentences and bind the paragraph into a single, coherent unit. The most common transitional devices are presented here.

Pronouns.   Since each pronoun must refer to an antecedent, a pronoun and its antecedent form a link. You can often make a paragraph cohere merely by using pronouns properly. On the other hand, incorrectly used pronouns can weaken coherence (see **51–53**). In the following examples, notice how pronouns in the second sentence of each pair provide coherence by referring to the important subjects in the first:

> *Self-help books* continue to proliferate. *They* appeal to the anxieties of our middle-aged society.

> *Patients* must fast for twelve hours before the test. *They* should also avoid red meats for seventy-two hours before coming in.

Repetition.   Substituting a pronoun for a noun is actually a kind of repetition. Direct repetition of a word or expression will give a similar effect:

> Exposure to too much sun can *damage* the skin. This *damage* is irreversible and can result in skin cancer.

Use direct repetition with care. Overdoing it will give an awkward, immature ring to your writing (*"Daily receipts* are taken to the central office. *Daily receipts* are then tallied . . ."). You can get much the same transitional effect by using synonyms or slightly altered forms of the repeated expressions:

> *George Bush* has been somewhat distant since leaving the White House. *The former President* has settled into a life of privacy.

18

Transitional terms. Transitional terms make a paragraph coherent by relating ideas. Like pronouns, many of these terms come to mind automatically, but you should carefully choose among them. Here is a partial list of common transitional terms:

1. *Time:* next, then, after, before, during, while, following, shortly, thereafter, later on, the next day, secondly, finally
2. *Place:* over, above, inside, to the left, just behind, beyond
3. *Contrast:* however, but, nevertheless, on the other hand, nonetheless, notwithstanding, on the contrary, conversely, yet
4. *Cause-effect:* so, therefore, thus, accordingly, consequently, as a result, hence, because of this
5. *Addition:* and, furthermore, moreover, likewise, similarly, in a like manner, too, also
6. *Emphasis:* indeed, in fact, especially, most important
7. *Summary:* in other words, in short, to sum up, in conclusion
8. *Example:* for instance, for example, that is, in particular

The following examples illustrate the use of transitional terms:

Indulgences developed from the medieval church's concept of penance as a substitute for

Time

punishment due to sin. *At first,* the penitent was required to make a pilgrimage or perform an act

Contrast

of charity. *But* such activities were only substitutes for the real punishment, and it was a simple step to make further substitutes for the original ones.

Example

For example, the sinner could make his penance by paying the cost of going on a pilgrimage rather than actually making a trip. In an age when travel was both expensive and dangerous,

Repetition

such a monetary substitution was sensible.

Effect

As a result, the sinner suffered financially, and the church could use his money for acts of charity.

Effect

Thus indulgences were born. The opportunities

Repetition

for abusing *this* practice of giving money in place

Contrast

of penance, *however,* were numerous.

Repetition

Indulgences were frequently criticized, and

Pronoun

Luther's famous attack on *them* was one among

Contrast

many. *Yet* the principle is sound and difficult to attack without undermining the entire theology of penance.

—*adapted from Donald J. Wilcox*

Sometimes it seems that Thomas Jefferson the

Example — man hardly exists for us. *That is, he* seems to be

Pronoun — mainly a symbol of what we as Americans are or

think we are. *He* appears almost to have been

invented so as to reveal something about

Emphasis — ourselves. *In fact,* no one else in our history

embodies so much of our democratic heritage

Contrast — and so many of our democratic hopes. *Yet* the

man himself has proved to be a fascinating,

complex character, the worthy subject of several

recent biographies.

18

Transitional sentences and paragraphs. Pronouns, repetition, and transitional terms can provide coherence within paragraphs and can even link two consecutive paragraphs, but to link two paragraphs that differ significantly in content, you occasionally will need a transitional sentence or even a short paragraph. If, for instance, you have devoted three or four paragraphs to the theories of one authority and are ready to shift to those of another, you will probably need a sentence to help the reader make the transition. For example: "However, a critic who approaches Shakespeare's plays differently is Maynard Mack, who. . . ."

If you have written three paragraphs on the ways in which your school district can provide better education for high school students and are now ready to shift to differing views on the subject, you might use a short transitional paragraph:

> However, several experts disagree with these conclusions and believe that the problem has been misinterpreted. As we will see, their views have one thing in common: parental responsibility.

Here are two versions of a student's paragraph. In the first, transitional devices are omitted. In the second, they have been inserted and italicized.

18

Less effective: There is no Nobel Prize for mathematics, and mathematicians rarely make the headlines. It is not a glamorous profession. There are no exotic, expensive pieces of equipment—no cyclotrons, body scanners, or electron microscopes—for the public to identify with. Research tools are plain. Pencil, paper, chalk, and a calculator are about all one needs. In a time when some scientists' names—Einstein, Jung, Freud, and others—have become household words, few people could name even one great modern mathematician. Mathematics is so basic to most scientific subjects that it has been called the language of all experimental dialogue.

More effective: There is no Nobel Prize for mathematics, and mathematicians rarely make the headlines. It is not a glamorous profession. *For example,* there are no exotic, expensive pieces of equipment—no cyclotrons, body scanners, or electron microscopes—for the public to identify with. *In fact,* research tools are plain. Pencil, paper, chalk, and a calculator are about all one needs. *And* in a time when some scientists' names—Einstein, Jung, Freud, and others—have become household words, few people could name even one great modern mathematician. *Yet* mathematics is so basic to most scientific subjects that it has been called the language of all experimental dialogue.

Note how the four transitional devices make explicit the connections between the ideas. The last transition—*yet*—clarifies the contrast between the final, climactic sentence and the preceding points.

dev

19 **Develop paragraphs fully.**

The main point of a paragraph must be clarified or supported if that paragraph is to be interesting and convincing. Effective development is quite different from "padding": think of development as growth and increasing depth, not as mere expansion. This section shows some of the various ways that writers, depending on their subject and purpose, develop effective paragraphs.

19

19a Examples

Including examples and details is one of the best ways to achieve good paragraph development. Examples provide readers with the specific information they need to understand the controlling idea. Merely asserting a point is never sufficient; each idea must be developed with facts and examples. Although too much detail is sometimes a problem, bad writing usually suffers from too little detail rather than too much. Short paragraphs often indicate lack of effort or thought.

In the following passage, notice how using the example of Japanese culture helps make the author's initial point concrete and convincing:

> Poetry provides an important outlet for expressing emotion. This is certainly true in Japan, where I lived as an exchange student for a year. In Japanese society, people are often reluctant to express their feelings directly, so poetry has become unusually popular. Millions of people write poetry regularly, buy best-selling books of poetry, and attend poetry meetings. Television programs have made some poets into national celebrities, and newspapers carry daily poetry columns on the front page. Nearly everyone, from the Emperor on down, enjoys the freedom and challenge of writing haiku and other forms of verse. Other arts that we think of as elite also flourish in Japan, but none as widely as poetry.
>
> —*Jason Clarke (student)*

In the following example, the weak paragraph is general, whereas the improved version is developed with specific illustrations:

19

Weak development: In many earlier cultures, salt was viewed not only as a preservative but also as a powerful religious and symbolic substance. Valued because it was essential to life, salt had such a symbolic significance that it came to represent health, virtue, and friendship. From biblical to medieval times, there are references to salt in many cultures. At the same time, this valuable substance contributed to a number of fascinating legends and superstitions.

Improved development: In many earlier cultures, salt was viewed not only as a preservative but also as a powerful religious and symbolic substance. Valued because it was essential to life, salt had such a symbolic significance that it came to represent health, virtue, and friendship. For example, Moses commanded the Israelites to sprinkle offerings of wheat with salt. And since covenants were usually made over a sacrificial meal, the expression "covenant of salt" was established. Arabs who shared bread and salt with guests were committed to protecting them, and the Persian expression "untrue to salt" means disloyal and ungrateful. This valuable substance also contributed to a number of superstitions. Some medieval Frenchmen said that the devil was often seen without a tail because courageous folk had once sprinkled it with salt. The devil was so agonized by the virtuous substance that he chewed his tail off.

19b   Comparison and Contrast

Comparison notes the similarities of two subjects; contrast notes the differences. Writers most often discuss both similarities and differences, following one of these two methods:

1. *Subject by subject* presents all the details of one side of the comparison or contrast first and then the details of the other side.

> Thomas Jefferson had an insatiable curiosity that made him a sort of Renaissance man. The third American president, author of the Declaration of Independence, and founder of the University of Virginia was also an architect, inventor, musician, and scholar of philology, meteorology, archeology, astronomy, chemistry, and anatomy, among other fields. The idea that such a man could master all knowledge and put it into practice was an invention of the Italian Renaissance, as seen in the career of Leon Battista Alberti, whose interests parallel Jefferson's. Alberti, also a self-confident innovator, studied languages, law, and mathematics and wrote treatises on painting, sculpture, and moving weights. In 1444, he wrote the first book on architecture since antiquity; a classical scholar, he was concerned with the practical application of his studies. His relaxations were the same as Jefferson's: music and horsemanship. Although Jefferson, unlike Alberti, was a politician and statesman, the similarities between the two men show that Jefferson's achievement owes much to the Italian Renaissance and its dream of the universal man.
>
> —*adapted from Kenneth Clark*

19

2. *Point by point* moves back and forth between the subjects, item by item:

> Generally, Americans who can be classed as liberals believe that government should be responsible for protecting the defenseless and for righting wrongs caused by inequities in wealth and privilege. However, conservatives believe that the government is an inefficient "protector" and causes more harm than good. Furthermore, they see large differences in wealth and privilege as part of the natural order. Liberals believe that

taxation of the wealthy is the logical method for government to finance its social programs, but conservatives, who disagree with liberals on both the cause of social problems and the possibility of fixing them, react angrily to having their incomes reduced by what they claim to be an ever-greedy federal government.

19c Definition

A definition explains the meaning of a word or concept by placing it into a general class and then supplying details that distinguish it from other items of the same class. Writers often expand upon historical definitions, using examples or comparison and contrast to distinguish one thing from another and thus provide a thorough explanation of an idea or term, as in this paragraph:

> The present debate over degrees of rape is nothing new: All through history, rapes have been divided between those that mattered and those that did not. For the first few thousand years, the only rape that was punished was the defiling of a virgin, and that was viewed as a property crime. A girl's virtue was a marketable asset, and so a rapist was often ordered to pay the victim's father the equivalent of her price on the marriage market. In early Babylonian and Hebrew societies, a married woman who was raped suffered the same fate as an adulteress—death by stoning or drowning. Under William the Conqueror, the penalty for raping a virgin was castration and loss of both eyes—unless the violated woman agreed to marry her attacker, as she was often pressured to do. "Stealing an heiress" became a perfectly conventional means of taking—literally—a wife.
>
> —*Nancy Gibbs*

19d Analogy

Writers use analogies to make comparisons of items that seem to have little in common. Analogies help make something that is unfamiliar or complex easier to understand, as in this example:

The South today might be compared to a man who has had a bad toothache for as long as he can remember. In fact, it has never occurred to him to imagine life without this constant pain. Then, suddenly, the pain disappears. At first, he doesn't know what has happened; then, realizing his good fortune, he enjoys his new, painless existence. But he soon discovers that he faces a new problem: what to do now that he no longer has the pain to worry about. In a similar way, Southerners have recently discovered that they are no longer obsessed with the problem of race that for so long was part of the very connotation of the word *South*.

—*adapted from Walker Percy*

19

19e Classification

Classification organizes material into categories to reveal the nature of each category. A writer might want to show the differences and relationships among the categories, as in explaining three types of instrumental music, or an author might outline several psychological theories before indicating which one she will discuss. In the following example, a student lists three reasons why student evaluations of faculty are biased:

Student evaluations of faculty are biased for several reasons. First, students' grade expectations influence their rating of an instructor. Those who are likely to receive a high grade will be more favorably disposed toward the instructor than those expecting low grades. A second area of bias is more subtle. It involves age, sex, and appearance. A study in the *Journal of Educational Psychology* found that unattractive, middle-aged female instructors and unattractive, elderly male instructors frequently received lower ratings than their younger, more attractive counterparts. Related to this is a third factor: that men generally are rated higher than women because of gender stereotyping that associates masculinity with success and authority. For these reasons alone, it is apparent that any effort to conduct student evaluations of faculty will be far from objective.

—*Cynthia Wilson (student)*

19

19f Cause and effect

Cause-and-effect paragraphs explain why something happened. They may proceed from cause to effects or may simply list the causes of an obvious effect. For example, a writer might explore the reasons for the stock market crash of 1929 without showing that the crash was disastrous. The following paragraph deals with some effects of the emergence of Adolph Hitler and Joseph Stalin, concentrating on the significance of those effects:

> Hitler and Stalin . . . were the makers of the world in which we have lived for the past forty-five years, and from which we are only now beginning to emerge. Without them, none of the slaughter that attended the Second World War, with the irreparable loss of forty million military and civilian lives, would have taken place; without them there would have been no divided Europe, no headlong dissolution of the European colonial empires, no cold war, no Korea and Vietnam; without them no debauching of the economies of great nations to support the burden of the nuclear arms race. It is easy enough to find, in the years that followed the First World War, general causes for the ills of European civilization, but its near destruction was the result of individual decisions, and the most baleful of these were made by Hitler and Stalin.
>
> —*Gordon A. Craig, "Above the Abyss"*

Writing Effective Sentences

Since the sentence is the primary means of expressing ideas, look carefully at each sentence you write to make sure that it is clear, emphatic, and mature. Chapter 8 focuses on correct grammatical patterns; this chapter focuses on effectiveness, describing ways to express your thoughts with skill and style.

The principal types of sentences (see also **84**) are as follows:

1. Simple sentence (one subject and one predicate)

I have never played tennis.

2. Compound sentence (two or more independent, or main, clauses)

I have never played tennis, but I hope to start taking lessons next year. (independent clauses joined by coordinating conjunction)

3. Complex sentence (one independent clause and at least one dependent, or subordinate, clause)

Although I have never played tennis, I hope to start taking lessons next year. (dependent clause + independent clause)

4. Compound-complex sentence (at least two independent clauses and one dependent clause)

Although I have never played tennis, I hope to start taking lessons next year; I really need the aerobic exercise that tennis provides. (dependent clause + two independent clauses)

Although I have never played tennis, I really need the exercise, so I hope to start taking lessons next year. (dependent clause + two independent clauses)

sub

20

 20   Use subordination to relate secondary details to main ideas and to improve choppy sentences.

Two or more ideas can be connected in a sentence by two means: *coordination* and *subordination*. Coordination gives the ideas equal grammatical emphasis; subordination presents one as the main idea and puts the other(s) in a dependent or deemphasized position relative to the main idea. Therefore, your sentence structure should depend upon the relationship you want to show between your ideas. Notice how the meaning subtly changes in the following sentences:

Two sentences: Comedians can make outrageous statements. They must make sure that no one takes the statements seriously.

Coordination: Comedians can make outrageous statements, but they must make sure that no one takes the statements seriously.

Subordination: Although comedians can make outrageous statements, they must make sure that no one takes the statements seriously.

Subordination: Comedians can make outrageous statements if they make sure that no one takes the statements seriously.

Subordination allows you to include a number of details in one sentence, some of which you need but do not want to emphasize. In this sentence, the emphasis is in the main clause, with the subordinate *(italicized)* elements adding additional information:

I started my car, *a white 1993 Buick with over 180,000 miles,* and drove to the lawyer's office, *which was not my favorite destination that summer.*

20

20a Use subordinate clauses to relate secondary details to your main idea.

Relative pronouns *(who, whom, which, that)* and subordinating conjunctions (such as *because, although,* and *since*—see others in the list below) introduce subordinate clauses and signal specific relationships between them and the main clause. Notice in the following examples how each subordinate clause has a different relationship to the main clause:

Effective: Antonio, *who* had slept for ten hours, still felt tired.

Effective: *Although* Antonio had slept for ten hours, he still felt tired.

Effective: *After* he had slept for ten hours, Antonio still felt tired.

Effective: *Because* Antonio had slept for only ten hours after working a double shift, he still felt tired.

The following list of subordinating conjunctions shows the variety of relationships that subordination can indicate:

Cause: since, because, if, so that, in order that
Contrast or concession: although, though, whereas, while

Time: when, whenever, as, before, since, after, as long as, once, until, while
Place: where, wherever
Condition: if, unless, whether, provided that, as long as
Manner: as, as though, as if, how
Similarity: as . . . as

Some subordinate clauses can be used in the same way as nouns (as subjects or objects):

Ms. Wallace argued *that command of a foreign language should be required for an advanced degree.* (clause as direct object)

Some subordinate clauses can also function as modifiers—as adjectives or adverbs. An adjective clause modifies (or qualifies) a noun or pronoun and most often begins with a relative pronoun:

Golf is a sport *that can reduce one to tears.* (The clause modifies *sport* and thus functions as an adjective.)

An adverb clause modifies a verb, adjective, adverb, verbal (such as a gerund or participle), or the rest of the sentence:

When Dr. Santiago speaks, people listen. (The clause modifies the verb *listen.*)

Be sure to place your main idea, the one you want to stress, in the independent clause. When possible, put the main clause last:

Since I started exercising, my health has improved.

Do not misplace the emphasis in a sentence by putting the main idea in a subordinate clause:

The American Medical Association issued a report *which warned that many doctors tend to ignore nutrition.*

Improved: According to an American Medical Association report, many doctors tend to ignore nutrition.

20b Use subordination to improve long, rambling sentences.

One mark of an inexperienced writer is frequent use of long, stringy sentences composed of a series of main clauses hooked together with *and* or some other coordinating conjunction. If you subordinate one or more clauses, you will usually make your meaning clearer and the sentence more readable:

Ineffective: Some business leaders are unhappy with the skills of the average entry-level applicant, *and* they argue that schools should better prepare students for the workplace *and* that college standards need to be raised in general.

Effective: Business leaders who are unhappy with the skills of the average entry-level applicant argue that schools should better prepare students for the workplace and that schools should raise their overall standards.

Ineffective: Ms. Zelinsky is a hard worker, *and* she is a good teacher, *and* she pushes her students to excel.

Effective: Ms. Zelinsky, who is a hard worker and a good teacher, pushes her students to excel.

Effective: Ms. Zelinsky, who pushes her students to excel, is a hard worker and a good teacher.

Ineffective: I watched the start of the movie and had the strange sense that I had seen it before, *and* I wondered if, in my haste, I had bought a ticket for the wrong film.

Effective: When I watched the start of the movie, I had the strange sense that I had seen it before, as if I had hastily bought a ticket for the wrong film.

20c Use subordination to improve a series of short, choppy sentences.

Numerous short, choppy sentences are another common sign of an inexperienced writer. Such sentences are awkward to

20

read and fail to show the relationships between their ideas. Notice in these examples how using subordination improves the short, choppy sentences:

Ineffective: Carl wanted a new truck very much. He took a second job. Then he went to his bank for a loan.

Effective: Carl wanted a new truck so much that he took a second job before he went to his bank for a loan.

Ineffective: Bettina expected to enjoy *The Remains of the Day.* She failed to understand it at first. Then she saw the movie.

Effective: Although she expected to enjoy *The Remains of the Day,* Bettina failed to understand it until she saw the movie.

20

20d   Avoid excessive subordination.

Although using subordination is a valuable strategy, too many subordinate structures in a sentence can make it awkward, monotonous, or even confusing:

Ineffective: Ms. Rivera works in Tropical Business Center, the new office park near Portside Mall on the south side of the interstate.

Improved: Ms. Rivera works in Tropical Business Center, the new office park near Portside Mall; TBC is on the south side of the interstate.

Ineffective: I caught a grayling, which is a kind of small salmon, which is found in Alaska and Canada.

Improved: I caught a grayling, the small salmon found in Alaska and Canada.

In these examples, notice how you can eliminate nonessential information (and wordiness) by deleting *which is, which are,* and so on at the beginning of a clause.

▼ EXERCISE

A. *Read the following sentences. Mark E for those that are effective and X for those needing less or more subordination.*

1. Feline leukemia is a deadly disease. It affects domestic cats. It is easily transmitted.

2. Mutual funds are becoming the most popular investment vehicle, and they are replacing individual stock purchases for investors and have a vast influence on the health of the stock market.

3. The realtor has bought a GIS system, which gives her an efficient way to pinpoint sites for new housing developments.

4. I did not finish my term paper, so I got an extension from my humanities instructor, so I'm off to the library.

5. The afternoon grew cold. Dusk was coming. Gloria sighed.

6. My friend Bobby is sick, and he could not accompany me to the races; I went with my friend Mario instead.

7. A national lottery has been debated for years, and its supporters believe that it would raise revenues and morale but that it would not cause problems for compulsive gamblers or open the door for organized crime.

8. At lunch I had a bacon cheeseburger, which is not real food but junk food, which is something that I'm trying to avoid.

9. Yuko specialized in the butterfly stroke, a style of swimming hard to master.

10. I find opera depressing. This is not because I have trouble following the story. It is because I have no appreciation for that style of singing.

B. *Rewrite the sentences that you marked X.*

20

C.   *In the following selection, a paragraph by a noted writer has been reduced to a series of short sentences. Combine as many of these as you think appropriate, using subordination whenever possible.*

Two summers ago I was camped alone in the Blue Ridge Mountains. They are in Virginia. I had hauled myself and gear up there to read. Among other things, I was going to read *The Day on Fire*. This is a novel by James Ullman. It is about Rimbaud. It made me want to be a writer when I was sixteen. I was hoping it would do it again. So I read every day. I was sitting under a tree by my tent. Warblers sang in the leaves overhead. Bristle worms trailed their inches over the twiggy dirt. The dirt was at my feet. I read every night by candlelight. Barred owls called in the forest. Pale moths seeking mates massed round my head. I was in the clearing. My light made a ring.

Compare your version with the original paragraph:

Two summers ago I was camped alone in the Blue Ridge Mountains of Virginia. I had hauled myself and gear up there to read, among other things, *The Day on Fire*, by James Ullman, a novel about Rimbaud that had made me want to be a writer when I was sixteen; I was hoping it would do it again. So I read every day sitting under a tree by my tent, while warblers sang in the leaves overhead and bristle worms trailed their inches over the twiggy dirt at my feet; and I read every night by candlelight, while barred owls called in the forest and pale moths seeking mates massed round my head in the clearing, where my light made a ring.

—*Annie Dillard*

co-ord

21 Use coordination to give equal emphasis to two or more points.

Two or more independent clauses may be joined by coordination to create one compound sentence that gives equal grammatical emphasis to each clause (see **48** and **83h**). A compound sentence is less choppy than two separate simple sentences that contain the same information. And compound sentences signal to the reader the similarity or equivalence of the material in the independent clauses.

Effective: Fame is temporary, but friends are permanent.

Effective: The horses entered the starting gate, and the crowd waited nervously.

Coordination implies an equal relationship between the clauses. If the content of one clause is more important than that of the other, subordinate the less important clause.

22

Ineffective: It was snowing, so we had to allow extra travel time.

Effective: Since it was snowing, we had to allow extra travel time.

comb

 22   Use coordination to combine sentences.

Parallel coordinate phrases can help you develop mature, expressive sentences. Instead of constructing separate sentences, skillful writers often combine and relate sentence elements so that a single sentence carries more weight.

You can add colorful or clarifying details to a sentence by adding modifiers to the subject, to the predicate, or to the sentence as a whole. You can add modifiers in front of the main clause to form a periodic sentence (see **23c**), or you can pile up modifiers after the main clause to avoid using a string of short, choppy sentences.

Ineffective: Computerized inventory systems have many uses. They allow businesses to monitor supplies.

Businesses can also make efficient purchases from wholesalers. Shoplifting will be reduced. Employees will be less likely to steal.

Effective: Computerized inventory systems have many uses, allowing businesses to monitor supplies, to make efficient purchases from wholesalers, and to combat shoplifting and employee theft.

Effective: By allowing businesses to monitor supplies, to make efficient purchases from wholesalers, and to combat shoplifting and employee theft, computerized inventory systems have many uses.

22

The repetition in sentences that all begin alike can be eliminated by creatively combining them into one richer, more complex sentence. However, too many modifiers can overload a sentence and make it hard to read; also, not every sentence need be developed in this way. But combining can be especially valuable in generating effective descriptive and narrative sentences.

Ineffective: Steven stands on the bridge. He drops pieces of wood upstream. He times how long it takes them to come out the other side and calculates the rate of flow.

Effective: Steven stands on the bridge, dropping pieces of wood upstream, timing how long it takes them to come out the other side, calculating the rate of flow.

—*Margaret Atwood*

1. *Noun phrases* can develop a sentence by vividly restating a noun in the main clause:

   Nancy bought a 1963 Corvette Stingray, a beautiful car that is a true collector's item.

2. *Verbal phrases* can provide details of the action, object, or scene mentioned in the main clause. In a narrative sentence, verbal phrases enable a writer to picture simultaneously all the separate actions that make up the action.

The following sentence is broken to distinguish the verbal phrases from the main clause that follows them:

Working more than eighty hours per week,
trying desperately to support her three small children,
  Terri somehow managed to stay ahead of the bill
  collectors.

3. *Absolute phrases,* like the indented phrases in the sentence below, can also add details to a single sentence, often by developing one aspect of the subject:

The waterfall loomed ahead,
  its rocks forbidding,
  its force tremendous,
  and its sound deafening.

Note that the use of coordinate modifiers requires parallelism (see **28**).

22

▼ EXERCISE

A. *Develop each of the following into one sentence, using coordinate noun, verb, or absolute phrases.*

1. The old man came to the door. His smile was kind. His voice was friendly.

2. The strip mall was abandoned. Its stores were boarded up. Its parking lot was covered with trash.

3. I once wanted to be a pirate. I saw myself standing in the wind on the bow of my ship. I dreamed of boarding the ships of the evil king's fleet and taking the plunder back to my island fortress.

4. Harry was seventeen when he got his first car. It was a fifteen-year-old sedan. Its doors would not lock. Its radio was broken.

5. My mother glared at the mess I had made. Her frown was severe. Her silence indicated that I was in real trouble this time.

B. *Combine the following groups of sentences, using whatever method works best, to form effective sentences.*

22

Ineffective: Jerry's room was a mess. The floor was littered with empty beer cans. The bed was piled high with dirty clothes. The desk was stacked with books.

Effective: Jerry's room was a mess, its floor littered with empty beer cans, its bed piled high with dirty clothes, and its desk stacked with books.

1. Some of the stranded travelers were quiet. They read or dozed in their seats. Others seemed angry. They talked about suing the airline.

2. The rain fell in sheets. It lashed the barn and the utility shed. The two buildings looked like the last survivors of some terrible weather war.

3. The movie took me to a place I had never been before. It was a place where technology was king. The people in the movie were the slaves of their machines.

4. Ann's cat is about five pounds above the average. It is a torteiseshell. It is mostly black. Its eyes are very green.

5. My grandfather's feed store was very small. It was in a cinder-block building. The floor was made of hard pine. The walls were covered with manufacturers' advertisements.

emp

 23 **Vary word order and sentence length for emphasis.**

23

Effective writing not only expresses ideas clearly and relates them to one another appropriately but also emphasizes the most important ideas. In addition, skillful writers vary the structure of their sentences to avoid relying on the same patterns.

23a Emphasize an important word by placing it at the beginning or end of the sentence.

The most emphatic position in most essays, paragraphs, or sentences is at the end. The next most emphatic position is at the beginning; therefore, you can emphasize key words by starting and ending sentences with them. Since semicolons operate much like periods, words immediately before and after semicolons also receive emphasis. Notice how altering the key words in the following examples improves the emphasis:

Ineffective:	All the villagers were killed, as Bob reported. (leaves the reader thinking about Bob, not about the tragedy)
Ineffective:	It was Bob who reported that all the villagers were killed. (empty words at the beginning of sentence)
Effective:	Bob reported that all the villagers were killed.

| Ineffective: | For us, time was brief and money was a problem. |
| Effective: | We had little time; we had little money. |

23b Use an occasional short sentence.

A very short sentence contrasting with longer sentences stops the flow and catches the reader's attention. You can also use a short sentence to emphasize an especially important point. Notice how effective the short sentences are in the following passages:

| Effective: | In the middle of a block of tasteful, quiet homes stood a two-story house with green paint and lavender trim, diamond-shaped windows, and gargoyles perched to strike. It was ghastly. |

| Effective: | If we read of one man robbed, or murdered, or killed by accident, or one house burned, or one vessel wrecked, or one steamboat blown up, or one cow run over on the Western Railroad, or one mad dog killed, or one lot of grasshoppers in the winter, we never need read of another. One is enough. |

—*Henry David Thoreau*

If you have written three or four long sentences, use a short one for variety. If you find that every sentence begins the same way, following the subject-verb-object pattern, for example, vary the word order and use subordination to express the relation among ideas.

| Weak: | People suffering from depression sometimes find it difficult to confront their problem. It is easier to let life slide by. But this medical condition will worsen if not treated. Depression requires prompt medical attention. |

| Improved: | Although people suffering from depression sometimes find it difficult to confront their problem, preferring to let life slide by, this medical condition will worsen if not treated. Depression requires prompt medical attention. |

23c   Use an occasional balanced or periodic sentence.

Most English sentences are *loose* or *cumulative* sentences—that is, the main clause comes first, followed by details supporting the main idea. The order is reversed in a *periodic* sentence, in which the main idea follows the subordinate details. Because it saves the most important idea for last and because it is less commonly used, the periodic sentence is more emphatic. However, do not overuse the periodic sentence; save it for those ideas you especially want to emphasize.

Loose: *The family farm is becoming an endangered species,* criticized by agricultural economists as inefficient, scorned by banks as a poor credit risk, and threatened by huge, multinational food producers.

Periodic: Criticized by agricultural economists as inefficient, scorned by banks as a poor credit risk, and threatened by huge, multinational food producers, *the family farm is becoming an endangered species.*

In a *balanced* sentence, coordinate structures are enough alike that the reader notices the similarity. You can use a balanced sentence to emphasize a comparison or contrast:

Balanced: Many of us resent shoddiness in cars, food, and services; few of us resent shoddiness in language.

Balanced: We expect our young children to obey us; we should not expect them to read our minds.

23d   Use a climactic word order.

By arranging a series of ideas in order of importance, you can gradually build emphasis:

Climactic: Like all great leaders, Lincoln was hated by many; like all strong presidents, he was embattled by Congress; and, like many heroes, he was popular only after death.

23e   Write primarily in the active voice.

In most active-voice sentences, the subject does something:

Vanessa → started → the car.

In passive-voice sentences, the subject receives the action of the verb:

The car ← was started ← by Vanessa.

The active voice is usually more direct, natural, and economical:

Passive: Great care should be exercised by anyone coaching youth sports.

Active: Anyone who coaches youth sports should exercise great care.

Passive: On May 7, a bill to establish permanent curfews for minors was introduced to the legislature by its sponsor, Representative Cooke. The issue at hand was discussed by legislators, and criticisms were offered by members from small towns and rural districts. It was suggested by Representative Blythe that the bill be sent back to committee. A vote on this motion was held, but a decision was not made due to an objection by Representative Cooke.

Active: On May 7, Representative Cooke, the sponsor of a bill to establish permanent curfews for minors, introduced the bill to the legislature. Legislators discussed the issue, and members from small towns and rural areas offered criticisms. Representative Blythe suggested that the bill be sent back to committee. The legislature voted on this motion but did not make a decision due to Representative Cooke's objection.

There are appropriate uses for the passive, as in these examples:

Passive: Franklin D. Roosevelt was elected to an unprecedented fourth term.

Passive: Jane Martin's article will be published next summer.

In each case, to rewrite the sentence in the active voice, the writer has to reconstruct the subject:

Active: American voters elected Franklin D. Roosevelt to an unprecedented fourth term.

Active: *Current Anthropology* will publish Jane Martin's article next summer.

If the writer is discussing Roosevelt or the article (or its author), not voters or *Current Anthropology,* the passive voice is more logical. But, in general, writing in the active voice is best. Passive-voice sentences tend to be artificial, wordy, and dull. They are less emphatic, especially when they obscure the doer of the action:

23

A tax increase was announced yesterday.

Passive-voice sentences can also lead to dangling modifiers (see **25f**):

To be a CPA, a college education and a state exam are needed.

By doing a few simple blood tests, the cause of the patient's illness can be isolated.

Finally, the passive is not an effective way to vary your style. Unnecessary shifts from active to passive can be distracting for the reader (see **58a**).

▼ EXERCISE

A. *Study the following sentences. Mark X for those that need rephrasing for emphasis, E for those that are effective.*

   1. It was suggested by Professor Cho that the biology curriculum needs to be revised.

2. Although not everyone agrees about the afterlife, many people claim not to fear death.

3. One of the most important battles of the American Revolution was fought at Saratoga, an upstate New York village now known for its horseracing season.

4. For the experiment to be successful, detailed procedures must be followed.

5. Women students today constitute roughly half of college populations, a large increase since 1930, when men predominated.

6. One possible effect of global warming is the loss of beaches, and the extinction of certain animal species is another.

7. In the first half of this century, African Americans were prohibited from playing Major League Baseball, but this ban was lifted in 1947.

8. Gas mileage is usually not improved by fuel additives, which are available at all auto parts stores.

9. Sam Snead was a great golfer, Jimmy Demaret was a good one, but Ben Hogan was outstanding.

10. Breathing large amounts of gasoline vapor may cause cancer, according to various studies.

B.   *Rephrase the sentences that you marked X.*

awk

 24   **Avoid awkward repetitions and omitted words.**

Awkward sentences are difficult to read. They may or may not be clear, but they always require extra effort and usually interrupt the flow of thought. In this section we discuss two common causes of awkwardness. But many awkward sentences do not fit into neat categories; they often result from the ineffective choice or arrangement of words, as described in this chapter and in Chapter 9. If awkwardness is a problem for you, try reading your sentences aloud: an awkward sentence usually does not *sound* right.

24a   Repeat words only for emphasis or transition.

Repeating a prominent word or expression can provide an effective transition between sentences or paragraphs (see **18b**). Occasional repetition of a key word can also emphasize an idea. But use repetition sparingly, for too much can create awkward sentences:

24

Awkward repetition:	A writer who writes about teenagers must be careful with slang.
Improved:	A writer who concentrates on teenagers must be careful with slang.
Effective repetition:	An external audit is valuable because it allows a company's managers to verify the firm's accounting procedures, to verify the firm's financial stability, and to verify the firm's perception by stockholders.
Effective repetition:	Cormac McCarthy's *The Crossing* is a great novel as well as a great read.

One especially confusing type of repetition is the use of two different senses of the same word in the same or adjoining sentences. Find a synonym for one instance of the word.

Awkward repetition:	No one knew the major reason for the major's sudden retirement.
Improved:	No one knew the principal reason for the major's sudden retirement.

24b Include all necessary words.

Many sentences are awkward because they use unnecessary words, but many others are awkward or confusing because they omit words. Below are some of the more common types of omissions:

Awkward omission:	I could see almost all the puppies were active and healthy. (*That* has been omitted after *see*. Omitting *that* will often produce a confusing and awkward sentence.)
Improved:	I could see that almost all the puppies were active and healthy.
Awkward omission:	The children were happy and talking freely. (*Were* has been omitted before *talking*. *Happy* and *talking* are not parallel.)
Improved:	The children were happy and were talking freely.
Awkward omission:	In her will, Mrs. Johnson left money to Myra Rhodes, a neighbor; Charles Johnson, her nephew; and Paula J. Stephens, her granddaughter. (*To* is omitted before *Charles Johnson* and *Paula J. Stephens*. Repeating the preposition shows the parallel elements more clearly.)
Improved:	In her will, Mrs. Johnson left money to Myra Rhodes, a neighbor; to Charles Johnson, her nephew; and to Paula J. Stephens, her granddaughter.

When you use two verbs that require different prepositions, be sure to include both prepositions:

Awkward omission:	Richard could neither comply nor agree to the proposal. (*With* has been omitted after *comply*.)

24

Improved: Richard could neither comply with nor agree to the proposal.

▼ EXERCISE

Mark X for sentences that are awkward and E for those that are effective. Rewrite the awkward sentences.

1. I felt my leg injury would keep me from training for the marathon.
2. Modern travelers frequently search and try to visit unspoiled destinations.
3. After the race, Lance was cold but talking a mile a minute.
4. For supper, we ate langostinos with wine as our beverage.
5. Dr. Hernandez is esteemed for her interest in her patients and her sense of them as individuals.
6. I delayed going to college so my brother won't have to.
7. The review board is willing to hear your demands and to comply with them, if at all possible.
8. The human rights team published a study that treated the plight of the refugees; the study focused on the refugees' treatment by the military at the border.
9. I advised my nephew to study, save his money, and to explore all available scholarship offers.
10. The governor could neither agree nor approve of the legislature's astounding proclamation.

24

mm dg

 Place all modifiers so that they clearly modify the intended word.

The meaning of English sentences depends largely on word order. If you move words and expressions around, you will often change what a sentence means:

> Nancy Ruiz recently published the poem she wrote.

> Nancy Ruiz published the poem she wrote recently.

The rule of thumb is to place modifiers as near as possible to the words that they modify.

25a   Place an adjective phrase or clause as near as possible to the noun or pronoun it modifies.

Single adjectives usually come immediately before the noun or pronoun they modify, adjective phrases and clauses immediately after. When other words come between an adjective and the word it modifies, the sentence may sound awkward, and its meaning may be obscured:

Misplaced: Vincent needed to see a doctor with a sprained ankle.

Improved: With a sprained ankle, Vincent needed to see a doctor.

Often you have to do more than move the modifier; you have to revise the whole sentence:

Misplaced: Unless completely anesthetized, surgeons cannot operate on cardiac patients.

Revised: Surgeons cannot operate on cardiac patients who have not been completely anesthetized.

Misplaced: The sick plant was placed in a new building, which needed all the help it could get.

Revised: The sick plant, which needed all the help it could get, was placed in a new building.

25b   Place a limiting adverb, such as *only* or *just,* immediately before the word it modifies.

In speech, most of us are casual about where we place adverbs such as *only, almost, hardly, just,* and *scarcely.* But writing should be more precise:

Misplaced: Tram almost completed all of her lab experiment.

Revised: Tram completed almost all of her lab experiment.

Notice how moving the modifier can change the meaning of a sentence:

I had five dollars only yesterday.

I only had five dollars yesterday.

I had only five dollars yesterday.

25c   Make certain that each adverb phrase or clause modifies the word or words you intend it to modify.

An adverb phrase or clause can appear at the beginning of a sentence, inside the sentence, or at its end:

After the awards ceremony, Irina Clarke found two new friends.

Irina Clarke, after the awards ceremony, found two new friends.

Irina Clarke found two new friends after the awards ceremony.

However, be careful that the adverb modifies only what you intend it to modify:

Misplaced:	A woman found dead behind a local bar was thought to be murdered by the city police.
Revised:	According to the city police, a woman found dead behind a local bar was thought to be murdered.
Misplaced:	On Tuesday, Michael swore that he was going to quit his job three times.
Improved:	On Tuesday, Michael swore three times that he was going to quit his job.

25d   Move ambiguous (squinting) modifiers.

If you find that you have placed a modifier so that it refers to more than one word, move it to avoid the ambiguity:

Ambiguous:	The woman who was asked the question sincerely considered her response.
Clear:	The woman who was asked the question considered her response sincerely. *Or:* The woman who was asked the sincere question considered her response.
Ambiguous:	The student whom Professor Walker answered shortly left the room.
Revised:	The student whom Professor Walker shortly answered left the room. *Or:* The student whom Professor Walker answered left the room shortly.

25e   Avoid awkwardly split infinitives.

Conventional usage avoids inserting an adverb between *to*—called the sign of the infinitive—and its verb form (for example, *to quickly run*). In some instances, splitting the infinitive is natural; many writers would prefer the following sentence to an alternative: "To suddenly stop accepting discount coupons might upset our customers." But the following example is awkward:

The veterinarian proposed *to,* if Ms. Jones agreed, *postpone* the dog's surgery until August.

Revised: The veterinarian proposed to postpone the dog's surgery until August, if Ms. Jones agreed.

25f   Make certain that introductory verbal phrases relate clearly to the subject of the sentence.

Modifiers are said to *dangle* when they do not logically modify a word or expression in the sentence. Most often, a *dangling modifier* does not correctly refer to the subject of the sentence:

Dangling: Driving to the old house, my left ear started to hurt.

25

In this sentence, the reader will mistakenly assume that the subject of the sentence *(ear)* is also the understood subject of the verbal *(driving)*. The result is absurd: Did the ear drive? The writer should have written the following:

Improved: *While I was* driving to the old house, my left ear started to hurt.

The improved sentence illustrates one way of correcting a dangling modifier: supply the necessary words to make the phrase into a complete dependent clause. It is relatively easy to supply missing words when the dangling modifier is an *elliptical phrase* (a predicate with the subject and part of the verb implied but not expressed):

Dangling: While watching the movie, their car was stolen.

Corrected: While *they* were watching the movie, their car was stolen.

At other times, the best way to correct a dangling modifier may be to revise the independent clause, as in the following examples:

| Dangling: | *Driving recklessly,* Allen's Miata crashed into a city bus. (dangling participial phrase) |
| Corrected: | Driving recklessly, Allen crashed his Miata into a city bus. |

| Dangling: | *To prosper,* a great deal of hard work and luck are needed. (dangling infinitive) |
| Corrected: | To prosper, one needs a great deal of hard work and luck. |

These examples illustrate two common causes of dangling modifiers. In the first sentence, the word that the phrase is intended to modify is not the subject of the sentence but a possessive modifying the subject *(Allen's).* In the second sentence, the independent clause is in the passive voice (see **23e**). Note that the revisions are both logical and more direct.

Some verbal phrases (called *absolute constructions*) refer not to a single word but to the whole idea of a sentence; hence, they do not dangle.

| Acceptable: | *Generally speaking,* most families have problems. |

| Acceptable: | *Considering the cost of gasoline,* the bus fare looks quite reasonable. |

25g   Be certain that concluding clauses and phrases modify the word intended.

| Illogical: | Anthony Hopkins won an Oscar for *The Silence of the Lambs,* his greatest role. (Was the movie his role?) |
| Corrected: | Anthony Hopkins won an Oscar for his greatest role, Hannibal Lecter, in *The Silence of the Lambs.* |

▼ EXERCISE

Rewrite the following sentences, correcting any dangling or misplaced modifiers.

1. Without money or prospects, Jonathan's future was dim.

2. While swimming in the mist of happy memories, my finger started to twitch.

3. She is only happy when she establishes a clear schedule for a project.

4. Jeremy nearly finished the race in 23 seconds, a school record.

5. Be it stupid or sublime, a reader should be able to experience a story's conclusion without having to wait for the next issue of the magazine.

6. I considered what Mr. Perkins had told me carefully .

7. To succeed at golf, a good grip is required.

8. Peering into the future, trouble was expected.

9. Yesterday, Roberta only worked three hours.

10. Considering all the time and expense that went into decorating the Christmas tree, the results are disappointing.

25

pred

26 Make subject and predicate relate logically to each other.

As a main verb, *be* links a subject with a complement: "The *piano is* an old *Steinway*; The *news is good*." A common error called *faulty predication* occurs when the subject and complement cannot be logically joined:

> **Faulty:** His job was a reporter for the *Sun Times*.
>
> **Correct:** He worked as a reporter for the *Sun Times*. (he = reporter)
>
> **Faulty:** The art competition is a chance to prove what a painter can do.
>
> **Correct:** The art competition provides a chance to prove what a painter can do. *Or:* The art competition is an event that proves what a painter can do. (art competition = event)

In general, avoid following a form of *be* with adverb clauses beginning with *where, when,* and *because:*

> **Faulty:** Someone said that diplomacy is when one lies gracefully for his country.
>
> **Correct:** Someone said that diplomacy is lying gracefully for one's country.
>
> **Faulty:** The reason I got a new CD player was because my old one was stolen.
>
> **Correct:** The reason I got a new CD player was that my old one was stolen.

Faulty predication can occur with verbs other than *be* whenever the subject and predicate do not fit together logically:

> **Faulty:** Neglected children must be dealt with severely.
>
> **Correct:** Child neglect must be dealt with severely.

▼ EXERCISE

A. *Mark E for those sentences in which the subject and complement are compatible, X for those with faulty predication.*

1. A malfunctioning computer is a ghastly experience for a writer working on deadline.

2. Atlanta is where the 1996 Summer Olympics were held.

3. The city was a mob of athletes, media figures, and spectators.

4. September was when the city got back to normal.

5. Justin's new executive position is much better compensated than was his old one.

6. Exceeding the posted speed limit is the most common criminal violation in the United States.

7. The reason is because motorists believe these restrictions to be absurd.

8. Actual battle conditions are when the military can evaluate a soldier's ability.

9. However, virtual reality offers one way to test a soldier prior to military conflict.

10. A good detective novel is an evening well spent.

B. *Reword the sentences that you marked X.*

26

comp

27 Compare only things that are logically comparable.

A common fault involves comparing a characteristic of one thing with another thing instead of with its corresponding characteristic:

Faulty: Disney's theme parks are visited by more people than any other company. (comparing *parks* to *company*)

Correct: Disney's theme parks are visited by more people than *those of* any other company.

Faulty: A technician's income is generally lower than a scientist. (*income* compared to *scientist*)

Correct: A technician's income is generally lower than a scientist*'s*. *Or:* A technician's income is generally lower than *that of* a scientist.

Many comparisons are faulty because the word *other* has been omitted:

Faulty: Miranda is smarter than any child in her class.

Correct: Miranda is smarter than any *other* child in her class.

Many faulty comparisons are ambiguous:

Faulty: Tim likes Amy much more than George. (Who likes whom?)

Correct: Tim likes Amy much more than George does. *Or:* Tim likes Amy much more than he likes George.

Faulty: Pensacola is farther from Chicago than Miami.

Correct: Pensacola is farther from Chicago than it is from Miami.

Many comparisons are incomplete because words such as *that* and *as* are omitted.

Faulty:	Reggae is as good if not better than other types of popular music.
Correct:	Reggae is as good *as,* if not better than, other types of popular music. *Or:* Reggae is as good *as* other types of popular music, if not better.
Faulty:	The poetic style of Vaughan is much like Traherne.
Correct:	The poetic style of Vaughan is much like *that* of Traherne. *Or:* . . . is much like Traherne's.

27

▼ EXERCISE

A. *Mark E for those sentences with effective comparisons and X for those with ineffective comparisons.*

1. On one dismal Saturday, my golf score was higher than any golfer's in the tournament.

2. Bobby loves pork chops more than his wife.

3. Plagiarism is as serious if not more so than any other problem involving academic integrity.

4. Technically, failure to yield the right-of-way causes more accidents than speeding does.

5. Cats have an easier life than any animal on the planet.

6. The baseball cap is more common in the United States than any other type of hat.

7. The swimmer's graceful stroke was like a swan.

8. Ed could never tell Karen's voice from Anne.

9. The traffic flow is better this summer than it has been for years.

10. I am much colder than yesterday.

B. *Reword the sentences that you marked X.*

comp

28 **Use parallel structures effectively.**

When you express two or more ideas that are equal in emphasis, use parallel grammatical structures: nouns with nouns, infinitives with infinitives, adverb clauses with adverb clauses. Parallel structures clearly and emphatically indicate parallel ideas.

Effective: The old man was haunted by his past, tortured by his failures, confused by his successes, and terrified by his future. (verb phrases)

Effective: It is better, Hippocrates said, for a doctor to do nothing than to do harm to the patient. (infinitive phrases)

Effective: Because of its acute hearing, because of its playful imagination, and most of all because of its amazing intelligence, the porpoise is a rare creature of the sea. (introductory phrases)

28a   In parallel structures, use equal grammatical constructions.

A common error among inexperienced writers is faulty parallelism—treating unlike grammatical structures as if they were parallel. This practice upsets the balance that the reader expects in a coordinate structure. Below are some of the more common types of faulty parallelism:

Faulty: Albert has two great ambitions: running a business and to become a millionaire.

Correct: Albert has two great ambitions: running a business and becoming a millionaire. *Or:* . . . to run a business and to become a millionaire.

Faulty: Andrea is intelligent, charming, and knows how to dress.

Correct: Andrea is intelligent, charming, and well dressed.

28b   Repeat necessary words to make parallels clear to the reader.

28

Awkward, confusing sentences often result if you do not repeat needed prepositions, signs of infinitives *(to),* auxiliary verbs, or other words needed to make a parallel clear:

Faulty: North Carolina is well-known for its beautiful mountains, found in the western region of the state, and its beaches, rivers, and farms.

Correct: North Carolina is well-known for its beautiful mountains, found in the western region of the state, and *for* its beaches, rivers, and farms.

Faulty: I told my daughter that she should be more realistic and driving two more miles to work would not be a huge problem.

Correct: I told my daughter that she should be more realistic and *that* driving two more miles to work would not be a huge problem.

28c   Always use parallel structures with correlative conjunctions such as *both . . . and* or *neither . . . nor.*

Correlative conjunctions can join two closely related ideas, but both ideas should be in the same grammatical form. The most common correlatives are *both . . . and, either . . . or, not only . . . but also, niether . . . nor, whether . . . or.*

Faulty:	Jack Nicklaus is well respected both for his outstanding career in golf and as a shrewd businessperson.
Correct:	Jack Nicklaus is well respected both for his outstanding career in golf and for his shrewd business sense.
Faulty:	He is admired not only by those who recognize his amazing athletic skills, but also financial analysts applaud his new career.
Correct:	He is admired not only by those who recognize his athletic skills but also by financial analysts, who applaud his new career.

28

▼ EXERCISE

A. *Mark with E those sentences that are effective and with X those containing faulty parallelism.*

1. I have three desires: to succeed, to marry, and have children.

2. To follow the letter of the law is not the same as following the spirit of the law.

3. "Son, you need to decide whether to fish or to cut bait," said my father.

4. Driving into the sun can lead to fatigue, headaches, and is irritating.

5. The summer camp for children is safe, convenient, and to the benefit of working mothers.

6. Most people enjoy having a meal cooked for them, their food served, and someone to clean up the aftermath.

7. In my first year with the company, I received many financial bonuses and several new clients for the firm.

8. The students of this campus should be opposed to and protest this blatant disregard for their freedoms.

9. Ellen wants to be a teacher and develop her skills as a consultant.

10. The new car that I want is beautiful, fast, but costs an arm and a leg.

B. *Reword the sentences that you marked X.*

28

P A R T

Editing Your Writing

Editing for Punctuation and Mechanics

Punctuation marks represent much of the information we transmit in speaking when we pause and raise or lower our voices—information such as where a sentence ends and whether the sentence is a question or a statement. Punctuation marks also signal things that we cannot communicate easily in speech, such as quoting someone directly. Although we can often "hear" when we need a punctuation mark, such as when we hear where we need commas in this sentence, we cannot always tell which mark to use. The only sure way to punctuate correctly is to know the conventions.

29 Use commas to separate certain elements of a sentence.

The comma is the most widely used—and misused—mark of punctuation. One of its most common uses is to separate clauses and phrases, as in these patterns: (1) commas used with coordinating conjunctions to form compound sentences, (2) commas used after introductory elements, (3) commas used to separate items in a series, and (4) commas used to separate coordinate adjectives.

29a Place a comma before a coordinating conjunction joining two independent clauses.

Use a comma before a coordinating conjunction (*and, but, or, nor, for, yet,* or *so*) when it joins two independent clauses to form a compound sentence. A comma without a coordinating conjunction between independent clauses is not enough and will cause a major error (see comma splice, **49**).

Incorrect: The taxation mechanisms of the United States are unjust but none of the proposed alternatives seem much better.

Correct: The taxation mechanisms of the United States are unjust, but none of the proposed alternatives seem much better.

Incorrect: Jack read innumerable warnings about smoking so he gave up reading.

Correct: Jack read innumerable warnings about smoking, so he gave up reading.

Be careful with *so* as a connector:

Incorrect: I took another job, so my wife could finish her degree.

Correct: I took another job so [that] my wife could finish her degree.

As mentioned in Chapter 6, the subordinator *that* is frequently left out of sentences. The incorrect sentence above is a good example of a problem that can result from this habit. The sentence *looks* like a compound, but in reality it is made up of an independent clause followed by a dependent clause.

If the clauses are very short and closely related, you may omit the comma, but it is generally safer to include it. (Why take chances?)

Acceptable: It is dark and I am alone.

Better: It is dark, and I am alone.

Note the difference between a compound sentence (one with two independent clauses) and a sentence containing a compound predicate (double verb):

Correct: Ms. Faul *graded* the tests and *entered* the scores in her database.

Correct: Ministers *write* and *preach* many sermons each year.

In each of these sentences, no comma is used before *and* since it does not join two independent clauses.

29b   Place a comma after an introductory dependent clause or a long introductory phrase.

29

A dependent clause resembles an independent clause in that it has a subject and a verb. However, an introductory dependent clause always begins with a subordinating conjunction (*although, because, since, while, after,* for example—see the list on page 362). Written alone, a dependent clause is a sentence fragment (see **48**); it is properly used in conjunction with an independent clause. A phrase, on the other hand, is missing a subject, a verb, or both.

Incorrect: Although murder is seen as a crime this prohibition is largely voided during military combat.

Correct: Although murder is seen as a crime, this prohibition is largely voided during military combat.
(introductory dependent clause—requires comma)

Incorrect: When the statistics instructor refused to mark the tests on a curve the students became indignant.

Correct: When the statistics instructor refused to mark the tests on a curve, the students became indignant.
(introductory dependent clause—requires comma)

Incorrect: Fighting hard against the crashing waves and shifting currents the small boat barely managed to avoid capsizing.

Correct: Fighting hard against the crashing waves and shifting currents **,** the small boat barely managed to avoid capsizing. (long introductory phrase—requires comma)

Incorrect: Although it was hard to believe the story was true. (dependent clause incorrectly used as sentence fragment)

Correct: Although it was hard to believe **,** the story was true.

Commas are optional after brief introductory phrases. However, including the comma is a more conservative approach, and if there is any possibility of confusing the reader, use the comma. Also, always include a comma after an introductory element that comes before an imperative.

Acceptable: After this month all my bills will be paid.

Better: After this month **,** all my bills will be paid.

Acceptable: In 1989 the Berlin Wall became an anachronism.

Better: In 1989 **,** the Berlin Wall became an anachronism.

Comma needed: In 1995 **,** 438 new employees joined our corporation.

Comma needed: After today **,** start parking your car in its assigned place.

There is usually no need for a comma when an adverb clause *follows* the independent clause:

No comma: He walked as if he owned the whole town.

A comma is needed before clauses that follow the independent clause and add a contrasting idea or are loosely connected to the independent clause:

Comma needed: Mr. Walker decided to apply for the programming position, although he had not touched a computer in two years.

Comma needed: An animal's habitat is the area in which that animal lives, whereas an ecosystem is made up of many habitats.

29c Place commas between items in a series.

Place a comma after each item except the last one in a series of words, phrases, or clauses unless all the items are joined by conjunctions. In a series with the last two items joined by a conjunction (a, b, *and* c), make sure that you place a comma before the conjunction to prevent a possible misreading. Some writers omit this comma, but the safer practice is to use it.

29

Incorrect: My father's pickles are made from a combination of cucumbers vinegar and dill.

Correct: My father's pickles are made from a combination of cucumbers, vinegar, and dill.

Incorrect: In mountainous areas, hikers should dress carefully plan an exact route and let friends know how long the excursion will take.

Correct: In mountainous areas, hikers should dress carefully, plan an exact route, and let friends know how long the excursion will take.

Incorrect: Consider the feeding habits of the following mammals: bears wolves wildcats rabbits foxes and cats and dogs.

Correct: Consider the feeding habits of the following mammals: bears, wolves, wildcats, rabbits, foxes, and cats and dogs. (Since the *and* before *cats* makes *cats and dogs* a single item, no comma is placed after *cats*.)

29d   Use commas to separate coordinate adjectives.

Coordinate adjectives modify a noun equally:

long, windy speech   cold, dark, muddy waters

You can check for coordinate adjectives by placing *and* between them or by reversing their order:

long and windy speech   muddy, dark, cold waters

Do not place commas between cumulative adjectives, those in which one adjective modifies the rest of the expression:

severe economic difficulties

In the above example, *severe* modifies not just *difficulties* but *economic difficulties. And* could not be inserted between *severe* and *economic,* nor could the adjectives be reversed. Therefore, no comma is used.

Incorrect: One of the dusty, battered, antique violins sold for $23,000.

Correct: One of the dusty, battered antique violins sold for $23,000.

Incorrect: We replaced our old, food processor.

Correct: We replaced our old food processor.

▼ EXERCISE

Delete unnecessary commas and add commas where necessary in the following sentences. If the sentence is correct, mark it C.

1. Maria Rodriguez was born in Puerto Rico but she moved to Atlanta with her family.

2. Maria liked Atlanta very much but her family moved to Florida when she was nine.

3. Although Maria spoke only Spanish before the move, she learned English very quickly.

4. There were many Hispanic American children in Maria's new school so she felt comfortable there.

5. Even though Eastwood Elementary was small it was well funded and carefully managed.

6. In fourth grade, Maria was taught by Ms. Karnes Mr. Rivera and Mrs. Ogletree.

7. Because Maria made very high grades in her first year at Eastwood Elementary the principal asked her parents about allowing Maria to go directly to sixth grade.

8. Despite the fact that Mr. Rodriguez thought that the idea was a good one his wife convinced him that Maria was better off staying in class with her friends.

9. Maria's mother was concerned that Maria would have been anxious about skipping a year that she still needed to adjust to the area and that she would have been a year younger than most of her classmates.

10. Maria was happy, and proceeded to do even better in fifth grade.

29

30 ▼ Use commas to set interrupting elements apart from the rest of the sentence.

Commas are also used to set apart groups of words that interrupt the normal flow of a sentence. Four such interrupters are especially common: (1) nonrestrictive modifiers, (2) nonrestrictive appositives, (3) parenthetical expressions, and (4) transitional adverbs or phrases.

30a Use commas to separate a nonrestrictive modifier from the rest of the sentence.

A **restrictive modifier** defines or restricts the noun or pronoun that it modifies. For example, the noun *candidate* can refer to any of those people seeking office, but *candidate who supports higher taxes* refers to someone from a much more limited group. In the sentence "A candidate who supports higher taxes cannot get elected in this state," the modifier *(who supports higher taxes)* is needed to limit the noun *(candidate)* so that it refers to someone in the smaller group. If the modifier is removed, the sentence is no longer accurate: "A candidate cannot get elected in this state."

A **nonrestrictive modifier,** on the other hand, is not needed to restrict the noun or pronoun it modifies: "Phil Spender, *who supports higher taxes,* cannot get elected in this state." Here the subject already refers to just one person, so the modifier simply adds information. Thus, the modifier is nonrestrictive.

Enclose a nonrestrictive modifier in commas:

Incorrect: My father who was born in Alabama retired in California.

Correct: My father, who was born in Alabama, retired in California.

Do not set off a restrictive modifier with commas:

Incorrect: Children, who are hyperactive, should be examined regularly by a pediatrician.

Correct: Children who are hyperactive should be examined regularly by a pediatrician.

Incorrect: Stores, which have electronic checkpoints at exits, have noticed a decrease in shoplifting.

Correct: Stores that have electronic checkpoints at exits have noticed a decrease in shoplifting. (restrictive)

Correct: O'Brien Stores, which have electronic checkpoints at exits, have noticed a decrease in shoplifting. (nonrestrictive)

The pronoun *that* is normally used to begin restrictive modifiers, and *which* is used to introduce nonrestrictive modifiers. (If the subject is a person or people, *who* is used, whether the modifier is restrictive or nonrestrictive.) The usage of *that* and *which* can cause problems; in Standard English, *which* can replace *that* in a restrictive context:

Correct: The car *that* is at the end of the parking lot is mine.

Correct: The car *which* is at the end of the parking lot is mine.

However, *that* cannot replace *which* in a nonrestrictive context:

Incorrect: My apartment, *that* is located at the corner of Vine and Illinois, is being renovated.

Correct: My apartment, *which* is located at the corner of Vine and Illinois, is being renovated.

As much as possible, avoid using *which* to introduce a restrictive modifier. Your decisions about punctuation will be made easier.

It is often difficult to determine whether a modifier is restrictive or nonrestrictive. Study the sentence both with and without the modifier. If the meanings are substantially different, the expression is restrictive and no commas are needed.

30

Correct: The exam for a driver's license is a traumatic experience for many people who have severe vision problems.

Note: Be careful to place a comma at both ends of a non-restrictive element (unless, of course, the element ends the sentence).

30b Use commas to separate a nonrestrictive appositive from the rest of the sentence.

An appositive is a noun or a noun phrase that restates, explains, or supplements a preceding noun:

The newcomer, *a friend of Rita,* is from Montreal.

Most appositives are nonrestrictive (see **30a**) and can be deleted from the sentence without changing its meaning. Enclose them in commas:

Incorrect: Flannery O'Connor the great American writer who lived in Georgia died at age thirty-nine in 1964.

Correct: Flannery O'Connor, the great American writer who lived in Georgia, died at age thirty-nine in 1964.

Incorrect: When I need to relax, I turn on Lyle Lovett my favorite singer.

Correct: When I need to relax, I turn on Lyle Lovett, my favorite singer.

A restrictive appositive, like a restrictive modifier, is essential to the meaning of the sentence and so should not be set off with commas:

Correct: My sister *Karen* always avoids laughing at children's errors.

In this sentence, the writer is a person with more than one sister. If, however, the writer had only one sister, the appositive would be nonrestrictive and would require commas:

Correct: My sister, *Karen,* always avoids laughing at
             children's errors.

30c   Use commas to separate a parenthetical element from the rest of the sentence.

Parenthetical elements are words, phrases, or clauses inserted into a sentence to clarify or emphasize a point or to give extra information. They interrupt the basic sentence structure, so they should be set off with commas:

Correct: My husband, as I had predicted, hated the shirt I
             bought him for Christmas.

Correct: Reckless driving, of course, is something to be feared.

Correct: A vast number of exhibits, large and small, will be
             featured in the Exposition Building.

Use commas to set off nouns that name the reader or listener in direct address:

Correct: We've already gone over that, Bob.

Correct: Charles, Anne, and Sara, please see me after class.

Use commas, too, for mild interjections:

Correct: Well, I guess I have no choice in the matter.

Commas also prevent misreadings:

Incorrect: From forty five were selected.

Correct: From forty, five were selected.

30d   Use commas to set off conjunctive adverbs and transitional expressions.

Words such as *however, moreover,* and *nevertheless* and phrases such as *for instance* and *on the other hand* are of-

ten used as parenthetical expressions to provide transition between independent clauses, sentences, or paragraphs. (See the lists on page 360.) Set them off with commas:

Correct: Hemingway's Americans sound more like Hemingway
than Americans; *on the other hand,* they could not be
anything other than Hemingway Americans.

Correct: *Therefore,* many readers find Hemingway's style
American in a special way.

If the transitional word or phrase appears within the independent clause, use a pair of commas:

Correct: Many viewers, *for example,* object to the lack of
character development in action films.

30

▼ EXERCISE

*Delete any unneeded commas in the following sentences, and add
commas where needed. If a sentence is correct, mark it C.*

1. One class Maria found difficult however was physical
   education.

2. Children like Maria who was small for her age are likely
   to find physical competition to be difficult.

3. Maria, who would undergo a growth spurt two years
   later, tried to be patient.

4. On the other hand the hour-long gym class seemed to
   take forever.

5. Everything Mrs. Rodriguez said will work out for the
   best.

6. Most children, at that age, hate mathematics.

7. Maria, however, found math intriguing.

8. Maria's best friend April stated that if math were to disappear, the world would be a better place.

9. Math, biology, and English April believed were ridiculously difficult.

10. Young students, who develop an aversion to one or more subjects, are likely to carry that aversion throughout their academic career.

31 Use commas in numbers, addresses, titles, and quotations.

Separate the day of the month from the year with commas:

October 24**,** 1957   December 23**,** 1996

When only a month and year are given, the comma is not used:

February 1941

The inverted form (for example, *1 December 1996*) also requires no commas.

Commas separate numbers into thousands, millions, and so on:

3**,**916   4**,**816**,**317**,**212

Within sentences (not on envelopes), items in addresses are separated by commas. Notice that no comma appears between the state name and the Zip code:

Toledo, Ohio

400 7th Street, New Kensington, PA 15068

121 87th Street, Brooklyn, NY 11209

In sentences, the final item of an address or a date is also followed by a comma:

Working in Phoenix, Arizona, has many compensations.

March 12, 1972, was a day he never forgot.

Use commas to separate titles and degrees from proper names:

Jane B. Nelson, Ed.D.

Joseph Hernandez, M.D.

Stephanie Pew, Ph.D., C.D.P., C.D.E.

Albert M. Johnston, Jr., took over as chief clerk.

Exception: Michael Raleigh III is our family attorney.

Use commas to introduce direct quotations and to separate quoted material from the rest of the sentence:

Dr. Guber asked, "When is her test scheduled?"

"I'm not sure," I answered, "that I really know."

Use commas to set off expressions such as *he said* and *she replied:*

He said, "I pull habits out of rats."

"No, you don't," she replied.

"The future," she wrote, "is just the past getting younger."

If the original quotation ends with a period, change the period to a comma when the quotation is followed by non-quoted material. In all cases, place the comma *inside* the quotation marks. Omit the comma if the quotation ends with an exclamation point or question mark:

"Do you want to register?" *[no comma]* Ms. LaPorte asked.

▼ EXERCISE

Supply needed commas in the following sentences. If a sentence is correct, mark it C.

1. The principal of Maria's new middle school located in Clickville was Lionel Jones M.Ed.

2. Maria started seventh grade on August 23 1988.

3. When Maria first saw the school, she said, "What a dump," even though she eventually came to like it.

4. Mrs. Rodriguez, not happy to hear Maria's comment, said "I hope you're not developing an attitude."

5. Andrea Walsh, Maria's biology teacher was born in Minneapolis, Minnesota on July 7 1951 and moved to Clickville Florida on August 3 1978.

6. After the first biology class, Maria said "Ms. Walsh is the coolest old person I've ever met."

7. On February 5, 1989, Ms. Walsh took her biology class on a field trip to the Reynolds Wildlife Preserve in Gidneyville, a nearby town.

31

8. February 1989 was a month Maria would remember.

9. Her father was promoted on 17 February.

10. Mr. Rodriguez's new contract started on March 1 1989, and continued through February 28 1991.

no ,

32   Omit all unnecessary commas.

Unnecessary commas will make your reader pause needlessly or look for connections that are not there. Use a comma only when any of the guidelines above calls for one or when you are certain that a comma is necessary to prevent misreading.

Do not use a comma to separate a subject from its verb:

Incorrect: The cholesterol problem caused by eating too many eggs, involves the yolk more than the white.

Correct: The cholesterol problem caused by eating too many eggs involves the yolk more than the white.

Do not use a comma to separate a verb from its object:

Incorrect: Ed always believed, that the weather was a farmer's enemy.

Correct: Ed always believed that the weather was a farmer's enemy.

Do not use a comma before a coordinating conjunction except when the conjunction precedes the last item in a series or joins two independent clauses:

Incorrect: Walking through the park, and lying in the shade of the water oaks are some of my favorite leisure activities.

Correct: Walking through the park and lying in the shade of the water oaks are some of my favorite leisure activities.

Do not separate a restrictive modifier from the rest of the sentence (see **30a**):

Incorrect: The two bills**,** that had the greatest popular support**,** failed in the Senate.

Correct: The two bills that had the greatest popular support failed in the Senate.

Do not use a comma before the first item or after the last item of a series:

Incorrect: History, language, and culture**,** are prized elements of all cultures.

Correct: History, language, and culture are prized elements of all cultures.

32

▼ EXERCISE

Delete any unnecessary commas in the following sentences. If a sentence is correct, mark it C.

1. Initially, Maria said, that she didn't like middle school.

2. Her mother pointed out that you can't always judge a book, by its cover.

3. This is especially true, Mrs. Rodriguez pointed out, in terms of schools.

4. Mr. Rodriguez had just finished reading an article titled, "School Funding Problems in the Eighties."

5. Then he read a book, about the same subject, titled *Public Schools and Their Trauma*.

6. Mrs. Rodriguez, likes to say, that schools are a hundred times more important than sports stadiums.

7. Mr. Rodriguez both knows, and respects her beliefs.

8. Schools, that were built before 1970, have aged badly.

9. The problem of funding new schools, was debated at a public meeting in Click County.

10. Dr. Edwina Wallace, superintendent of schools, said, new state funds, and matching federal funds, were essential to the funding issue.

33

33   Use periods after statements or commands and in abbreviations and decimals.

The period ranks second to the comma as the most common mark of punctuation. It is one of the easiest to use properly, serving three basic functions: to end sentences, to end abbreviations, and to separate decimals.

33a   Use a period after a sentence that is not a direct question or an exclamation.

The examples below show three types of sentences ended by periods:

Direct statement:	Spiritualism is alive and flourishing.
Indirect question:	I wonder why Miguel looks so happy.

Instruction or command: Cut the chatter, please.

33b   Use periods according to conventions in abbreviations and decimals.

Periods are required after most abbreviations, as shown below. See **45** for help in using abbreviations.

Ms.   Mrs.   Mr.   Jr.   Dec.   a.m.   p.m.   e.g.
i.e.   A.D.   B.C.

Do not use periods in acronyms (abbreviations pronounced as words) and abbreviations of company names and governmental agencies:

NATO   CORE   ITT   FBI   CIA   NOW

Most writers omit periods from capitalized abbreviations:

JFK   USA   NJ

Use a period as the decimal point in a decimal fraction, between a whole number and decimals, and between dollars and cents:

.007   .95   98.6°   3.1416 $.19 $36,500.48

Include the period *inside* quotation marks (see **40c**):

Incorrect: When asked about his lateness, George said, "Ask my teenage son".

Correct: When asked about his lateness, George said, "Ask my teenage son."

34   Use a question mark to indicate a direct question.

Question marks are end stops for direct questions; they can also be used within sentences, as shown here:

Correct: Why has Frank Herbert's *Dune* remained so popular through the years**?**

Correct: I want to go, but how can I**?**

Correct: "When will we get there**?**" she asked.

Correct: Mr. Walsh called in three backup units (who knows why**?**) after the situation had been resolved.

Correct: You actually like Sean**?** (Notice that the question mark here shows the reader how to read the sentence; a period would produce an entirely different meaning.)

Use a period after an indirect question:

Correct: Brad asked if he could turn in his essay a day late**.**

35   Use an exclamation point to show extreme emphasis.

An exclamation point shows extreme emotion or disbelief and can end a sentence, an interjection, or a clause or phrase. Do not overuse the exclamation point; instead, try to achieve emphasis through your choice of appropriate words. Do not use a comma or period following an exclamation point.

Correct: What a night we've had**!**

Correct: Get out of my way! Now!

Correct: You can't be serious!

▼ EXERCISE

Correct any punctuation errors in the following sentences. If a sentence is correct, mark it C.

1. Maria told April that she really liked history class!

2. April wondered how someone as old as Mr. Salinger could be such an interesting teacher?

3. "Why is age such a big deal," Maria inquired?

4. "I guess I don't know many older people—do you?"

5. "Just my parents, and they're almost forty!"

6. Maria learned that her grandfather—or was it her great-grandfather—lived to be ninety-seven.

7. "That's impossible," she shouted when her father told her the story.

8. "No one lives to be *that* old!"

9. "Did he really live that long?"

10. Maria asked her father to tell her more.

35

36   Use semicolons to separate independent clauses and punctuated items in a series.

The semicolon is an intermediate mark, stronger than a comma but weaker than a period. It is used only between grammatically equal units—two or more independent clauses or two or more items in a series.

36a   Use a semicolon to connect two independent clauses not joined by a coordinating conjunction.

In a compound sentence (two or more independent clauses), join the clauses with a semicolon unless you use a coordinating conjunction (*and, or, nor, for, but, yet,* and *so*) and a comma (see **49**):

Incorrect: I need another notebook, this one is almost full. (comma splice)

Correct: I need another notebook; this one is almost full.

Incorrect: The student parking lot is half empty at 3:15 P.M. this must be a commuter campus. (fused sentence)

Correct: The student parking lot is half empty at 3:15 P.M.; this must be a commuter campus.

Incorrect: Personal safety is threatened not only in the home, it is also threatened on the highways and at the workplace.

Correct: Personal safety is threatened not only in the home; it is also threatened on the highways and at the workplace.

Use a semicolon before a conjunctive adverb (*however, hence, therefore,* etc.) or transitional phrase (*on the contrary,* etc.—

see the lists on page 356) that introduces an independent clause:

Incorrect:	The casual sports fan will always be interested in big-name athletes, however, their greed is threatening to destroy professional sports.
Correct:	The casual sports fan will always be interested in big-name athletes; however, their greed is threatening to destroy professional sports.
Incorrect:	My opponent's so-called tax overhaul is not a carefully designed and equitable system, on the contrary, it is clearly meant to appease the special interests that my opponent has always served.
Correct:	My opponent's so-called tax overhaul is not a carefully designed and equitable system; on the contrary, it is clearly meant to appease the special interests that my opponent has always served.

Before a coordinating conjunction joining two long independent clauses that already contain internal punctuation, it is acceptable to use a semicolon rather than a comma:

My father never mentioned Louis Armstrong, except to forbid us to play his records; but there was a picture of him on our wall for a long time.

—*James Baldwin,* Notes of a Native Son

Do *not* use a semicolon after a dependent clause when it precedes an independent clause:

Incorrect:	Although the skies looked threatening; the race began on time.
Correct:	Although the skies looked threatening, the race began on time. (dependent clause with independent clause)
Correct:	The skies looked threatening; nevertheless, the race began on time. (both independent clauses)

36

36b   Use semicolons to separate items in a series when the items themselves contain commas.

When punctuating a series of items that contains commas, such as dates or cities and states, use semicolons between the items to avoid confusion with the internal commas:

Incorrect:	Bonnie has already attended colleges in Fort Collins, Colorado, Tempe, Arizona, and Galesburg, Illinois.
Correct:	Bonnie has already attended colleges in Fort Collins, Colorado; Tempe, Arizona; and Galesburg, Illinois.
Incorrect:	Vicky met several uninvited guests at the door: Bruno, her older brother, Tina, her former roommate, and Robert, her secretary.
Correct:	Vicky met several uninvited guests at the door: Bruno, her older brother; Tina, her former roommate; and Robert, her secretary.

36

▼ EXERCISE

In the following sentences, replace incorrectly used commas with semicolons, and replace incorrectly used semicolons with commas. If a sentence is correct, mark it C.

1. For her research paper in Mr. Salinger's class, Maria decided to write about the history of Click County; choosing the subject after hearing Mr. Salinger speak at the PTA.

2. Maria started work on her essay, April, however, was undecided.

3. Although the paper was not due for five weeks; Maria wanted to give herself plenty of time.

4. Click County was named after Major Ezekiel Click, who was born in Chattanooga, Tennessee; and joined the military during the Civil War.

5. Major Click traveled with his regiment to a small town in Florida; called Gidneyville.

6. The major was separated from his troops, he had been caught in a powerful storm while hunting in a swamp.

7. Searching for Click were Myron Parker, a sergeant, Obidiah Welles, a corporal, and Johnson Baker, a private.

8. Click eventually became frustrated, he abandoned his military career and bought a farm.

9. Everyone thought that nothing could be grown in the area of Click's farm, on the contrary, the soil was perfect for rutabagas.

10. In terms of the military, Click was a failure; as a farmer, however, he was a success.

11. Not only did Click become a wealthy man; he also became an author.

12. Despite the fact that Click was a horrible speller; he devoted his later years to his writing career.

13. Overall, Click published seven books; such as *The Virtues of Becoming Lost* and *Rutabagas and Moral Health*.

14. His books, however, did not find a wide audience.

36

15. Click continued writing until his death in 1918, he finished his last title, *Rutabagas and the War Effort,* three days before he died from indigestion at the age of seventy-five.

:

▼ **37** **Use a colon to call attention to what comes next or to follow mechanical conventions.**

The colon is a formal mark that calls attention to words that follow it. It also has special uses in titles, scriptural references, time references, and formal letters. Do not confuse it with the semicolon, which separates grammatically equal elements.

37a **Use a colon to introduce a list, an explanation or intensification, an example, or (in certain cases) a quotation.**

Place a colon at the end of an otherwise grammatically complete sentence to introduce a list of items, an explanation of the first part of the sentence, or an example.

Correct: As project coordinator, my boss always followed the same policy: do what is right today; justify it later.

Correct: In my old neighborhood we lived lives of plenty: plenty of relatives, boarders, landlords, cats, fights, and cockroaches.

Do not use a colon after *such as* or after a verb. Also, do not place a colon before a list unless the list is introduced by an independent clause.

Incorrect: I enjoy a variety of sports, such as: baseball, swimming, tennis, and soccer.

Correct: I enjoy a variety of sports, such as baseball, swimming, tennis, and soccer.

Incorrect: The students who applied for the job were : Thomas, Sims, and Watkins.

Correct: The students who applied for the job were Thomas, Sims, and Watkins.

Incorrect: Peter is interested only in : his guitar, his motorcycle, and his girlfriend.
(The words before the colon do not form a grammatically complete sentence.)

Correct: Peter is interested only in his guitar, his motorcycle, and his girlfriend.

Colons may separate two independent clauses when the clauses are very closely related and the second explains or intensifies the first:

Correct: Reynaldo couldn't decide what to do or where to turn : he was stymied.

Correct: Yesterday I realized my age : my son asked if I remembered an old-time singer named Jim Morrison.
(The second part of the sentence explains the first part; the colon = *that is.*)

Use a colon to introduce a long quotation (more than one sentence) or a shorter quotation not introduced by a word such as *said, remarked,* or *replied:*

Correct: I remember my reaction to a typically luminous observation of Kierkegaard's : "Such a relation which relates itself to its own self (that is to say, a self) must either have constituted itself or have been constituted by another."

—*Woody Allen, "My Philosophy"*

Correct: Consider the words of John Donne: "No man is an island entire of itself. . . . "

37b Use a colon between title and subtitle, between Bible chapter and verse, between hours and minutes, and after the salutation of a formal letter.

Scripture:	Genesis 1:7	John 3:16
Time references:	3:00	1:17 p.m.
Salutations:	Dear Ms. Jones:	Dear Sir or Madam:
Subtitles:	*Greek Tragedy: A Literary Study*	
	The Fields of Light: An Experiment in Critical Reading	

37

▼ EXERCISE

In the following sentences, mark any incorrectly used punctuation and insert colons where necessary. If a sentence is correct, mark it C.

1. Maria found that Click County had one characteristic in common with the surrounding counties, its economy was based on agriculture.

2. Ezekiel Click had given the county its motto "The family farm is where the food is grown."

3. He believed the most important crop was, of course: rutabagas.

4. Maria planned to give copies of her report to: her mother, her father, and her Aunt Agnes.

5. Her essay was titled "Ezekiel Click's Obsession with an Obscure Vegetable."

--

38 Use dashes to signal sharp changes or to set apart emphatic parenthetical elements.

The dash is a strong, dramatic mark that has several important uses. Unfortunately, it is often misused and overused. In college- and job-related writing, it should be used sparingly, not overused as a substitute for other punctuation.

38a Use a dash to signal a sharp change in thought or tone.

Correct: "There is a simple solution to every complex problem--the wrong one."

—*H. L. Mencken*

Correct: Kendricks' treatment of urban health problems is poorly researched, inaccurately documented, badly written--but why go on?

38b Use dashes to separate and emphasize a parenthetical element or to set off a parenthetical element that contains commas.

The dash is a stronger mark than the comma, indicating a longer pause in reading. It is used to give extra emphasis to parenthetical elements. It is also useful when parenthetical elements themselves contain commas:

Correct: Oviparous mammals--those that lay eggs--are strange descendants of the past.

Correct: The real Lawrence of Arabia--vain, secretive, obsessive, manipulative--remains both fascinating and infuriating.

In printed text, the dash is shown as a continuous line. With most word processors, however, you will need to use two hyphens together with no space before or after. For hyphens, see **43**.

39 Use parentheses to set off parenthetical material that is long or strictly supplementary.

Unlike dashes, which *emphasize* parenthetical material, and unlike commas, which relate parenthetical material to the rest of the sentence, parentheses set such material apart from the rest of the sentence and *de-emphasize* it. Use parentheses for material that is not essential to the meaning of the sentence, material that could just as well appear in footnotes. Notice in the first example below that the period is inside the parentheses: the parenthetical material is a complete sentence and is not included in another sentence. Otherwise, put end punctuation after the final parenthesis.

Correct: Milton lived well into the Restoration period. (He died in 1674.)

Correct: Only one of the thirteen studies (see Appendix A) showed even minor irregularities.

Correct: *Cajun* (from the word *Acadian*) refers to Louisiana culture and cuisine.

▼ EXERCISE

In the following sentences, replace any incorrectly used parentheses or dashes with the proper punctuation. If a sentence is correct, mark it C.

1. Maria wrote her essay on her new PC (personal computer).

2. Her young cousin Roberto the one with the hyperactivity disorder was staying with the Rodriguez family that week.

3. Roberto's mother Mr. Rodriguez's youngest sister believed that Roberto's condition would improve over time.

4. Roberto's sisters (Xiomara, Tatiana, and Consuelo) all had to be treated for the same condition.

5. Maria believed that revising her essay should take around three hours (if she could have some privacy).

40 **Use quotation marks to indicate direct quotations.**

Quotation marks enclose words quoted directly from another source. Use them only when you quote the exact words of your source. Indirect quotations, which report the gist of a message but not the exact words, do not need quotation marks.

40a Enclose direct quotations in double quotation marks.

Put double quotation marks around the exact words spoken or written by your source; do not enclose introductory or interrupting information, such as *she said.*

Correct:	According to Samuel Kaplan, "The social and economic segregation of suburbs also is resulting in the political segregation of suburbs."
Also correct:	Samuel Kaplan said that "the social and economic segregation of suburbs also is resulting in the political segregation of suburbs."
Correct:	"I'll beat you to the barn," Uncle Gene said, jumping onto his horse.

Do not enclose an indirect quotation in quotation marks:

Direct:	According to *Robert's Rules of Order,* "The subsidiary motion to Amend . . . requires only a majority vote, even in cases where the question to be amended takes a two-thirds vote for adoption."
Indirect:	*Robert's Rules of Order* says that an amendment needs only a simple majority, even when the main motion needs a two-thirds vote.
Combined:	*Robert's Rules of Order* says that an amendment needs only a simple majority, "even in cases where the question to be amended takes a two-thirds vote for adoption."

For quotations of four or more typed lines, double-space, indent ten spaces from the left margin, and do not add quotation marks:

Correct:

Roger Taylor comments on women writers:

The Equal Rights Amendment has stimulated community interest in the issues of women's rights. Both men and women are taking a second look at the roles and expectations of women in society. The subject of women and "women writers," therefore, moves to the forefront of what should be offered to the community. (21)

In quoting poetry of more than three lines, indent each line ten spaces from the left margin, double-space, and do not add quotation marks (shorter quotations of poetry can be included within the text):

I write it out in a verse—

McDonagh and MacBride

And Connolly and Pearse

Now and in time to be,

Wherever green is worn,

Are changed, changed utterly:

A terrible beauty is born.

—*William Butler Yeats*

40b Use single quotation marks to enclose a quotation within a quotation.

Correct: As John Ehrlichman wrote, "Nixon is the 'Man of a Thousand Facets' to me."

40c Place other punctuation marks inside or outside closing quotation marks, according to standard conventions.

Place periods and commas *inside* closing quotation marks.

Correct: "No," she replied, "I wouldn't consider joining your company for that salary."

40

Correct: His favorite short story is Faulkner's "That Evening Sun."

Exception: The hero asserted, "Patience conquers all" (Joyce 21). (The period follows the source of the direct quotation; see **77a** and **78a**.)

Place question marks, exclamation points, and dashes inside the closing quotation marks when they apply directly to the quoted material:

Correct: My mother asked her favorite question, "Where do you think you're going, young lady?"

Correct: My response was, "Oh, no!"

40

When a question mark, exclamation point, or dash is not part of a direct quotation, place it outside the closing quotation marks. (If both an entire sentence and the quoted material are questions or exclamations, place the question mark or exclamation point inside the quotation marks.)

Correct: Was it Pete Seeger or Woody Guthrie who wrote "This Land Is Your Land"?

Correct: It was Guthrie, but wasn't Seeger the one who wrote "Where Have All the Flowers Gone?"

Correct: Why did Jim Hubbard submit a theme with the title "An Immodest Proposal"?

Place all colons and semicolons *outside* closing quotation marks.

Correct: In his first conference he stated emphatically, "We will finish by July 30"; in his second conference he hedged a bit.

Correct: His first pronouncement was "I am not yet ready to quit": he resigned the next day.

40d Use an ellipsis (. . .) to indicate material omitted from a quotation.

An ellipsis consists of three spaced periods and is used to show that a word or words have been deleted from a quoted passage. It is usually unnecessary to use an ellipsis at the beginning of a quotation; the ellipsis is normally used in the middle or at the end of a quoted sentence. When you omit material at the end of a sentence, use four dots (period plus ellipsis), with no space before the first one:

Correct: According to Dr. Peter LeWitt, "the brain may record short-term and long-term memory differently. . . . Long-term memory might be recorded more permanently."

Correct: "As soon as sensible birth control devices became widely available, women . . . began to use the new methods—when the front office allowed them to."

—*Richard Cornuelle,* De-Managing America

40

40e Use brackets ([ ]) to mark an insertion into a quotation.

Brackets have only one commonly accepted function in text: to enclose editorial comments or other information inserted into a direct quotation. *Do not confuse parentheses with brackets.* Parentheses appear within quotations only when they are part of the quotation itself.

Correct: His response was a mild "Well, I do the best I can [debatable], but sometimes that isn't good enough."

Correct: "They [the staff] are all conscientious, honest people."

Always quote your original exactly, including errors. Insert *sic*—meaning *thus*—in brackets [*sic*] after an error to indicate that the error appears in the original:

Correct: "The civil rights movement picked up steam after President Kennedy's assassination in 1953 [*sic*]."

▼ EXERCISE

Correct any errors in punctuation in the following sentences. Mark C if the sentence is correct.

1. In her essay, Maria quoted this passage: "One who becomes lost finds himself in a world of pure possibility. . . . Whilst others believe themselves to be in a secure environment, the one who is lost waits for Fortune's blessing."

2. Click defined the rutabaga as "a tuber [root] from heaven".

3. Maria wrote that "the rutabaga was much more important to Click than to anyone else".

4. When Maria finished her essay, her father said, "Congratulations!."

5. Mr. Rodriguez said that it was "the best thing she had ever written," Mrs. Rodriguez had some minor criticisms.

6. She asked Maria, "Don't you know how to spell *receive*"?

7. Maria found this error in one of Click's books: "The Civil War lasted seven (*sic*) years."

8. The error was in the chapter titled "Who Knows the Future?"

40

9. Later in this chapter, Click wrote that "harm [is] in the eye of the beholder".

10. "The future is the pudding" Click wrote, "that makes us appreciate the salad of life."

ital

 Use underlining (italics) or quotation marks to designate titles and special types of words.

41

Enclose titles of articles, chapters, poems, short stories, musical compositions, or paintings in quotation marks:

Correct: Stan thinks that John Updike's best short story is "A&P."

Correct: I just read a helpful article titled "Theftproof Your Cellular Phone."

Correct: The best essay in the magazine is "Faulkner's Women."

Use italics to designate the title of a book, newspaper, periodical, play, motion picture, or television program. In handwritten or typed materials, use underlining to indicate italic print.

Correct: Dave Barry's humor column originates in the *Miami Herald.*

Correct: Cheryl always keeps *The American Heritage Dictionary* and the *Information Please Almanac* close at hand.

Correct: After becoming popular in the television series *Bosom Buddies,* Tom Hanks starred in such movies as *Philadelphia* and *Apollo 13.*

Avoid using both italics and quotation marks to indicate a title:

Incorrect: One of my favorite paintings is *"The Naked Maja."*

Correct: One of my favorite paintings is "The Naked Maja."

Do not use italics or quotation marks to refer to the Bible or parts of the Bible:

Correct: Genesis is the first book of the Bible, Revelation the last.

41

Use italics to indicate a foreign word that is not yet a standard part of English; a scientific name of a plant, animal, disease, etc.; a word mentioned as a word; or letters or numbers used as examples:

Correct: The word *liberal* comes from Latin *liber,* meaning free.

Correct: *Gauge* is now spelled *gage* in some professional journals.

Correct: *Dracaena marginata* is an easy plant to propagate by mound layering.

Correct: Social Security numbers beginning with *3* come generally from the Midwest.

Some writers use italics or quotation marks to give a word or phrase special emphasis, but you should do so very sparingly. Avoid enclosing slang in quotation marks as a form of apology. Using emphatic wording is a much more effective approach.

▼ EXERCISE

Correct any sentences in which italics or quotation marks are improperly used. If a sentence is correct, mark it C.

1. Click always carried a copy of the "New Testament."

2. Maria saw a copy of one of Click's letters and realized that his capital F's and T's were almost impossible to distinguish.

3. Click's writing style was modeled on that of T. R. Williams, editor of the "Florida Harvester."

4. *My Beginnings* is the first chapter of "The Virtues of Becoming Lost."

5. At a used bookstore, Maria found a biography of Click titled "Clickville's Pioneer."

6. Maria called this book a wonder.

7. She learned that Click's lucky number was 8.

8. "Lost in the Swamp," the fourth chapter of the biography, tells of Click's belief that moss always grows on the north side of trees.

9. This mistake was the coup de grace to Click's plan to get out of the swamp.

10. Maria was bothered by the biographer's constant use of "per se" and "ipso facto".

41

42 ▼ Use apostrophes to form contractions, certain plurals, and the possessive form of nouns and indefinite pronouns.

42a Use an apostrophe to indicate the possessive of nouns and indefinite pronouns.

Add an apostrophe and *s* to form the possessive of indefinite pronouns (*everyone, someone, somebody,* etc.) and of most singular nouns:

> Sally's coat   Ms. Cullom's office
> anybody's game   one's chances
> a dollar's worth   a cat's life

The same rule applies if a one-syllable singular noun ends with an -*s* sound:

> boss's relatives   class's performance

But in words of more than one syllable, the -*s* following the apostrophe is optional when it might not be pronounced:

> Sophocles' *or* Sophocles's   Perkins' *or* Perkins's

Add only the apostrophe to plurals ending in -*s*. Add an apostrophe and *s* to plurals not ending in -*s*:

> girls' jumpers   cats' lives
> ladies' shoes   two months' work
> children's clothes   mice's cages

Add an apostrophe and *s* to the last word of a word group or compound:

> the editor-in-chief's office   the chief of staff's car

Add an apostrophe and *s* to each name to indicate individual ownership; add the apostrophe and *s* to the last name to show joint ownership:

Jo's and Arnie's cars   David and Linda's apartment

42b Use an apostrophe to indicate the omitted letters in a contraction. Use it also to indicate omitted parts of dates or other numerals.

they'll (they will)   it's (it is)   can't (cannot)   class of '65

Note that the apostrophe is used only where letters are left out and not between the words joined in a contraction:

wouldn't   can't

42

42c Use an apostrophe to form the plural of lowercase letters and of abbreviations followed by periods. Use it also to prevent confusion in forming plurals of other abbreviations, of capital letters, of symbols, and of words used or singled out as words.

M.S.'s	*j*'s	*miss*'s
J's *or* Js	UFO's *or* UFOs	@'s *or* @s

Note that the *s* is not italicized.

Never use an apostrophe to form a simple plural:

Incorrect: Three dog's barked.

Incorrect: Three Mazda Miata's were parked in a row.

▼ EXERCISE

Correct the use of apostrophes in the following sentences. If a sentence is correct, mark it C.

1. When Maria started Mippallaupa High School, she found that it's environment was different.

2. Mippallaupa contains three *a*'s, three *p*'s, two *l*'s, and one *m*.

3. The school's locker's were more than a foot wide.

4. Each lockers' door was painted a different color than the one adjacent to it.

5. The assistant principals job was one of the most crucial in the school.

6. Her situation was made worse by her father-in-law's illness.

7. The Johnson's spent all their evenings at the hospital.

8. Ms. Johnson had planned to spend the time reviewing a proposed course in womens' studies.

9. Its true that the course could wait for a semester.

10. The lives of the Johnsons were put on hold.

42

-

43 Use a hyphen to join two words into a single adjective, to join a root word to a prefix or suffix, and to write out a fraction or compound number.

Compound words are sometimes written separately, sometimes hyphenated, and sometimes together as one word. When in doubt, consult a college-level dictionary.

43a Use a hyphen to join two or more words serving as a single adjective before a noun.

up-to-date information
seventeen-year-old son
well-intentioned actions

energy-related problems
late-night meeting
claw-like arms

But do not hyphenate such adjectives following the noun:

The information was clearly not up to date.

His son was seventeen years old.

The agency's actions were well intentioned.

Do not use a hyphen between an adverb ending in *-ly* and an adjective:

unusually fine wine

carefully developed plot

43b Use hyphens to write out fractions and compound numbers between twenty and one hundred.

twenty-two
a two-thirds majority

three hundred sixty-one
one-fourth complete

43

However, do not hyphenate a fraction used as a noun:

one fourth of a cup   two thirds of the members

43c Use hyphens to join root words to certain prefixes and suffixes.

The suffix *-elect* and the prefixes *pro-, anti-, ex-, self-,* and *great-* are normally joined with hyphens to root words. Check your dictionary when you are uncertain whether to use a hyphen with a prefix or suffix.

ex‑convict   self‑confessed   great‑grandmother
anti‑abortionist   pro‑abolitionist   congressman‑elect

43d Use a hyphen to avoid a confusing combination of letters or syllables.

43

re‑creation (*not* recreation)

steel‑like (*but* froglike, etc.—the idea is to avoid using double *l*)

43e Use a hyphen to divide a word at the end of a line of print.

Do not divide a one-syllable word:

dined   tenth   strength

Divide only between syllables. Consult your dictionary. Most dictionaries indicate syllabication with dots:

in · ti · mi · date   wis · dom   an · i · mal

Do not put a single letter at the beginning or ending of a line of print; do not put a two-letter ending at the beginning of a line:

Improper: thick- ly   ax- es   a- brupt   fox- y

▼ EXERCISE

Correct any misuses or omissions of hyphens in the following sentences. If a sentence is correct, mark it C.

1. As a healthy, intelligent, fourteen year old girl, Maria found high school interesting.

2. The school was painted a light rosy-beige.

3. The exterior color was an attempted recreation of the appearance of the old Clickville Academy.

4. In Maria's sophomore year, Ms. Johnson, assistant-principal and self-described workaholic, was named as the new principal-to-be.

5. Thirty-seven teachers, more than three-quarters of the faculty, signed a petition supporting her promotion.

44

cap

44 **Always capitalize the first word of a sentence and the word *I*; capitalize proper nouns and important words in titles according to conventional practice.**

Appropriate capitalization is a matter of convention. This section will show you basic conventions, but conventions vary, and expert writers often disagree on what should be capitalized. Consult your college dictionary for specific problems; words commonly capitalized will be shown that way in the dictionary entry.

44a   Capitalize the first word of a sentence and *I*.

Correct: He advised our club on energy-saving devices.

Incorrect: I would go if i could.

Correct: I do not know whether I want a root beer or a milk shake with my lunch.

44b   Capitalize the names of persons, races, and nationalities.

Also capitalize derivatives of such words:

English	Maxwell R. Folger	Ms. Tucker
Chicano	Americanize	Cuban
Caucasian	Russian	Kentuckian

44

Neither *black* (African American) nor *white* (Caucasian) is capitalized; however, *Hispanic* is capitalized.

44c   Capitalize place names.

Puerto Rico	Amazon River	Orange County
Zaire	Nile Valley	North Carolina

44d   Capitalize the names of organizations, historical events, holidays, days of the week, and months.

World War II	Xerox	Thursday
Chrysler Corporation	Yom Kippur	Thanksgiving
the Renaissance	NAACP	July

44e   Capitalize titles preceding a name.

Professor Elizabeth Kirk

Chairman Dick Fisher

Titles following a name are capitalized in addresses and typed signatures of letters, but not in sentences:

Elizabeth Kirk, Professor of Chemistry

Dick Fisher, Chairman of the Board

The chairman of the board called the meeting to order.

Elizabeth Kirk is a professor of chemistry.

44f Capitalize common nouns such as *street, company, river,* or *aunt* only when they are part of a proper noun. Capitalize *north, south, east,* and *west* only when they refer to specific regions.

Huskey Company	my brother's company
Kirkman Road	on the road
Roosevelt University	at a university
Atlantic Ocean	in the ocean
American Airlines	a major airline
Uncle George	my favorite uncle
Oak Ridge High School	my old high school
the Midwest	go west
East Texas	toward the east

44

44g Capitalize the first word and all important words of the title of a book, periodical, article, report, or other document. Also capitalize the titles of chapters and other major divisions.

The Scarlet Letter	*Macbeth*
"Chapter Six: Projected Revenue"	*Writers on Writing*
Newsweek	"Methods Used"

A, an, the, conjunctions, and prepositions of fewer than five letters should not be capitalized unless they are the first or last word in a title or subtitle.

▼ EXERCISE

Correct any errors in capitalization in the following sentences. If a sentence is correct, mark it C.

1. After the High School year was over, Maria wondered what she would do that Summer.

2. Her family planned a picnic for the July 4 Holiday.

3. Some of their Puerto Rican relatives planned to come up to join them.

4. The picnic was to be held on the banks of the Gidney river.

5. In August, Maria planned to visit Clickville's rutabaga festival.

6. The rutabaga Queen would be crowned after an extensive Pageant.

7. This year's Queen was born in Mary Sherman hospital in Sullivan, Indiana, a small town South of Terre Haute.

8. For cultural reasons, many people considered it inappropriate to have a midwesterner win a north Florida Pageant.

9. Maria's mother said that it just proved that Clickville was moving out of the middle ages and into the early renaissance.

10. The pageant was hosted by a member of the Gidney Family, prominent republicans who owned a great deal of farmland in Click county.

44

ab

45 Capitalize and punctuate abbreviations according to conventional practice.

Abbreviations and figures are widely used in technical reports, tables, footnotes, and bibliographies. However, only a few abbreviations and figures are commonly used in the text of college writing.

45a Use only conventionally accepted abbreviations in college and general writing.

The following abbreviations are recommended:

45

Mr.	M.D.	Rev. (Rev. Jane Smith or the Rev. Mr. Jones)
Mrs.	M.S.	
Ms.	S.P.A.	Col. and other military titles
Dr.	A.D. or B.C.	
St. (Saint)	a.m. or p.m.	Ph.D. and other degrees
Jr.	no.	CIA, IBM, NAACP, and other groups commonly known by initials
Sr.	D.C.	

45b Spell out the following in college writing:

Units of measure:	pounds, feet
Place names:	Arkansas, New York
Parts of addresses:	Street, Avenue, Road
Corporate identities:	Company, Incorporated (except in official titles)
Parts of written works:	page 3, Chapter Seven, Volume 14
Personal names:	Charles (not Chas.)
Names of courses:	English 101 (not Eng. 101)

Check your college dictionary for the proper spelling, punctuation, and capitalization of abbreviations.

▼ EXERCISE

In the following sentences, correct any improper abbreviations or supply abbreviations as needed. If a sentence is correct, mark it C.

1. Maria found the capt. of her swim team to be an interesting case.

2. Edna Smith was born in Texarkana, Ark., on a Tues. morn.

3. She weighed three pounds, four oz.

4. Her family then moved to Washington, District of Columbia.

5. When Edna was five, her parents took her to a Dr., Kenneth Perkins, for a checkup.

6. Ken.'s clinic was named Healthy Children, Inc.

7. Doctor Perkins wanted to be an M.D. ever since he could remember.

8. His clinic is described on p. 367 of Vol. 4 of *America's Great Physicians*.

9. After Perkins started treating E. S., she grew seven in. and gained fifty pounds in the year before the Smith family moved to Fla.

10. Edna's father, Robt., bought a big house on State St. in Clickville.

45

46 **Spell out one- and two-word numbers in most situations.**

Use figures for page numbers, numbers with units of measure, time followed by *a.m.* or *p.m.,* percentages, decimals, identification numbers, and numbers that cannot be written in one or two words. Otherwise, write out numbers.

Use Figures	Write Out
428 5,687,414	eleven twenty-two
	seventeen thousand
$3\frac{3}{4}$	three-quarters
	one third of the population
East 181st Street	East Eighty-first Street
Channel 3	
page 17	seventeen-page report
85°F 12 meters	eighty-five cadets
6:30 p.m.	six-thirty that afternoon
38% 10 percent	
3.1416 .005	
U.S. 66 I-84	
4 B.C. 1996	

46

Avoid beginning a sentence with a number, but if it is unavoidable, write out the number:

> Four hundred twenty-eight people attended the opening ceremonies.

In a series, if one number must be written in figures, write all the numbers in figures:

Incorrect: Of the students who responded to the questionnaire, thirty had never used the university tennis courts, twelve had used them once, and 123 had used them more than once.

Correct: Of the students who responded to the questionnaire, 30 had never used the university tennis courts, 12 had used them once, and 123 had used them more than once.

▼ EXERCISE

Correct any errors in number usage in the following sentences. If a sentence is correct, mark it C.

1. In the summer of Nineteen Seventy Nine, Clickville found itself in the national news for the 1st time.

2. A controversy occurred on County Road 546 near Interstate ninety-five.

3. 9 farmworkers went on strike against Gidney Farms.

4. Over twenty percent of the county deputies arrived and arrested the strikers.

5. The group became known as the Clickville 9.

6. A petition in support of the strikers was signed by 37 people and was printed on page two of section 2 of the *Clickville Clarion*.

7. Surveys revealed that only a third of area citizens believed the strikers to be guilty of a crime, but another 1/4 feared the powerful Gidney family.

8. Channel Thirteen covered the story extensively, but Channel 5 had other concerns.

9. Temperatures that summer were broiling, averaging just under ninety-four degrees.

46

10. The 16-page investigative report was completed by the District Attorney's office in thirteen days.

sp

47 Proofread for proper spelling, and work on your spelling weaknesses.

Unfortunately, there is no easy shortcut to effective spelling. Some writers who are otherwise very skillful struggle all their careers with poor spelling. If you are a poor speller and cannot seem to improve much, allow extra time to look up spellings. If you frequently misspell the same words, make a list of them. The suggestions below should help you with some of the more common spelling problems; however, for many words, only memorization or reference lists will help.

ie or ei. Place *i* before *e,* except after *c* and in words pronounced with other than the long *e* sound:

Correct:			
field	ceiling	sleigh	height
grief	conceit	vein	stein
niece	deceive	weigh	foreign
relief	conceive	neighbor	heir

Exceptions: fiery, seize, species, weird, neither

Final e. Drop a silent final *e* before suffixes beginning with a vowel; keep it before suffixes beginning with a consonant:

Correct:		
writ*ing*	hope*ful*	guid*ance*
love*ly*	nine*teen*	sincere*ly*

Exceptions: dye*ing* (clothes), nin*th,* tru*ly,* courage*ous*

Changing y to i. When adding a suffix, change a final *y* to *i* except before a suffix beginning with *i:*

Correct: fly, flying, flier
rely, reliance
forty, fortieth

Plurals.   Most plurals add -s to the singular; plurals of nouns ending in s, ch, sh, or x add -es.

Correct: girls   tables   typists   spoonfuls
dishes   taxes   churches   bosses

Singular nouns ending in y preceded by a consonant change the y to i and add -es.

Correct: cities, tragedies, replies, supplies

Singular nouns ending in o preceded by a consonant usually add -es, but note the exceptions:

Correct: potatoes, tomatoes, heroes, zeroes, hypos, pros, jumbos

ghettos or ghettoes, mosquitos or mosquitoes

The Glossary of Usage at the back of this handbook (page 380) lists some words easily confused because of similar spelling. Here are a few others:

advice, advise   inequity, iniquity
ascent, assent   paradox, parody
censor, censure   passed, past
decent, descent, dissent   prophecy, prophesy
definite, definitive   stationary, stationery
device, devise   to, too
idea, ideal   weather, whether

Here is a list of one hundred commonly misspelled words:

absence	disastrous	occasionally
accommodate	dissatisfied	occurred
acquaintance	embarrass	omitted
adequately	environment	parallel
aggravate	exaggerate	permissible
alleviate	existence	personnel
all right	familiar	possess
a lot	feasible	preceding
altogether	February	predominant
amateur	forth	prejudice
analysis	gauge	prevalent
apparent	government	privilege
argument	grammar	procedure
athletic	guard	proceed
becoming	harass	prominent
bureaucracy	hindrance	psychology
calendar	hurriedly	questionnaire
category	hypocrisy	receive
cemetery	imitation	recommend
committee	incredibly	repetition
competition	independent	rhythm
condemn	intelligence	ridiculous
conscience	irrelevant	schedule
conscientious	irresistible	separate
conscious	knowledge	sergeant
consistent	leisure	succeed
continuous	license	supersede
criticize	loneliness	susceptible
definitely	maintenance	temperament
description	maneuver	thorough
desirable	mischievous	unanimous
desperate	necessary	undoubtedly
develop	noticeable	villain
disappoint		

47

▼ EXERCISE

Underline the correctly spelled words. Write out the proper spelling of the words that are incorrect.

1. independent
2. resistence
3. indispensable
4. heighth
5. occurrance
6. mispell
7. preceed
8. procede
9. compatible
10. chastise
11. evidentally
12. larnyx
13. seperate
14. column
15. incidently
16. reciept
17. accidently
18. develope
19. sieze
20. hurriedly

47

Editing for Grammar

The principles of grammar are means to an end: effective communication. They express the conventional practices followed by experienced speakers and writers of Standard English. Not following these conventions often results in writing that is not only technically incorrect but also confusing or misleading. Most of the time we follow the conventions of English without thinking about them. However, some errors are almost inevitable, and knowing the rules makes correcting those errors much easier.

If you find that you need to review any of the parts of speech discussed here, see Chapter 12.

48   Use grammatically complete sentences.

A group of words that is punctuated as a sentence but that is not a grammatically complete sentence is called a *fragment* or *sentence fragment*. Although experienced writers sometimes use fragments intentionally, fragments are usually unacceptable in college writing. Unintentional fragments can create misunderstanding and distract your readers. A fragment is usually either a *phrase* or a *dependent clause*.

167

Complete sentence: David is a talented artist.
                         (independent clause)

Fragment: Because David is a talented artist.
                (dependent clause)

Fragment: Like a talented artist.
                (prepositional phrase)

Most fragments result from chopping a phrase or clause from the end of an adjoining sentence. It is usually a simple matter to correct them. You can reconnect the fragment to the previous or following sentence, or you can add the necessary elements to make the fragment a grammatically complete sentence. Subordinating conjunctions such as *although, because, if,* and *when* (see the list on p. 362) introduce subordinate (dependent) clauses, and such clauses cannot stand alone as sentences. The following examples show the most common types of clauses or phrases used incorrectly as fragments:

48

Incorrect: Although being left-handed has been seen as a minor misfortune. Many great athletes, artists, and political leaders have succeeded in adjusting to a right-handed world.
(The subordinate clause introduced by *although* is not a sentence.)

Correct: Although being left-handed has been seen as a minor misfortune, many great athletes, artists, and political figures have succeeded in adjusting to a right-handed world.
(subordinate clause connected to independent clause)

Incorrect: Science owes its system of plant classification and its double Latin names for flora and fauna to Linnaeus. The eighteenth-century Swedish botanist.
(final noun phrase not a sentence)

Correct: Science owes its system of plant classification and its double Latin names for flora and fauna to Linnaeus, the eighteenth-century Swedish botanist.
(noun phrase as an appositive connected to preceding sentence)

Incorrect: The Rattlers were disappointed once more. Having finished second in the city baseball tournament for the fifth year in a row.
(participial phrase as fragment)

Correct: The Rattlers were disappointed once more, having finished second in the city baseball tournament for the fifth year in a row.
(phrase connected to preceding sentence)

Correct: The Rattlers were disappointed once more. This was the fifth year in a row that they had finished second in the city baseball tournament.
(phrase expanded to independent clause)

Incorrect: Collectively, they vowed to combine their efforts toward one goal. To win first place next year.
(infinitive phrase as fragment)

Correct: Collectively, they vowed to combine their efforts toward one goal: to win first place next year.
(infinitive phrase connected to previous sentence)

Incorrect: Practice sessions will begin immediately and will be held during the whole year. On the second Saturday of each month.
(prepositional phrase as fragment)

Correct: Practice sessions will begin immediately and will be held on the second Saturday of each month during the whole year.
(prepositional phrase inserted in previous sentence)

48

▼   EXERCISE

A.   *Mark with S any word group that is a grammatical sentence; mark with X those that are sentence fragments. Explain why those marked X are fragments.*

1. Maria's friend Jeff Reynolds who joined the football team.

2. Because the coach urged him to do so.

3. Good hands combined with better than average speed.

4. Jeff became a wide receiver, an assignment that he welcomed.

5. Although the quarterback and the running backs get the most publicity.

6. Because they are the ones who score most of the points.

7. Although Jeff was a sophomore, he started every game for Mippallaupa High.

8. Scoring five touchdowns on twenty-seven receptions.

9. Coach O'Reilly's philosophy of using rushing to set up the pass.

10. Coach O'Reilly believed in a balanced attack.

11. Hoping to keep the opponents on their toes.

12. Although, some teams handled the Mippallaupa Rattlers fairly easily.

13. Lake Parson High beating Mippallaupa four years in a row.

14. Absolutely Mippallaupa's most feared rival.

15. Gidneyville Consolidated, however, being something less of a challenge, losing to Mippallaupa 73-6.

B. *Rewrite as sentences the fragments that you identified above.*

fs cs

49 Separate two independent clauses with a period, semicolon, or comma and coordinating conjunction.

If you fail to separate independent clauses properly, you will create one of two structural problems: a *fused sentence* (or *run-on*) or a *comma splice*.

An independent clause is a group of words that can be punctuated as a complete sentence. Whenever a sentence contains two independent clauses, those clauses must be separated by a semicolon or by one of the coordinating conjunctions (*and, or, nor, for, but, yet,* or *so*) plus a comma. A comma alone is not adequate punctuation, even if it is followed by a conjunctive adverb such as *furthermore, however,* or *moreover.*

Fused sentence: The arresting officer did not attend the trial the case was dismissed.

Comma splice: The arresting officer did not attend the trial, the case was dismissed.

49

Once you learn to identify fused sentences and comma splices, you can easily avoid them. Some of the most common ways are shown here:

1. Make each clause a separate sentence:

The arresting officer did not attend the trial. The case was dismissed.

2. Place a semicolon between the clauses:

The arresting officer did not attend the trial; the case was dismissed.

3. Insert a conjunctive adverb between the clauses. The adverb should be preceded by a semicolon and followed by a comma:

The arresting officer did not attend the trial; **therefore**, the case was dismissed.

4. Place a comma and coordinating conjunction between the clauses:

The arresting officer did not attend the trial, **so** the case was dismissed.

5. Convert one clause into a dependent clause by beginning it with a relative pronoun (*whoever, whomever, whichever, whatever,* for example) or with a subordinating conjunction such as *because, after, since,* or *while:*

Because the arresting officer did not attend the trial, the case was dismissed.

6. Rearrange the entire sentence into another pattern:

The case was dismissed due to the absence of the arresting officer.

49

All of these revisions are grammatically correct. You will find that choosing the best correction is a matter of style. Note that each of the following fused sentences and comma splices can be corrected in ways other than the one shown:

Faulty: My old car has become too unreliable, I'm going to have to start looking for another one soon. (comma splice)

Corrected: My old car has become too unreliable; I'm going to have to start looking for another one soon. (semicolon)

Faulty: The old rancher perceived that a storm was imminent he turned his horse around and headed home. (fused sentence)

Corrected: The old rancher perceived that a storm was imminent, so he turned his horse around and headed home. (comma plus coordinating conjunction)

Faulty:	There is one major problem with exercise, it is addictive. (comma splice)
Corrected:	There is one major problem with exercise; it is addictive. (semicolon)
Faulty:	I've paged your father three times, he still hasn't called me. (comma splice)
Corrected:	I've paged your father three times, but he still hasn't called me. (comma plus coordinating conjunction)
Faulty:	Many Americans believe that they are victims of the tax laws this attitude causes income tax returns to be highly creative. (fused sentence)
Corrected:	Many Americans believe that they are victims of the tax laws, a belief that causes income tax returns to be highly creative. (sentence rearranged)

▼ EXERCISE

49

In the following sentences, mark C for those that are correct and X for those that are fused sentences and comma splices. Then correct those marked X.

1. The district football tournament was held at Xanadu High the stadium was called the Pleasure Dome.

2. In the first round, Mippallaupa beat Gidneyville, Xanadu beat Lake Parson.

3. Maria attended the game with her parents, and they all sat in the visitors' section.

4. The Xanadu Kublas hadn't lost a game all season, however, their star running back was out with a broken ankle.

5. Maria could hear the chant of the Xanadu cheerleaders "Beware! Beware! His flashing eyes, his floating hair!"

6. The game was tied at fourteen at the end of the third quarter, nevertheless Xanadu had a first down and goal to go at the Mippallaupa seven-yard line.

7. But the Mippallaupa defense dug in, Xanadu scored two plays later.

8. The Kublas missed the extra point, with a Rattler linebacker coming through to block the kick.

9. Jeff Reynolds caught three passes in the Rattlers' final drive he would have scored a touchdown if he had not been caught by the free safety after the third catch.

10. The Rattlers were stopped, however, by an interception.

50

s/v agr

50 Make each verb and its subject agree in number.

Use the singular form of a verb with a singular subject and the plural form of a verb with a plural subject:

Singular	*Plural*
She watches.	They watch.
The watch runs fast.	The watches run fast.
The team is playing.	The teams are playing.
The plan has changed.	The plans have changed.
He was especially kind.	They were especially kind.

Notice that the *-s* or *-es* ending makes nouns plural but makes present-tense verbs singular, except in the first and second person:

> She goes.
> I go.
> You go.

Making subjects and verbs agree is usually easy in short sentences, but it can be more difficult in longer, more complicated sentences. Make sure that you do not let a prepositional phrase or other modifier influence your decision. Be careful to identify the subject so that your verb agrees with the correct word or words:

Incorrect: Ms. Gabriel's attention to time, efficiency, and savings deserve favorable consideration.

Correct: Ms. Gabriel's attention [subject] to time, efficiency, and savings *deserves* favorable consideration.

Incorrect: My supervisor's first priority in cutting departmental expenses are reducing overtime and sick pay.

Correct: My supervisor's first priority [subject] in cutting departmental expenses *is* reducing overtime and sick pay.

In a sentence beginning with *there,* the subject follows the verb:

Correct: There *is* an extra *pair* [subject] of shoes in the hall closet.

Correct: There *are* no good *concerts* [subject] at the Civic Center anymore.

Forms of the verb *be* agree with the subject of the sentence, not the complement, even when the subject is plural and the complement is singular, or vice versa:

Correct: Unsafe working conditions [subject] *were* the primary cause [complement] of the government investigation.

50

Correct: Mr. Jefferson's reason [subject] for early retirement *was* his health problems [complement].

Correct: Earning [subject] extra money *is* her only reason [complement] for babysitting.

50a   With compound subjects joined by *and,* use a plural verb.

Incorrect: The movement of the tropical fish and the bubbles from the filter entrances the young cat.

Correct: The movement of the tropical fish and the bubbles from the filter *entrance* the young cat.

However, when *each* or *every* precedes the compound subject, use a singular verb:

Incorrect: Every boy and girl are required to have parental permission to go on the field trip.

Correct: Every boy and girl *is* required to have parental permission to go on the field trip.

Note: The phrase *as well as* is used as a preposition, not as a conjunction. It does not create a compound subject.

The Indian diplomat as well as the Pakistani *was* upset by the U.N. vote.

50b   With compound subjects joined by *or* or *nor,* make the verb agree with the subject nearer to the verb.

Use a singular verb when two singular subjects are joined by *or* or *nor:*

Incorrect: Either *Hamlet* or *Othello,* rather than the usual *Macbeth,* are going to be performed this year.

50

Correct: Either *Hamlet* or *Othello,* rather than the usual *Macbeth, is* going to be performed this year.

Use a plural verb when two plural subjects are joined by *or* or *nor:*

Incorrect: Neither Stephen King's novels nor Lawrence Block's seems to lose popularity.

Correct: Neither Stephen King's novels nor Lawrence Block's *seem* to lose popularity.

When *or* or *nor* joins a singular subject and a plural subject, the verb agrees with the subject nearer to the verb:

Incorrect: Gail could not decide whether her math class or her two science classes was harder.

Correct: Gail could not decide whether her two science classes or her math class *was* harder.

Also correct: Gail could not decide whether her math class or her two science classes *were* harder.

Incorrect: Neither the clerks nor the assistant manager were watching the register.

Correct: Neither the clerks nor the assistant manager *was* watching the register.

Also correct: Neither the assistant manager nor the clerks *were* watching the register.

50

In the last two examples, note that of the two correct sentences shown, the second sentence sounds much better. In this type of situation, placing the plural nearer the verb will produce a more natural-sounding sentence.

50c *Each, either, neither, one, everybody, somebody, nobody,* and *anyone* require singular verbs.

Incorrect: Each of the development team's twelve members were given a portion of the bonus money.

Correct: Each of the development team's twelve members *was* given a portion of the bonus money.

Incorrect: Nobody from inside the company are ever given serious consideration for the top positions.

Correct: Nobody from inside the company *is* ever given serious consideration for the top positions.

50d Quantitative words such as *some, half, all, part, most,* and *more* are singular or plural depending on the nouns to which they refer.

50

Correct: All of the members *were* notified, and most *have* arrived.

Correct: All of the cake *has* been eaten.

Correct: Most of the committee's time *was* wasted in senseless wrangling.

Correct: One third of all meals eaten in this country *are* purchased in restaurants.

Correct: Two thirds of his diet *is* starch.

None usually obeys the same rule, although some writers consider the word's origin ("not one") and treat it consistently as singular:

I left messages for all of the members, but none *has* returned my call.

50e A collective noun that refers to a group as a unit takes a singular verb.

Nouns such as *class, committee, team, family, crew, jury, faculty, majority,* and *company* take singular verbs when they refer to a group acting as a unit:

Correct: The company *has* tried to diversify its investments.

Correct: If a majority *votes* in favor of adjournment, no further motions are allowed.

Occasionally you may need a plural verb to show that members of a group are acting as individuals:

Incorrect: If a majority votes according to their consciences, these amendments will be defeated.

Correct: If a majority *vote* according to their consciences, these amendments will be defeated.

In the incorrect sentence, the writer has been forced to shift from a singular verb *(votes)* to a plural pronoun *(their)*. Once you have decided whether a collective noun is singular or plural, treat it consistently within the sentence as one or the other. Another example:

50

Correct: The jury votes by secret ballot, with twelve votes required for indictment. *(jury* treated as a whole)

Correct: The jury have taken their seats. *(jury* treated as individuals)

Incorrect: The jury has taken their seats.

Many writers of American English avoid using collective nouns in the plural. They say "members of the jury" when they treat the jury as individuals acting separately, or they use the singular: "The jury *is* seated."

50f   Some singular subjects may look like plurals.

Certain nouns look like plurals but function as singulars and require singular verbs. *News, economics, politics, physics,* and *mathematics* are common examples of words that cannot be made singular because they already are.

Correct: Politics, unfortunately, often *affects* hiring decisions.
(not plural verb *affect*)

▼   EXERCISE

A.   *Study the sentences below for subject-verb agreement. Mark those that are correct with C and those that have faulty agreement with X.*

1. In her junior year, Maria found that physics were a very difficult subject.

2. Neither her mother nor her father were able to help her.

3. All of the students in the class was having trouble.

4. Maria, as well as April and Jeff, were planning to form a study group.

5. The group were composed of those three and April's friend Liam, who was making the best grades in the class.

6. Every one of them were responsible for checking the day's assignment.

7. Mr. Sterne, who had taught physics and chemistry for more than thirty years, were feared by generations of Mippallaupa students.

50

8. Liam believed that at least one of the study group members were going to fail.

9. A wide variety of problems was expected on the final exam.

10. However, most of the problems were based on those in earlier tests.

B. *Correct the sentences above that you marked with X.*

pn agr

 51 **Use singular pronouns to refer to singular nouns and plural pronouns to refer to plural nouns.**

Make each pronoun agree in number—singular or plural—with the noun or pronoun to which it refers. (This noun or pronoun is called the **antecedent.**)

51

The flight instructor [singular antecedent] finished her [singular pronoun] lecture, but the pilots [plural antecedent] remained in their [plural pronoun] seats.

It is usually easy to recognize an antecedent as singular or plural and to decide whether the pronoun should be singular or plural, but some sentences are complicated. The antecedent may be compound, or it may be a collective noun or an indefinite pronoun.

51a Collective nouns such as *team, committee, chorus,* and *class* can be either singular or plural depending on how they are used.

Avoid treating a collective noun as both singular and plural:

Incorrect: The interview committee *is* going to finish *their* deliberations tomorrow.

Correct: The interview committee *is* going to finish *its* deliberations tomorrow.

Incorrect: Our soccer team *has* not won yet, but Saturday *they* will be doing *their* best.

Correct: Our soccer team *has* not won yet, but Saturday *it* will be doing *its* best.

See **50e** for a fuller discussion of collective nouns.

51b Indefinite antecedents such as *a person, each, neither, either, someone, anyone, no one, one,* and *everybody* almost always take singular pronouns.

Incorrect: There are too many issues raised by this petition for the officials to give each one the attention they deserve.

Correct: There are too many issues raised by this petition for the officials to give each one the attention *it* deserves.

Incorrect: When a student first registers for classes, they risk making embarrassing errors.

Correct: When a student first registers for classes, *he or she* risks making embarrassing errors.

Correct: When *students* first register for classes, they risk making embarrassing errors.

Avoid using *he, him,* or *his* with an indefinite pronoun unless the pronoun refers to an exclusively male group. Use *he or she, him or her,* or *his or her* instead, or rewrite the sentence so that the plural *they, them,* or *their* is appropriate. See **64a** for more on sexist language. See **50c** and **50d** for more on indefinite pronouns.

51c   Compound antecedents with *and* take plural pronouns.

Correct: Beth and Eileen won *their* awards in tennis and swimming.

51d   If a compound antecedent is joined by *or* or *nor,* the pronoun agrees with the antecedent nearer to the pronoun.

If both antecedents are singular, use a singular pronoun:

Incorrect: Neither the television station nor its radio affiliate had their license revoked because of the charges of corruption.

Correct: Neither the television station nor its radio affiliate had *its* license revoked because of the charge of corruption.

If both antecedents are plural, use a plural pronoun:

Correct: It was impossible to blame either the reporters or the editors. *They* did all they could to verify the story.

If one antecedent is singular and one plural, make the pronoun agree with the antecedent nearer to the pronoun:

Correct: Either the instructor or the students are responsible for turning off *their* classroom lights and audiovisual equipment.

Avoid wasting time puzzling over intricate agreement problems with subjects or antecedents joined by *or* or *nor*. If following the rules in this section and in **50b** results in an absurd or awkward sentence, simply rewrite it. You may be able to join the subjects or antecedents with *and*:

Awkward: Neither Amanda nor Bob will be in [his? her? their?] office this afternoon.

51

Rewritten: Both Amanda and Bob will be out of their offices this afternoon.

▼   EXERCISE

A.   *Mark with X those sentences with pronoun agreement errors. If the sentence is correct, mark it* C.

1. Mr. Rodriguez announced plans to learn how to cook: "Every man should know their way around a kitchen."

2. After some reading, he found that each cookbook has a style of its own.

3. He soon discovered that one cookbook publisher aimed their books at men who were just learning.

4. He realized that an expert chef wouldn't waste their time on such a book.

5. Either Mr. Rodriguez or Mrs. Rodriguez cooked each night for his family.

6. In May, the Clickville Bake-off was going to be held, and their entry rules were published in the *Clarion*.

7. Mrs. Rodriguez urged her husband to submit his recipe for Rutabaga Surprise.

8. "Anyone who submits their entry has a chance," Mrs. Rodriguez argued.

9. Neither Mr. Rodriguez nor Mrs. Rodriguez expected their recipe to win, however.

10. Both of them were pleased when a letter arrived in his mailbox stating that his recipe had won second place, losing only to Rutabaga Milano.

B. *Correct the sentences above that you marked with X.*

ref

52   **Make each pronoun refer clearly to one antecedent.**

Since a pronoun takes the place of its antecedent, a pronoun's meaning is clear only when it points clearly to that antecedent. Two or more plausible antecedents will confuse your reader:

52

Ambiguous:	Alex told Rafael that he should be earning more money.
Clear:	Alex told Rafael, "You should be earning more money." *Or:* Alex told Rafael, "I should be earning more money." *Or:* Alex complained to Rafael about being underpaid.
Ambiguous:	As soon as Mrs. Kennedy christened the ship, she was set afloat in the Thames.
Clear:	As soon as Mrs. Kennedy christened her, the ship was set afloat in the Thames.

In the second pair of examples, sensible readers will know that the ship, not Mrs. Kennedy, was set afloat; but since they will notice the comical ambiguity, the sentence is still ineffective.

52a   Make each pronoun refer to a noun or to an earlier pronoun.

To keep references clear, make each pronoun refer to a noun used as a subject, object, or complement, not as a modifier or a possessive:

Ineffective:	Mrs. Valdez questioned the investigator's honesty even though he had helped her.
Effective:	Even though the investigator had helped her, Mrs. Valdez questioned his honesty.

Ineffective:	At Sybil's office, she is the manager.
Effective:	Sybil is the manager of her office.

Also be sure that a pronoun can logically refer to its antecedent:

Ineffective:	I had tonsillitis when I was eight, so my doctor removed them.
Effective:	I had tonsillitis when I was eight, so my doctor removed my tonsils.
	Or: When I was eight, my doctor removed my tonsils because they were continually inflamed.

52b   Make each pronoun refer to one word or to a specific group of words rather than to an implied idea.

Except in informal writing, use *you* when referring directly to your reader, not when referring to any person in general. Substitute *one* or an appropriate noun:

Ineffective:	Many people believe that college should help you earn a better living.
Effective:	Many people believe that college should help a person earn a better living.

Or: Many people believe that college should help one earn a better living.

Except in idiomatic expressions such as "It is cold," use *it* and *they* only to refer to specific nouns:

Ineffective: On page 381 of our text, it says that Henry Clay was "the great compromiser."

Effective: On page 381 of our text, the author says that Henry Clay was "the great compromiser."
Or: On page 381, our text says that Henry Clay was "the great compromiser."

Ineffective: They do not have many Catholics in Iraq.

Effective: Iraq does not have many Catholics.
Or: There are few Catholics in Iraq.

52c   Insert nouns to clarify the antecedents of *this, that,* and *which.*

52

This, that, and *which* are often vague when they refer broadly to an idea expressed or implied in a preceding clause. To avoid confusion, change the pronoun to a noun or add a noun.

Vague: The young residents did the actual cutting even though the surgeon received credit and payment for the operation. This is common in many hospitals.

Clear: The young residents did the actual cutting even though the surgeon received credit and payment for the operation. This practice is common in many hospitals.

Vague: The CPA reviewed tax returns after her interns prepared them, which is quite common.

Clear: The CPA reviewed tax returns after her interns prepared them, a common arrangement.

▼ EXERCISE

Underline all pronouns used inappropriately in the following sentences.

1. Maria enjoyed studying sociology, which led her to consider it as her major in college.

2. "It says in the newspaper that a degree in sociology can be used in many ways," Maria commented.

3. Maria told April that she could choose a major if she weren't so busy.

4. When Maria's father brought home a book that evaluated American colleges, she read it eagerly.

5. "They charge more for tuition in the North than they do in the South," Maria said.

6. One of the reasons Maria liked choosing sociology was that it would gain the approval of her parents.

7. She might need to go through graduate school to finish her education, but she didn't mind this.

8. After Maria finished reading the book on American colleges, she gave it to April.

9. April was in no hurry to plan her career; this is common in young people.

10. Maria and April agreed that she was not getting any younger.

52

53 Determine the correct case of a pronoun by the word's function in the sentence.

The personal pronouns (*I, we, you, he, she, it, they*) appear in different case forms depending on their function in the sentence: "I liked *her,* but *she* hated *me.*"

	Nominative	**Objective**	**Possessive***
First Person:	I, we	me, us	my, mine, our, ours
Second Person:	you	you	your, yours
Third Person:	he, she, it, they	him, her, it, them	his, her, hers, its, their, theirs

*Note that no apostrophe is used for the possessive pronouns.

53

The **nominative** (also called **subjective**) case forms are used for the subject and predicate nominative functions:

We were turned away. (subject)

This is *she.* (predicate nominative)

The **objective** case forms are used for direct objects, indirect objects, and objects of prepositions:

The modem gave *us* trouble all night. (indirect object)

The Cougars beat *us* badly in both games. (direct object)

Next year we will be ready for *them.* (object of preposition)

The **possessive** case forms are used to show possession:

Their product was no better than *ours.* (possessives)

Be especially careful of the pronoun case in compound structures. Note the following:

Incorrect: Him and his older brothers learned to play canasta.

Correct: He and his older brothers learned to play canasta.
(compound subject)

Incorrect: Mr. Edwards may try to get you and I in trouble.

Correct: Mr. Edwards may try to get you and me in trouble.
(object of *get*)

Incorrect: The judge was unsympathetic to my mother and I.

Correct: The judge was unsympathetic to my mother and me.
(object of *to*)

A pronoun used as an appositive (an explanatory word, phrase, or clause that clarifies a noun) should be in the same case as the noun or pronoun it refers to:

Correct: The culprits, Alice and I, were caught at midnight.

Correct: The police quickly apprehended the culprits, Alice and me.

Incorrect: Three contestants won prizes at the finale: Karen Turner, Kris Bercov, and me.

Correct: Three contestants won prizes at the finale: Karen Turner, Kris Bercov, and *I*.

Use the possessive form immediately before a gerund:

Incorrect: My parents are concerned about me working while carrying fifteen credit hours.

Correct: My parents are concerned about *my* working while carrying fifteen credit hours.

However, you can normally use a nonpossessive common noun before a gerund, especially if the noun is plural:

Correct: The officials attributed the rise in unemployment to *women entering* the job market.

Use the nominative case for the subject of an implied verb form:

Incorrect: No one on their team is as tall as me.

Correct: No one on their team is as tall as *I.* (understood: "am tall")

Use the nominative form as the subject of a clause regardless of the function of the clause:

Incorrect: Most Americans still show great respect for whomever is President.

Correct: Most Americans still show great respect for whoever is President. (*Whoever* is the subject of *is* in the final clause.)

In formal writing, such as research papers and theses, always use *whom* as you would *me* or any other objective form. Many people have stopped using *whom,* especially in speech and informal writing, but in most college writing it is best to use *whom* whenever it is called for.

53

Incorrect: Whom did you say was calling?

Correct: Who did you say was calling? (*Who* is the subject of *was.*)

Correct: Whom did you call? (*Whom* is the object of *call.*)

Correct: To whom was that call made? (*Whom* is the object of the preposition *to.*)

A quick way to determine the case is to rephrase such questions as statements—for example, "You did call whom."

As a relative pronoun, *whom* is often dropped from the sentence:

Correct: Commissioner Jackson is the only one [whom] we should reelect. (*Whom* is the direct object of *reelect*.)

▼ EXERCISE

A. *Study the following sentences. Mark X for those with improper pronoun case and C for those sentences that are correct.*

1. Maria believed that, out of her senior class, no one else wanted to go to college as much as her.

2. Few of the other students were as conscientious as she.

3. However, Bob and Marge Walker, the parents of April, believed that their daughter going to college was in doubt.

4. The school counselor was the person to whom they inquired.

5. The counselor could not find a record of April taking a college preparatory test.

6. "Who do you think is responsible for this problem?" Mrs. Walker asked.

7. "Her parents, Bob and me, would like to know."

8. The counselor replied that he would look through the records again and would call Marge and Bob to inform they about anything that turned up.

9. "Whom will we talk to if you don't succeed?" Mrs. Walker asked.

53

10. The counselor replied that him losing anything that came into his office would be a rare event.

B. *Correct the sentences above that you marked with X.*

adj/adv

 54 **Use adjectives to modify nouns and pronouns, and use adverbs to modify verbs, adjectives, or other adverbs.**

Both adjectives and adverbs are modifiers; they limit or describe other words.

Adjectives: The *radical* changes of personnel were *unpleasant* but *necessary.*

Adverbs: The *highly* complex steering mechanism turned the glider *smoothly.*

54

Adverbs are usually distinguished by their *-ly* endings *(rapidly, formally),* but many adjectives, such as *ghastly* and *heavenly,* also end in *-ly,* and many adverbs, such as *often* and *well,* do not. If you are in doubt whether a word is an adjective or adverb, check a dictionary.

   In very informal writing and speaking, certain adjectives— such as *sure, real,* and *good*—are often used in place of the adverbs *surely, really,* and *well.* In more formal writing, however, the safer practice is to use the adverb forms to modify verbs, adjectives, and other adverbs and to use adjectives to modify only nouns or pronouns:

Very informal: I did so *bad* on my first calculus test that I thought about dropping the class.

More formal: I did so *badly* on my first calculus test that I thought about dropping the class.

Use adjectives for complements after verbs such as *feel, look, smell, sound,* and *taste,* which function like forms of the verb *be;* use adverbs to modify these verbs. A quick test to make sure that the complement is correct is to substitute *is, was,* or other appropriate forms of the verb *be.*

Complement:	He was obviously upset, but he did not look *angry.* (Substitute *was not* for *did not look.*)
Adverb modifying verb:	He looked *angrily* at us, then stalked off.
Complement:	I felt *nervous* as I approached the dark building. (Substitute *was* for *felt.*)
Adverb modifying verb:	I felt *nervously* in my pocket for a match.

54a   Use the correct comparative and superlative forms of adverbs and adjectives.

54

Most short adjectives add *-er* for the comparative and *-est* for the superlative. Longer adjectives and most adverbs use *more* and *most.* A few have irregular comparative and superlative forms. Check a dictionary when you are in doubt.

Positive	*Comparative*	*Superlative*
strong	stronger	strongest
happy	happier	happiest
surprising	more surprising	most surprising
happily	more happily	most happily
good	better	best
well	better	best
bad	worse	worst

Use the comparative form when comparing two items, and use the superlative for three or more:

Incorrect:	Bill and Kathy were both excellent troubleshooters, but Kathy had the most even temperament.
Correct:	Bill and Kathy were both excellent troubleshooters, but Kathy had the *more* even temperament.
Incorrect:	Diamonds are the better sellers among the three stones most often picked for engagement rings.
Correct:	Diamonds are the *best* sellers among the three stones most often picked for engagement rings.

▼ EXERCISE

A. *Mark the following sentences with C if they are correct; mark with X those containing incorrectly used adjective or adverb forms.*

1. Maria sent applications to two schools, Harvard University and Click Memorial Union; Harvard was a great school, but C.M.U. was the closest of the two.

2. She felt pretty good about her chances of getting in either one.

3. However, the letter she got back from C.M.U. was worded very strange.

4. "Click Memorial Union accepts only the better students out of those who apply."

5. "Applicants who do good on their preparatory exams have the best chance of acceptance."

6. "We eagerly await further evidence of your skills."

7. Maria had the sudden thought that of her choices of attending Harvard, attending Click, or staying home,

54

the last was not the worse option.

8. However, she knew that C.M.U. had to be better than it first seemed.

9. She felt nervously about her choice of C.M.U.

10. But her parents were nervous about her going all the way to Massachusetts, so Maria chose C.M.U.

B. *Correct those sentences above marked X.*

†

55   Use the verb tense appropriate to the time of an action or situation.

Although English relies heavily on adverbs and adverbial phrases and clauses to refer to time *(now, tomorrow, yesterday morning, after the play had already started),* English also indicates time by changes in the verb. By using verb tenses accurately, you can help your reader keep track of time relationships in your writing.

English verbs have only two primary tenses—present and past—but by using auxiliary verbs we can create complex verb forms. Thus, we can list three simple tenses, three perfect tenses, and progressive forms for all six tenses.

Simple tenses.   The **simple present tense** is far from simple in the ways that it is used:

Present time:	I *hear* you calling. He *looks* anxious.
Habitual time:	I *hear* the train go by every morning. He *repairs* his old Volkswagen himself.
Historical present:	Brutus *hears* the mob hailing Caesar.

Literary present: In "The Man That Corrupted Hadleyburg," Twain *exposes* the ability of money to corrupt us.

Future action: The case *goes* to court next week. When the defense attorney *finishes* her remarks, the jury will retire.

In the present tense, verbs of third-person singular subjects require an *-s* ending.

The **past tense** is formed by adding *-ed* to regular verbs or by changing the spelling of most irregular verbs. The **future tense** uses the auxiliary *shall* or *will*. Traditionally, *shall* has been reserved for use with first-person subjects (*I shall go), will* with second- and third-person subjects (*you will go; she will go),* except when the writer reverses the usage to show strong emphasis: "I *will win.* You *shall* obey me." Today, only the most formal writing observes that distinction, and *will* is regularly used with all persons.

The following table shows the forms for a regular verb *(play)* and for the most irregular and most often used English verb, *be:*

55

	Regular Verb	*Be*
Present:	I play you play he, she, it plays we, you, they play	I am you are he, she, it is we, you, they are
Past:	I played you played he, she, it played we, you, they played	I was you were he, she, it was we, you, they were
Future:	I will [shall] play you will play he, she, it will play we, you, they will play	I will [shall] be you will be he, she, it will be we, you, they will be

Perfect tenses. The perfect tenses indicate a relationship between two times. The **present perfect** refers to an indefinite time in the recent past or to a time beginning in the past and continuing to the present:

> Representative Green *has voted* with the conservatives more often than with the liberals.

> This five-dollar watch *has kept* perfect time for two years.

The **past perfect** indicates a time before some other specified or implied time in the past:

> The teams *had met* twice before the play-offs.

	Regular Verb	Be

Present Perfect:	I have played
	you have played
	he, she, it has played
	
	we, you, they
	  have played
		I have been
		you have been
		he, she, it has
		  been
		we, you, they
		  have been

Past Perfect:	I had played
	you had played
	he, she, it had played
	
	we, you, they
	  had played
		I had been
		you had been
		he, she, it had
		  been
		we, you, they
		  had been

Future Perfect:	I will [shall] have
	  played
	you will have played
	
	he, she, it will
	  have played
	we, you, they will
	  have played
		I will [shall] have
		  been
		you will have
		  been
		he, she, it will
		  have been
		we, you, they
		  will have been

55

Similarly, the **future perfect** may be used to indicate a time before some other stated or implied time in the future:

Before they return, the astronauts *will have broken* the record for time spent in space.

Note that *return* in the previous example is a typical case of the present used for future time. This use of the present is very common in dependent clauses.

The perfect tenses combine a form of the auxiliary *have* with the past participle of the main verb:

Progressive tenses. Progressive forms of verbs indicate continuous actions:

Present Progressive:	I am playing he, she, it is playing we, you, they are playing
Past Progressive:	I was playing he, she, it was playing we, you, they were playing

Future Progressive:	I, he, she, it will [shall] be
	    playing
	we, you, they will [shall] be
	    playing

Present Perfect Progressive:	I have been playing he, she, it has been playing we, you, they have been playing
Past Perfect Progressive:	I, he, she, it had been playing we, you, they had been playing

Future Perfect Progressive:	I, he, she, it will [shall] have
	    been playing
	we, you, they will [shall] have
	    been playing

The candidates *are waiting* for the results of the election.

I *was running* toward the corner when my knee gave way.

I *shall be working* on my tax return all day tomorrow.

Mr. Velkoff told me last week that I *had been using* the wrong database for at least six months.

There are progressive forms for all six tenses:

Tenses of verbals. Verbals (infinitives, gerunds, and participles) have present and present-perfect forms. Each participle also has a past form:

Present infinitive:	to sink, to be sinking
Perfect infinitive:	to have sunk
Present gerund:	sinking
Perfect gerund:	having sunk
Present participle:	sinking
Perfect participle:	having sunk, having been sinking
Past participle:	sunk

Use the past or perfect form of a verbal to indicate a time before the main verb in the clause:

Amelia would like [now] *to have seen* last night's fireworks.

He could not get over *having failed* his teammates.

Having signed all the letters, she went home early.

But: The woman *addressing* the assembly will retire next month. (The present participle here indicates the same time as the speaking or writing of the sentence.)

Use the past participle to indicate a time before that of the main verb or to describe a condition that began before the time of the main verb:

Angered by the story, the apartment owner sued both the newspaper and the reporter.

In most other cases, use the present forms of verbals:

Emily decided to *play* selections from Sondheim. (The playing follows the deciding.)

Emily enjoys *playing* selections from Sondheim. (The playing and the enjoying take place at the same time.)

Writing about *Dick Tracy,* Pauline Kael remarked. . . . (The writing and the remarking take place together.)

Voice. English verbs show active voice ("The butler *committed* the crime") or passive voice ("The crime *was committed* by the butler"). The forms presented in this section have all been in the active voice. Verbs in the passive voice combine a form of *be* with the past participle of the main verb:

	Active	*Passive*
Present:	I know	I am known
Past:	I knew	I was known
Future:	I will know	I will be known
Present Perfect:	I have known	I have been known
Past Perfect:	I had known	I had been known
Future Perfect:	I will have known	I will have been known

55

Progressive verbs are sometimes used in the passive voice: "I *am being followed.*" Careful writers generally avoid the passive voice because it is wordy, indirect, and less natural than the active. For a thorough discussion of voice and style, see **23e**.

▼ EXERCISE

A. *Mark these sentences with C if they are correct and with X if they contain errors in verb tense.*

1. In 1994 Click Memorial Union will have been operating for seventy years.

2. In 1974 the university was being celebrated as one of the South's leaders in the study of sociology.

3. C.M.U. invested a great deal of money in the sociology program after it had been described as lagging behind the other departments in Arts and Sciences.

4. When Maria took her first sociology class, she felt that she won't understand the instructor.

5. Edwin Click, a grand-nephew of Ezekiel, received his doctorate in 1985 and had started teaching at C.M.U. the next year.

6. Now Click puts his emphasis on teaching and decided to let his research wait a few years.

7. However, he still used a very abstract approach to sociology, and Maria had decided that he was hard to understand.

8. "My major problem at this point," she thought, "will be translating Clickese into English."

9. Professor Click had told the class that he will meet with students who had questions.

55

10. Having taken the midterm, Maria then faced the research paper.

B. *Correct the sentences marked X.*

56 **Use the correct principal parts of irregular verbs.**

You must know the principal parts of verbs in order to form all the tenses correctly. English verbs have three principal parts: the infinitive (or present stem), the past tense, and the past participle. For regular verbs, the past tense and past participle are formed by adding *-d* or *-ed* to the infinitive: *walk, walked, walked; move, moved, moved.* Other verbs—the irregular verbs—form the past tense and past participle by various means, usually by changing a vowel in the infinitive *(win, won).* The list below includes the principal parts of the most common irregular verbs and a few regular verbs often mistakenly treated as irregular. Your college-level dictionary also gives the principal parts of irregular verbs. If your dictionary does not list the past tense and past participle forms, you can assume that the verb is regular.

56

Infinitive	*Past Tense*	*Past Participle*
awake	awaked (awoke)	awaked (awoke)
beat	beat	beaten
become	became	become
begin	began	begun
bend	bent	bent
bite	bit	bitten
bleed	bled	bled
blow	blew	blown
break	broke	broken
bring	brought	brought

Infinitive	*Past Tense*	*Past Participle*
build	built	built
burst	burst	burst
buy	bought	bought
catch	caught	caught
choose	chose	chosen
come	came	come
cut	cut	cut
deal	dealt	dealt
dig	dug	dug
dive	dived (dove)	dived
do	did	done
drag	dragged	dragged
draw	drew	drawn
drink	drank	drunk
drive	drove	driven
drown	drowned	drowned
eat	ate	eaten
fall	fell	fallen
fight	fought	fought
fly	flew	flown
forget	forgot	forgotten (forgot)
freeze	froze	frozen
get	got	gotten (got)
give	gave	given
go	went	gone
grow	grew	grown
have	had	had
hide	hid	hidden
hold	held	held
keep	kept	kept
know	knew	known
lead	led	led
leave	left	left
lend	lent	lent
let	let	let
lose	lost	lost
mean	meant	meant
prove	proved	proven (proved)
read	read	read
ride	rode	ridden
ring	rang	rung

Infinitive	Past Tense	Past Participle
rise	rose	risen
run	ran	run
say	said	said
see	saw	seen
sell	sold	sold
send	sent	sent
sew	sewed	sewn (sewed)
shake	shook	shaken
shave	shaved	shaved (shaven)
show	showed	shown (showed)
shrink	shrank (shrunk)	shrunk (shrunken)
sink	sank (sunk)	sunk
speak	spoke	spoken
swear	swore	sworn
swim	swam	swum
take	took	taken
teach	taught	taught
tell	told	told
think	thought	thought
throw	threw	thrown
wear	wore	worn
win	won	won
write	wrote	written

56

A few verbs with two distinct meanings have different principal parts in each meaning:

bid (a price)	bid	bid
bid (an order)	bade (bid)	bidden (bid)
hang (execute)	hanged	hanged
hang (suspend)	hung	hung
shine (emit light)	shone	shone
shine (polish)	shined	shined

Three pairs of verbs are easily confused, especially in their past-tense and past-participle forms. The key distinction is that one of each pair is transitive (it takes an object) but the other is intransitive (no object).

Transitive

lay (place)	laid	laid
set (place)	set	set
raise (lift)	raised	raised

Intransitive

lie (recline)	lay	lain
lie (falsehood)	lied	lied
sit (be seated)	sat	sat
rise (rise up)	rose	risen

He *laid* his head on a rock and *lay* in the sun for an hour.

She *set* her pen on the desk and *sat* waiting for others to finish.

He *rose* from the bed and *raised* the window.

▼ EXERCISE

Underline the correct verb forms in the following sentences.

56

1. Maria decided that the best topic for her paper (lay, laid) in the work of Émile Durkheim.

2. Durkheim (lead, led) the intellectuals of the twentieth century to (see, seen) the importance of sociology.

3. Today, many people have (forgot, forgotten) that Durkheim (set, sat) up the study of deviance as a primary field of sociological inquiry.

4. Maria had (dived, dove) into her research with a vengeance.

5. She had (wore, worn) out two pencils while taking notes in the library.

6. Her efforts that semester (lend, lent) credence to her parents' theories about the value of hard work.

7. When she received an *A* on the assignment, her face (shined, shone) with pleasure.

8. She (hanged, hung) the paper on her bulletin board.

9. The memory of Professor Click's difficult lectures (shrank, shrunk) with time.

10. Maria realized that by the time she finished school, she would have (wrote, written) many more essays.

mo

57 **Use the mood required by your sentence.**

English has three moods: **indicative** for statements of fact and questions about facts, **imperative** for commands, and **subjunctive** for wishes and demands or for statements that are contrary to fact.

57

Indicative: I know who he *is.*

Imperative: *Be* yourself.

Subjunctive: If I *were* you, I would avoid that subject.

The subjunctive is used far less now than earlier in the history of the language, but there are some situations in which the subjunctive is still the only choice:

Correct: She demanded that Thomas *finish* the work. (Desired action. Less formally, this might be expressed, "She told Thomas to finish the work.")

Correct: It is essential that I *be seen* at the boss's party.

Correct: Eddie drank as if Prohibition *were* being reintroduced. (contrary to fact)

Correct: Eve wishes that she *were* more talented. (contrary to fact)

Only a few forms of the subjunctive are different from the indicative forms given in **55**. Those forms are shown here in bold type:

Present:	that I walk that he, she, it **walk** (no -*s*) that we, you, they walk	that I **be** that he, she, it **be** that we, you, they **be**
Past:	that I walked that he, she, it walked that we, you, they walked	that I **were** that he, she, it **were** that we, you, they were
Present Perfect:	that I have walked that he, she, it **have** walked that we, you, they have walked	that I have been that he, she, it **have** been that we, you, they have been

EXERCISE

Study the sentences below. Mark with C those that are correct and with X those that have errors in mood. Correct the sentences marked X.

1. Maria looked at her humanities class as though it was a harmless diversion.

2. However, the instructor, Mr. Santellini, insisted that humanities be seen as the "cultural repository of human memory."

3. If Maria were not interested at first, Mr. Santellini changed her mind.

4. He said, "If I was in your situation, I would explore the link between humanities and sociology."

5. He insisted that this connection be the topic of her research paper.

shift

58 ▼ Be consistent when using verbs and pronouns.

To present your information smoothly and clearly, be consistent in the tense, voice, and mood of verbs and in the person and number of nouns and pronouns. Unnecessary shifts—from past to present or from singular to plural, for instance—make awkward reading and can confuse your reader. Some shifts are necessary—to indicate passing time, for example—but it is best to make such shifts only when you have no other choice.

58a Avoid unnecessary shifts in tense, voice, and mood.

A change in **tense** usually signals a change in time, so be sure not to give your reader a false signal by switching tenses unnecessarily. A shift such as the following is often just the result of carelessness:

Shift in tense: As he *turned* the corner, he *became* aware that someone *is* following him.

Corrected: As he *turned* the corner, he *became* aware that someone *was* following him.

Be careful not to shift time when you are using one of the perfect tenses:

Shift in tense: We had paid our dues and are ready to begin attending meetings. (past perfect with present)

Corrected: We have paid our dues and are ready to begin attending meetings. (present perfect with present) *Or:* We had paid our dues and were ready to begin attending meetings. (past perfect with past)

See **55** for a discussion of verb tenses.

Active and passive **voice** can be mixed in one sentence ("She *ran* for senator twice and *was defeated* twice"), but an unnecessary shift in voice can spoil the focus of a sentence:

Shift in voice: Electrolysis is used by Dr. Lambiase, and he also performs minor surgery.

Improved: Dr. Lambiase uses electrolysis and also performs minor surgery.

58

Shift in voice: The report showed that white-collar criminals almost never serve hard time, while long sentences are served by petty burglars.

Improved: The report showed that white-collar criminals almost never serve hard time, while petty burglars serve long sentences.

Active voice is usually more direct and natural than passive voice (see **23e**).

A change in mood should reflect a change in the way the writer views the action or situation being described: "If I *were* willing to lie, I *would tell* you I enjoyed the story, but I *am* not willing to lie." Unmotivated shifts are distracting:

Shift in mood: If I were the President, I would take action, not act as if I was still in Congress.

Corrected: If I were the President, I would take action, not act as if I were still in Congress.

See **57**.

58b   Be consistent in the number and person of your nouns and pronouns.

Shift the number of nouns and pronouns (singular or plural) only to show a valid change: "I wanted to go to Europe, but *we* could not afford the trip."

Faulty: The class of 1996 was academically outstanding, but they were unusual.

Improved: The class of 1996 was academically outstanding, but it was unusual.

Faulty: The jury was given instructions by the judge before they were asked to start their deliberations.

Improved: The jury was given instructions by the judge before it was asked to start its deliberations.

Similarly, keep the person of your pronouns consistent. Be especially careful to avoid slipping into the universal *you* (second person) when you are writing in the third person *(she, he, they, it)*:

58

Faulty: Deer hunters in the Ocala National Forest must wear bright clothing so you will not get shot.

Improved: Deer hunters in the Ocala National Forest must wear bright clothing so they will not get shot.

Faulty: Other hunters will shoot at you if they see movement in the brush.

Improved: Often other hunters will shoot carelessly if they see movement in the brush.

▼ EXERCISE

A. *Mark C for sentences without awkward shifts and X for those with awkward shifts.*

1. Maria was leery about her instructor for Sociology II, Ms. Chan, because students always have trouble with her class.

2. If a student had trouble early on in Chan's class, he or she is on a downhill path.

3. The class met in a building that was known by students as "Afterthoughts," and it is located near the Student Center.

4. The building had no air conditioning nor any other amenity that invites attendance at classes.

5. Maria decided that if the class was held in any other campus building, the students would have a less difficult time.

6. Ms. Chan was feared by many of the students, but Maria excelled in Sociology II.

7. Each of her friends in the class struggled, but they were all passing at midterm.

8. The third exam was failed by seven students, but Maria received an *A*.

9. After the third exam had been successfully undertaken, Maria was ready for her next research paper.

10. If she had been allowed to choose her topic, Maria would have selected the work of Howard Becker, but Ms. Chan insisted that Maria work on the early writings of Max Weber.

B. *Reword those sentences above marked* X.

58

C H A P T E R **9**

Using Appropriate Diction

Diction refers to selecting and using appropriate language—putting the right word in the right place to say just what you intend. Effective writing requires a respect for words, an awareness of their various uses and the various effects they can have on readers. It requires using words that are specific and concrete, precise and forceful, vivid and clear. Finding such words may be your greatest challenge as a writer. To meet that challenge, you must know what words mean and how to use them. As you become more sensitive to words—to their ability to clarify or obscure and to their suitability for your purposes and audiences—you will use them with increasing confidence.

Words are "right" only when they have an appropriate effect in your sentence; therefore, choosing words always means considering the context in which they are used. We speak and write in various "languages": one for friends, one for family members, one for employers and instructors. Although you may speak of an *"awesome* evening," you will generally write *"enjoyable* evening" unless your reader would expect informality, as may be the case in a narrative essay. The writing context will usually require you to *submit* a report (not *hand it in*) or to provide *abundant* (not *a lot of*) facts.

A college-level dictionary will help you decide whether the word that you think is the right one actually expresses what you intend. It will also warn you if a word is considered slang, obsolete, or in some other way inappropriate for college writing. The following sections will help you use your dictionary more efficiently and will offer other advice about choosing words wisely.

lev

59   Write at a level appropriate to your subject and audience.

A writer's choice of words involves basic questions of style: How should I sound? Does my subject require a relaxed tone or a dignified tone? Should I talk directly to the reader? You can achieve an effective style by avoiding stilted, impersonal language and by using the appropriate person (see **58b**), using the active voice whenever possible (see **23e**), and using sentences that are properly emphatic (see **23**). In addition, effective writers are aware of various levels of usage when considering their audience's expectations.

Dictionaries generally classify words according to four types—formal, standard, informal, or slang:

Formal or learned words are more common in reading than in speaking and are serious and scholarly in tone. Some examples are *prevaricate* (to lie), *ameliorate* (to improve), and *altercation* (quarrel).

Standard or popular words are familiar to the widest group of educated speakers and writers. For instance, *truth* is the standard counterpart of the more formal *veracity*.

Informal or **colloquial** words are appropriate to spoken language and to writing that aims for a conversational effect.

Many good writers use colloquial terms for humor or for a casual, relaxed tone.

Informal	*Standard*
flunk	fail
mad	angry
guy	man
TV show	television program
job	position
to kid	to tease
to cook up	to invent, concoct

Slang is highly informal language that is used to add color and novelty to speech. Because it often does not last long enough to have a clearly established meaning, slang is inappropriate in most college writing.

Slang	*Standard*
cool	admirable
neat	wonderful
uptight	very nervous
chill	relax

The English language includes many dialects—different ways of communicating in particular geographic areas or among particular groups of people. The predominant dialect used by educated writers and speakers of American English is called Standard English. It is the variety of English expected in college essays, business reports, and books like this one. Most dictionaries mark the words not usually used in Standard English as *nonstandard, substandard,* or *dialect. Nowheres,* for example, is labeled *Dial.* in *Webster's New Collegiate Dictionary.* (*Note:* Some words may be standard in one sense but not in another. *Learn* is nonstandard when used to mean "teach.") The abbreviations for these labels vary; your dictionary will have a section at the front or back explaining its labels and abbreviations.

59

Standard English is written and spoken in many styles, which we can arbitrarily divide into three "levels": formal, informal, and general. Each level is appropriate in some situations but not in others.

Formal English is found in technical reports, scholarly books and articles, and many types of professional or academic writing. It uses an extensive, elevated vocabulary and sentences more complex than those found in other levels of writing. It avoids contractions and colloquial expressions and therefore sounds different from the way people speak:

> Money and the habitual resort to its use are conceived to be simply the ways and means by which consumable goods are acquired, and therefore simply a convenient method by which to procure the pleasurable sensations of consumption; these latter being in hedonistic theory the sole and overt end of all economic endeavor. Money values have therefore no other significance than that of purchasing power over consumable goods, and money is simply an expedient of computation.
>
> —*Thorstein Veblen*

Informal English, on the other hand, has a more conversational tone. Writers of Informal English regularly use contractions, colloquial expressions (*a couple of* instead of *two, really* instead of *very*), and slang. They usually write in loose sentences with more *and*'s and fewer subordinate clauses than are used in other levels of writing. Informal English is popular in journalism but is usually inappropriate in most college writing:

> Tattoos may not be good for your mainstream image, but they can make you feel a lot better about yourself. You might think that people get tattooed because they like the way it looks or the way it feels, and that's true, but what really happens, at least for many people, is that the pain and the permanence of the tattoo are like a test of your willingness to face where you've been and where you're going. Fake tattoos that go on with water and come off with alcohol just don't cut it.

59

General English follows a middle course between formal and informal. Most of its sentences are less complex than those of Formal English but tighter than those of Informal English. In the right circumstances, General English might use such relatively formal words as *haughty* and *vilify* or informal words such as *stuck-up* and *trash,* but most of the time it uses such words as *proud* and *slander.* General English is usually the best choice for college or business writing.

> Beginnings are apt to be shadowy, and so it is with the beginnings of that great mother of life, the sea. Many people have debated how and when the earth got its ocean, and it is not surprising that their explanations do not always agree. For the plain and inescapable truth is that no one was there to see, and in the absence of eyewitness accounts there is bound to be a certain amount of disagreement.
>
> —*Rachel Carson*

▼ EXERCISE

A. *Label each of the following paragraphs F for Formal, I for Informal, or G for General English. Be prepared to discuss the circumstances in which each paragraph would be appropriate.*

59

1. It is the contention of some philosophers that the aforementioned moral scheme was the historical antecedent of the idea of virtue as it is defined here, the same moral scheme which, in a variety of diverse forms and with numerous rival theories, came to dominate the thinking of the European Middle Ages, at least from the twelfth century onwards, a scheme which included both classical and theistic elements.

2. It used to be you started college with a portable typewriter and maybe even a tape recorder, and you thought you were ready for a run at the dean's list. But if you look at today's college students, who grew up around computers, you find gadgets and gizmos

that their parents' generation would connect to *Star Trek* but that, in fact, are absolutely needed for the high-tech learning that goes on.

3. Not too long ago, *multimedia* meant looking at a film-strip, accompanied by a scratchy record explaining the wonders of nature. More recently, computer technology has given a whole new meaning to the word *multimedia*. Now text, music, and spoken words, once stored separately, are in digital form, allowing them to be interwoven and recombined in a new format that allows students to interact with information in all its various guises.

B. *Complete the following exercises by using a college-level dictionary.*

1. Check your dictionary to see if the following words are considered slang, colloquial (informal), or standard: *crook, duds, exam, kid, jock, hacker, klutzy, nutty, sleaze, spin.*

2. Look up the word *gimmick* in your dictionary to see how it can be both colloquial (informal) and slang. Find another such example.

3. Determine which of these words is considered formal, informal (colloquial), slang, or standard: *hassle* (noun), *hassle* (verb), *hang-up, altercation, argument.* How do the meanings differ? Under what circumstances would each be appropriate?

4. List five slang terms, and write short, original definitions for each. Then compare your definitions with those in your dictionary.

d

60 **Keep your level of usage consistent.**

Appropriate diction requires a consistent style. Mixing formal and informal language can produce distracting and absurd results:

> The Governor's speech to the Legislature was not one that his opponents could blow off.

Here the slangy conclusion clashes with the standard level of the rest of the sentence. Just as you would not wear shorts with a dinner jacket, you do not want to call attention to yourself by inappropriately mixing styles of writing.

Inappropriate: The *New York Times* has this quote that goes, "All the news that's fit to print."

Appropriate: The *New York Times* has a motto that says, "All the news that's fit to print."

Keep in mind that *quote* is a verb, not a noun. The noun form is *quotation,* and this word refers to quoted text, not primary text.

60

▼ EXERCISE

Study the levels of usage in the following sentences. Rewrite in General English any sentences that are too informal for college writing or that combine slang with more formal usage. If a sentence is correct, mark it C.

1. Our trip to the museum was a surprisingly fun experience.

2. The English language, Orwell observed, is unquestionably hard up.

3. At the recent stockholders' meeting, the president made several off the wall remarks.

4. Studying history has never turned Jan on that much.

5. Many television viewers, disgusted with commercials, opt for public television channels.

6. TV ads tell you that remedies are instantly available for any conceivable hang-up.

7. Even after a whole year of studying Shakespeare, Jeff still finds the plays tough to relate to.

8. Two candidates withdrew from the current presidential primary when they were accused of not being sufficiently hard-nosed about crime.

9. The dean advised the faculty to chill-out after submitting their grades.

10. The computer science final exam is not one that you can expect to ace.

idiom

61 **Use the idiom of written English.**

An **idiom** is a customary expression peculiar to a language. For example, native speakers of English will say "with the naked eye," not "with a bare eye," though it is impossible to explain why. You may have difficulty with some of the idiomatic uses of certain prepositions: When do you say *differ from* instead of *differ with*? Do you say *to the contrary* or *on the contrary*? If your ear cannot guide you, a college-level dictionary usually can. Here are some troublesome phrases:

Unidiomatic	*Idiomatic*
absolve of	absolve from
accept to	accept by
accuse with	accuse of
accustom with	accustom to
adhere in (*or* by)	adhere to
adjacent of	adjacent to
agree in	agree to (a proposal)
	agree on (a course of action)
angry at (a person)	angry with (a person)
apologize about	apologize for
bored of	bored with (*or* by)
comply to	comply with
concur about	concur with (a person)
	concur in (a decision or action)
conform in	conform to (*or* with)
derived of	derived from
different than	different from
in accordance to	in accordance with
in search for	in search of
intend on doing	intend to do
interfere about	interfere with (= prevent)
	interfere in (= meddle)
oblivious about	oblivious of (*or* to)
plan on doing	plan to do
preferable than	preferable to
similar with	similar to
superior than	superior to

61

▼ EXERCISE

Reword any of the following sentences that contain unidiomatic expressions. If a sentence is correct, mark it C.

1. The mayor was not concerned for the ownership of the land.

2. Jason believes that all imported wines are superior to domestic ones.

3. Our new neighbors are trying hard to be different than everyone else on the street.

4. Sara was too angry at him to apologize about her own rudeness.

5. Nick graduated high school at sixteen, benefiting by an accelerated program.

6. Some people find themselves caught in a vicious cycle in which they cannot escape.

7. Women are more capable to hold high-stress military jobs than many people think.

8. Laura did not concur with the majority decision.

9. The story contains a warning on amassing wealth and being obsessed over power.

10. Because of today's attitudes of money, a desire for upward mobility is prevalent with many Americans.

vague

62 Use specific and concrete words.

Consider the following sentences:

> We protected all of the plants in the yard.

> We mulched the shrubs, mounded around the rosebushes, and covered the eucalyptus tree.

The second sentence is more specific; it identifies the plants and the ways of protecting them. It is longer, but the extra words give the reader a clearer picture.

Specific terms give more information than general ones. For example, *surgeon* implies *doctor,* but *doctor* does not identify a person as a surgeon. If you find yourself writing *people* when you mean *U.S. citizens* or *college students,* you are not asking yourself this important question: Am I identifying what I am referring to as specifically as I should? The following list shows how little effort it takes to become more specific:

General	*Specific*	*More Specific*
vehicle	car	Toyota Cressida
go	run	sprint
go	walk	shuffle
religion	Christianity	Roman Catholicism
officer	Cabinet officer	Secretary of State

The best choice is usually the most specific expression that says what you mean. In the following examples, notice how the specific sentences clarify the general ones:

General: The vegetables were prepared.

Specific: We chopped the celery, diced the carrots, and sliced the onions.

Specific: We steamed the carrots and baked the Idaho potatoes.

General: Jan worked.

Specific: Jan sold paint at her uncle's hardware store for two years.

Specific: Jan spent last weekend cleaning the windows, floors, and walls of her apartment.

Abstract terms often combine with general terms in dull writing. An abstract term names something intangible, such as an idea or a quality: *democracy, finance, linguistics.* A concrete term, on the other hand, points to something physically real: *desk, checkbook, motorcycle.* We could not communicate complex ideas without using abstract terms, but dull

62

writing tends to be unnecessarily abstract. Sentences filled with *aspects, cases, factors, circumstances,* and *instances* will weaken your writing. Many writers mistakenly convert verbs (*explain, prefer*) into abstract nouns (*explanation, preference*) and use those nouns with such vague verbs as *be, have,* or *make:*

> Jonathan offered no explanation for his preference for California wines.

We can improve the sentence by changing the abstract nouns back to verbs:

> Jonathan did not explain why he preferred California wines.

Notice how the following abstract sentence, taken from a newspaper report, is improved by avoiding the abstract nouns *decline* and *use:*

Abstract:	The U.S. Department of Agriculture statistics show a decline in the annual per capita use of eggs during the period 1974 to 1984.
More concrete:	According to U.S. Department of Agriculture statistics, the average American ate fewer eggs in 1984 than in 1974.

Often you may not be able to make your writing more concrete simply by changing a few words. If your sentences are filled with abstract and general terms, you may find that you need to add specific examples. Vague language often indicates vague or incomplete thinking.

Vague:	The government official visited the new company headquarters.
Specific:	Joan Wood Branham, the Secretary of Commerce, visited the new Southwestern Bell headquarters in suburban St. Louis.

62

▼ EXERCISE

Mark specific or concrete sentences with S and those that are vaguely worded with X. Rewrite those marked X with specific, concrete words.

Example: Plants can combat indoor air pollution.

Some common houseplants can scour the air of carbon monoxide, benzene, and other harmful chemical fumes.

1. The media are often blamed for too many things.
2. New paint will brighten this old building.
3. For many people, music is a major source of spirituality.
4. Married couples need many resources.
5. The space program continues to make a significant contribution to our society.
6. In many cases, consumers are misled by advertising.
7. Toy commercials on television easily manipulate young children's minds.
8. Alternative medicine has undergone considerable growth.
9. The new millennium offers the possibility of many interesting scenarios.
10. In the 1990s, rap has had a major influence on musical experiments in jazz, rock, and the blues.

63

ww

63   **Make sure that you understand the meanings of words.**

A well-chosen word, Eric Sevareid once said, is worth a thousand pictures. If you are to select the word that expresses precisely what you intend to say, you must understand its denotation—what it literally means. If you write *notorious* when you mean *famous,* or *erotic* when you mean *erratic,* you will confuse your readers and cause them to doubt your competence as a writer. The Glossary of Usage (page 384) lists a number of easily confused words.

Imprecise: Many English classes require at least one *analyzation* of a poem or story.

Precise: Many English classes require at least one *analysis* of a poem or story.

Imprecise: The 1993 article by Olsen *quotes* that "computer-aided literature studies have not yet had the impact many scholars expected."

Precise: The 1993 article by Olsen *states* that "computer-aided literature studies have not yet had the impact many scholars expected."

▼ EXERCISE

A. *Determine the difference between these paired words:*

63

1. apprehend—comprehend
2. simple—simplistic
3. notable—notorious
4. exceedingly—excessively
5. disinterested—uninterested

6. fortunate—fortuitous
7. feasible—possible
8. forceful—forcible
9. illusion—allusion
10. imply—infer

B. *Is the italicized word in each of the following sentences correct? If not, supply the correct word. If a sentence is correct, mark it C.*

1. Louise's office *services* disabled students.

2. Chemical research *includes* effort, time, and efficiency.

3. At the *onset* of the class, the instructor gave a pop quiz.

4. Bob did not wish to be *involved* in his ex-wife's problems.

5. In our *distraughtness* after the accident, we forgot to call our families.

6. Good teachers usually try to *elicit* involvement from students.

7. Before her death, Mrs. Wilson *dispersed* money to ten charities.

8. Medieval Christianity played an important *factor* in the lives of every European.

9. The author goes on to *express* that Lawrence is a powerful writer.

10. Five students, *disinterested* in the lecture, fell sound asleep.

 Make sure that the connotations of your words are appropriate.

64

We choose words for their literal as well as for their implied meanings. Whereas **denotations** (literal dictionary definitions) are neutral, **connotations**—the suggested or implied meanings of words—convey feelings and attitudes and include emotional overtones. For example, a dictionary will define *politician* as one who actively engages in politics. But if you describe a fellow student as a "real politician," you call up not the literal meaning of *politician,* its denotation, but its connotations: your fellow student is a smooth operator. Consider the differences in tone in each of these sentences:

The faculty senate *discussed* the proposed grading system.

The faculty senate *debated* the proposed grading system.

The faculty senate *argued about* the proposed grading system.

The faculty senate *quarreled over* the proposed grading system.

After three hours of *questioning,* the *detained protesters* were *released.*

After three hours of *grilling,* the *political prisoners* were *liberated.*

The dictionary can help you distinguish among various synonyms whose meanings overlap yet remain distinct:

—*rare* is applied to something of which there are not many instances or specimens and usually connotes, therefore, great value [a *rare* gem]; *infrequent* applies to that which occurs only at long intervals [his *infrequent* trips]; *uncommon* and *unusual* refer to that which does not ordinarily occur and is therefore exceptional or remarkable [her *uncommon* generosity, this *unusual* heat]; *scarce* applies to something of which there is, at the moment, an inadequate supply [potatoes are *scarce* these days].

—*Webster's New World Dictionary*

64

Many words have powerful social and political overtones. Because these words may evoke personal, emotional responses in those who hear or read them, you must be conscious of their connotations. *Loaded words,* used especially by propagandists and advertisers, appeal to emotion rather than to reason. These words are imprecise and biased. Words such as *un-American, radical, leftist, subversive,* and *reactionary* indicate prejudicial political stereotyping. Political commentators sometimes refer to liberals as "bleeding hearts" or to welfare payments as "government handouts."

64a   Avoid sexist language.

Among the changes occurring in contemporary usage is that writers are trying to avoid sexist language and are using less offensive, more inclusive terminology. Although much of this terminology was once exclusively male, the language preferred today is designed to include women. Good examples are the changes in job titles from *salesman* to *salesperson* and the change from the generic use of *man* or *mankind,* in referring to both men and women, to *human beings* or *humankind.* Other gender-neutral terms that prevent sex-role stereotyping are the following:

	rather than:	
chairperson, chair		chairman
member of the clergy		clergyman
firefighter		fireman
personnel		manpower
member of Congress, legislator		congressman
worker		workman
server		waitress, waiter
technician		repairman

You should also avoid using singular masculine pronouns *(he, him, his)* to refer to both men and women when you are unsure of the gender of the antecedent or when both sexes are involved (see **51b**). That is, you can change:

Every writer has *his* own story to tell.

to:

Every writer has *his or her* own story to tell.

However, because the use of *his or her* can become awkward, a better strategy is to use the plural:

Writers have *their* own stories to tell.

You can also rewrite sentences so that the issue of gender does not arise:

Before starting his practice, a physician must put in many long, hard years of work.

64

Before starting a practice, a physician must put in many long, hard years of work.

In some instances, the plural cannot be used, so you will have to write *he or she, him or her,* or *his or her.* But doing so indicates to your reader that you are aware of the problem of sexist language and are trying to avoid it.

▼ EXERCISE

A. *Complete the following sentences by selecting the most appropriate words.*

1. Under the circumstances, the cashier's attitude toward the robber was surprisingly _____ (lenient, reasonable, temperate).

2. Beginning drivers are often a bit too _____ (wary, cautious, discreet).

3. Because of some low grades, my plans to attend law school do not seem _____ (feasible, possible, practicable, probable).

4. Paloma attended only one of our _____ (scarce, rare, infrequent, unusual) meetings.

5. The new model-Z car is an unbeatable combination of European _____ (skill, genius, artistry, craftsmanship) and the traditionally _____ (courageous, bold, intrepid) American design. This accounts for its _____ (peculiar, distinctive, special) style.

B. *Rewrite these sentences, eliminating sexist language.*

1. The Western civilization course concerns the history of man's ingenuity and persistence.

2. Man-made lakes are created for the pleasure of boaters and fishermen.

3. The mayor requested two additional policemen to man the polling place.

4. Success for a law school student depends on his command of language skills.

5. A man alone is in bad company.

C. *How do the connotations of these paired words differ?*

1. cheap—inexpensive
2. design—shape
3. tough—durable
4. invincible—unbeatable
5. distinguished—distinctive

6. startled—shocked
7. spinster—bachelor
8. childish—childlike
9. brilliance—ingenuity
10. smart—elegant

65

fig

65 **Use figures of speech to create vivid images.**

Figurative language, or imagery, is not limited to poetry. Comparisons between the familiar and the less familiar are a basic part of everyday communication. When we talk about a politician playing hardball, we are not speaking literally about sports, but figuratively: we are comparing two unlike things that are similar in some often unexpected way. Figures of speech can clarify a point and make writing come alive by creating vivid pictures for your reader. The most commonly used figures are similes and metaphors.

Similes are direct, explicit comparisons, using *like* or *as:*

> Jake was as mean as a ferret with a hangover.
>
> Her laugh was loud and piercing, like hail on a copper roof.

Metaphors are indirect, implied comparisons, without *like* or *as*:

> "Churchill mobilized the English language and took it to war."
> —*John F. Kennedy*

> Memories are hard to control since the mind seldom stays on its leash but dashes randomly off into the past, digging up and retrieving old bones.

Personification is a type of metaphor that gives human qualities to inanimate objects or abstractions:

> "The bridge wears a necklace of twinkling lights."
> —*Student*

65

Compare these statements to see how a dull literal statement can be made more lively by using imagery:

Dull: His jaw was rigid.

Vivid: "His jaw was as rigid as a horseshoe."
> —*Flannery O'Connor*

Dull: This movie is empty and pretentious.

Vivid: "This movie is a toupee made up to look like honest baldness."
> —*Pauline Kael*

If, however, you cannot create a fresh metaphor that fits your subject, rely on an accurate literal statement. A dull, overused metaphor (see **67**) will demonstrate only that you are not original; a wildly inappropriate or strained metaphor will spoil what you have to say.

Strained: Each wave rolled in like a giant wall of emerald ice cream topped with whipped cream.

Strained: The rising sun, pushing aside the darkness, spit out a glowing welcome sign over the horizon.

▼ EXERCISE

A. *Complete each of the following sentences with an original metaphor or simile.*

1. The news of the divorce spread through the town like _____ .

2. The old woman's hair was so thin that _____ .

3. The usually cool detective was shaking like _____ .

4. The judge listened, as impartial as _____ .

5. After driving nonstop for seven hours, Kim was so exhausted that he _____ .

B. *List as many figures of speech as you can that are derived from baseball, such as ballpark figure.*

C. *Revise the following strained images so that they create clear and consistent pictures.*

1. The photographer's lens is riveted to life's passing parade.

2. The prosecutor hammered away at the witness, much like a butcher hacking away at a carcass.

3. The economy must not be nailed to the cross of the stock market.

4. The empty spaces on the library shelves grinned broadly, like a gap-toothed crone.

5. A bad law is like chewing gum stuck to the sole of a shoe.

65

fig

66   **Make your figures of speech consistent with each other and with your subject.**

Metaphorical language is so common that writers may be unaware of the comparisons their words evoke. For example, when you speak of "grasping" or "catching" rather than "understanding" what a writer is saying, you are making a simple comparison between the mind and hands. If you speak of being "flooded with memories," you are using another metaphor: the mind is the land, the memories the floodwaters. But if you were to say "When I grasped what he was saying, it flooded me with memories," you would have a **mixed metaphor,** two images that conflict with each other. Mixed metaphors are a sure sign that you are not thinking about the pictures that your words create:

Mixed: The idea blossomed, then quickly crept away like a thief in the night.

Mixed: The theater of life is often a valley of tears.

66

Revise trite figures of speech, whether they conflict with other images or not (see **67**), and make sure that your images call up pictures that fit your subject.

▼   EXERCISE

Explain why the figures of speech in the following sentences are ineffective.

1. The avalanche of statistics is hard for voters to swallow.
2. If differences can be ironed out between Congress and the President, the economy will receive a needed shot in the arm.
3. Our language seems to be coming apart at the seams because writers burn themselves out on a diet of clichés.

4. The bottom line on inflation boils down to some tough decisions that Congress may find hard to swallow.

5. Evelyn didn't have a leg to stand on after the judge warned her that she was skating on thin ice.

trite

 67 **Avoid trite expressions and unwarranted euphemisms.**

In conversation, we often use stale expressions without thinking about what they mean. But as a writer, you have time to think, so try to make the most out of your words.

Clichés. Many of the figures of speech that come most readily to mind were once fresh images. But, through overuse, they have lost their effectiveness. We too easily use these trite expressions, or **clichés**, in place of original thought. No reader will be impressed by such hackneyed images as *fresh as a daisy* or *dead as a doornail*. Here is a brief list of clichés that have lost their value as figures of speech:

67

acid test	frosting on the cake
beat around the bush	in a nutshell
by leaps and bounds	nipped in the bud
bit the dust	light as a feather
crystal clear	no stone unturned
explore every avenue	playing with fire

Fillers. Also common are useless phrases such as *all in all, so to speak, as it were, needless to say, it goes without saying,* and *as a matter of fact.* These phrases add words but no meaning. Here are some others to avoid:

better late than never	last but not least
each and every	point with pride
easier said than done	rain or shine

few and far between	safe and sound
first and foremost	short and sweet
golden opportunity	without rhyme or reason

Using an original metaphor, Richard Altick sums up the point: A writer should provide "traction for the readers' minds rather than allow them to slide and skid on a slippery surface paved with well-worn phrases."

Euphemisms.   A **euphemism** refers indirectly to something unpleasant or embarrassing. For example, many people use *pass away* or *expire* to mean *die.* A euphemism is sometimes the best way to avoid hurting someone's feelings; however, many euphemisms are trite, many are wordy, and many conceal truths that should be made plain.

Members of Congress seldom mention *bribes, graft,* and *expense-paid vacations;* they do mention *honorariums, campaign contributions,* and *travel reimbursement.* The result of such language is a dangerous double-talk that misleads readers and distorts truth.

Trite and wordy:	under the influence (drunk)
	stretch the truth (lie)
	kick the bucket (die)

Misleading:	civil disturbance (riot)
	protective reaction strikes (bombing)
	inoperative statement (false, retracted statement)
	revenue enhancement (tax increase)

67

▼ EXERCISE

A.   *To see how easily clichés come to mind, complete the trite expressions in the following "speech."*

"First and _____, as you travel down the

_____ to success, you will face many challenges

_____ and beyond the call of _____. If

you persevere, you will pass life's greatest tests with

_____ colors; and you can then point with

_____ to your achievement. For you will then be

truly in a class _____ _____. In the

_____ analysis, when all is _____ and

_____, it goes without _____ that each

and _____ _____ of you can succeed

only if you _____ the line and keep your

_____ to the wheel as well as your

_____ to the grindstone. Last but not

_____, I must remind you that all of this is

_____ said than _____."

B. *Find a euphemism for each of the following words.*

1. bossy
2. cheap
3. steal
4. spy
5. ugly

C. *Find equivalents for the following clichés and euphemisms.*

1. knowing the ropes
2. lap of luxury
3. bottom line
4. severe nutritional deficiency
5. electronic surveillance
6. skating on thin ice
7. bite the dust
8. nipped in the bud
9. wedded bliss
10. uphill fight

flowery

 Avoid pretentious and unfamiliar words.

In general, write in plain English. Although you should try to build a rich vocabulary, strive to use it precisely, not just to show it off. "Pomposity," "flowery diction," and "over-writing" are just some of the terms used to describe the common mistake of using big words when familiar words would be more appropriate to the audience and subject. Use a long, formal word only when it expresses your meaning exactly, and avoid falsely poetic, foreign, and artificially formal terms:

Pretentious: It is requested that superfluous illumination be extinguished upon exiting the premises.

Improved: Turn off the lights when you leave the room.

Pretentious: The unauthorized ignition of tobacco-containing substances on this site constitutes felonious behavior.

Improved: Smoking in this area is a felony.

68

▼ EXERCISE

Translate the following pretentious sentences into more direct English.

1. Individuals who inhabit domiciles composed of frangible substances containing silicon compounds should be wary of casting hard, nonmetallic mineral matter.

2. The sky's stellar sentinels signaled the termination of the day.

3. Percipient weather prognosticators indicate that significant amounts of precipitation are anticipated in these United States.

4. Harvey, albeit inebriated, was not guilty of prevarication when he asserted that his position had been terminated.

5. A not unimportant date to be borne in mind by any inhabitant of planet Earth is January 1, 2001.

jargon

 69 **When writing for the general reader, avoid jargon and highly technical language.**

Nearly every specialized field develops its own specialized language: psychologists speak of *syndromes* and *psychoses,* computer programmers discuss *core capacity* and *interface,* and art critics refer to *texture* and *value contrast.* Among specialists, a specialized vocabulary can convey exact meanings. Among nonspecialists, however, the same vocabulary is only jargon, usually pretentious and confusing. If you want to use a technical term, ask yourself two questions: Do I really need the term? Will my readers understand it? If you do need the term and your readers might not understand it, be sure to define it.

Jargon also refers to the many unnecessarily technical expressions that develop in most fields. Some of these expressions are euphemisms (see **67**), some just inflated language. Here are a few examples of educational jargon:

learning facilitator (= teacher)
exceptional student (= slow or fast learner)
underachiever (= slow student)
disadvantaged (= poor)
empower (= help)
enable (= help)

69

Big words such as the following are often misused to give a technical flavor to nontechnical writing:

ameliorate (improve)   exhibit (show)
endeavor (try)   factor (item, point, cause)
inaugurate (begin)   *per se* (in itself)
individual (person)   peruse (read)
initiate (begin)   presently (now)
maximum (most)   utilize (use)
optimum (best)   viable (workable)
finalize (finish)   conceptualize (understand)

Here is President Kennedy's famous statement, "ask not what your country can do for you; ask what you can do for your country," translated into modern jargon:

> It is not deemed appropriate to make inquiry as to those initiatives to be actualized by this nation on behalf of individuals but, contrariwise, to ascertain the methodologies by which said individuals can maximize their optimum contributions to said nation.

Such bloated language prevents communication.

▼ EXERCISE

Rewrite the following sentences, eliminating jargon.

1. A vast majority of the specimens presently under examination exhibit deteriorative tendencies suggestive of a virus as the causal factor.

2. Within the parameters of the social sciences, the thrust of much research is focused on ameliorating conditions which militate against the optimum adjustment of partners in a marital situation.

3. Commencing in the new year, I will endeavor to prioritize my debts.

4. The library's growth necessitates maximizing present resources to the optimum advantage.

5. The staff must initiate a program to utilize every visible mode of aerobic exercise for the employees.

69

wdy rep

 Avoid needless repetition and wordiness.

As you revise, look for ways to eliminate anything that does not add to your meaning. Writers often pad sentences with clichés (see **67**) and jargon (see **69**):

Wordy: As to the reason for the delay, it was not because of the absence of the governor.

Improved: The reason for the delay was not the governor's absence.

Wordy: It is our belief that the safety device in question possesses the capability of being used by the airlines.

Improved: We believe that airlines can use this safety device.

Note that verb phrases using *is, are, was,* and *were* can lead to wordiness; the same is true of sentences starting with *there is, there are,* etc.

Wordy: Jon is capable of cooking more than pasta.

Improved: Jon can cook more than pasta.

70

Wordy: There are some countries that limit or outlaw explicit and violent movies.

Improved: Some countries limit or outlaw explicit and violent movies.

Wordy: It is important for motorists to avoid the right-hand lane unless they want to turn right.

Improved: Motorists must avoid the right-hand lane unless they want to turn right.

Avoid long verb phrases (*give consideration to* or *come to a conclusion*); instead, use simple, concrete verbs (*consider* or *conclude*). Avoid unneeded intensives *(indeed, really, quite frankly)*, windy openers *(it is, there are)*, and stock phrases such as these:

due to the fact that (= because)
in all probability (= probably)
in excess of (= more than)
in many instances (= often)
in a similar fashion (= similarly)
in the neighborhood of (= about)
on a daily basis (= daily)
in the event that (= if)
on the part of (= by *or* among)
a large number of (= many)
a small number of (= few)
during the time that (= while)
small-sized (= small)

▼ EXERCISE

A.   *Reduce each phrase to one word.*

outside of	in the near future
plan ahead	advance forward
can possibly	future plans
recur again	possible likelihood
question as to whether	disappear from view
rectangular in shape	red in color
quite exact	absolutely essential
cease and desist	most unique
contain within	complete monopoly
visible to the eye	

70

B.   *Replace each of these phrases with a single verb.*

conduct an investigation
undertake the removal of
result in damage to
have a necessity for
take a measurement
place a call to

70a   Eliminate meaningless intensives.

We tend to fill our speech with words such as *very, so, certainly, quite, really,* and *simply.* In writing, however, you should eliminate most of these words because they are vague, insincere, or unnecessary. Clear thoughts do not usually need modifiers such as *very (clear), quite (clear),* or *really (clear).* It is also best to avoid such imprecise, extravagant modifiers as *fabulous, fantastic, terribly,* and *awfully.*

70b   Eliminate obvious repetition and redundancy.

Other forms of wordiness include obvious repetition, redundancy (expressing the same idea in different ways, as in *basic essentials* or *the reason is because*), and unnecessary negatives *(not unlikely).* See the Glossary of Usage (p. 384) for some common redundant expressions and **24a** for repetition in sentences.

Obvious repetition:	When any two items are compared, one must consider many aspects. Some of these aspects are readily discernible. These aspects involve similarities and differences.
Improved:	Any comparison must consider both similarities and differences.
Redundant:	Throughout the entire story, the young girl faces many dangers.
Improved:	Throughout the story, the young girl faces many dangers.
Needless negatives:	Not a few modern airports are not well equipped for large numbers of passengers.
Improved:	Many modern airports are not well equipped for large numbers of passengers.

70

▼ EXERCISE

A. *Improve the following sentences by eliminating unnecessary words. Reword the sentences if necessary.*

1. What Gail does is edit an electronic journal.

2. In my opinion, the artist employs the use of color and light very effectively.

3. The letter was written by someone whose name must remain anonymous.

4. In that time period, it was not uncommon to find husbands and wives in business partnership together.

5. The reason why we are gathered together here is because we are celebrating a special birthday.

6. In the first two paragraphs of the story, it indicates who the likely suspect is.

7. *The Zoo Story is* a play by Edward Albee. It is a play that is dealing with the subject of alienation.

8. There is truth to the contention that the causes of the Civil War were in a very real sense economic.

9. This particular device is hexagonal in shape.

10. One reason for the economic decline is because of the past history of the deficit.

B. *Explain the redundancy in each of the following.*

1. present incumbent
2. personal friendship
3. advance planning
4. past experience/history
5. throughout the entire period of time

A Practical Guide to Writing

Writing a Research Paper

The research paper is a documented essay containing citations to the sources you have consulted. It combines your own ideas, experiences, and attitudes with supporting information provided by other sources. These sources allow you to develop your topic with informed opinions, which you support with the evidence you have gathered. Using sources properly will help you write more authoritatively.

The process of research involves these principal activities:

1. Searching for a topic and for library sources
2. Reading to select an appropriate topic and to gather information
3. Evaluating information and ideas
4. Organizing and writing the paper

The process might be more fully outlined as follows:

Step 1. Beginning the research
   Choosing an interesting subject
   Selecting a limited topic
   Developing a working thesis
Step 2. Locating and skimming sources
   Searching for information relevant to your working thesis

249

            Eliminating irrelevant information
            Reexamining your working thesis
Step 3. Reading sources and drawing conclusions
            Reading selected sources carefully
            Taking detailed notes
            Analyzing the information
            Developing a thesis statement
Step 4. Writing the paper
            Composing the first draft
            Revising the paper
            Adding documentation
            Formatting, keying, and editing the final draft
            Preparing the Works Cited or References page
            Proofreading and submitting the paper

Taking the research paper assignment step by step, as outlined in this chapter, and giving yourself adequate time for each step in the process will make the task more profitable and manageable.

71   Select an interesting, manageable topic.

Research papers too often become long recitations of facts and opinions copied out of library books. The best way to avoid producing anything so unoriginal and to eliminate needless drudgery is to choose a subject that you already know something about and want to learn more about. As you read general reference books, consider aspects of the broad subject that experts differ on. And look for a topic that can be covered within the limits of your assignment. Then your research will not only satisfy your curiosity but will also allow you to write with authority about a topic that means something to you. By examining facts, sifting evidence, and comparing opinions, you will be able to arrive at your own conclusions and keep your own contribution at the heart of your paper.

If you are free to choose your own subject, do not try to read everything you can find on politics, nature, art, or whatever general field most interests you. You must focus on one small corner of that field: not politics but the problem of revenue sharing and social-welfare programs; not nature but the causes of weed pollution in local lakes; not art but the influence of Cézanne on Cubist painting. An argumentation topic—one that has at least two sides—or a topic involving a problem will let you approach the question in an interesting way. Your instructor may propose a general subject, such as "television advertising," and challenge you to develop your own topic. Out of that you might develop these:

> Types of deception used in television commercials
> Sexual stereotyping in television commercials
> Government regulation of television advertising
> Methods that advertisers use to influence programming

You can save yourself time if you avoid certain predictable kinds of unsuitable topics:

- Topics too complex or controversial to be handled in anything less than a book: "AIDS research"
- Topics so limited that you can find only a few brief sources: "developing Ektachrome prints"
- Topics so new that little has been published on them
- Topics so cut-and-dried that you can do little more than summarize your sources in a report on your reading: "the life of Abraham Lincoln"
- Topics about which you can write little that is not already known to most people: "drunk driving is harmful"
- Topics about which you have such strong feelings that you might not be able to evaluate what you read objectively: "the morality of abortion"

72   Explore library resources.

Before you settle on a topic, be sure that you can find enough material to develop that topic. First, decide on a research plan that suits your library resources, your topic, and your available time. A typical procedure is to read general reference books such as encyclopedias to get an overview of the subject and to help you narrow the focus to a manageable topic. You might then search for books (through the card catalog) and magazine and journal articles (through periodical indexes) that you can skim to see how relevant they are for your purposes.

As you develop a basic bibliography—a list of books, articles, and other sources that you will investigate—write on a 3″ × 5″ card the call number, author's full name, full title, and other pertinent information for each source. Being complete and using correct form (see **77b** and **78b**) will save you time later when you prepare your final paper.

72a Locating information

The library catalog. Whether your library is traditional or computerized, its main catalog of books—the card catalog—will be arranged by author, title, and subject. Use subject headings to locate material on your topic. To determine the headings under which books on your topic are likely to be cataloged, consult the two-volume *Library of Congress Subject Headings.*

Periodical indexes. Since some of the most current information is available in magazine and journal articles, using the various indexes to periodical literature is essential in almost every library research project. Just as the card catalog is the key to books, so the periodical guides are the keys to articles. Do not limit yourself to the best-known and most general of these indexes, the *Readers' Guide to Periodical Literature.* Note that many periodical indexes are also available as databases or on CD-ROM, allowing you to search for articles electronically by entering key words, words that would logically appear in titles of articles in a given area. Also note that there is a national network of research files. These include PAIS (Public Affairs Information Service), Newsearch (a daily index of news articles from 1,400 newspapers and periodicals), ERIC (Educational Resources Information Center), and many other specialized databases.

72

BIBLIOGRAPHY CARD: BOOK (MLA FORMAT)

Troyer, Ronald J., and Gerard E. Markle.
Cigarettes: The Battle Over Smoking.
New Brunswick, N J: Rutgers UP, 1983.

HV 5740. J 77

BIBLIOGRAPHY CARD: ARTICLE (MLA FORMAT)

Viscusi, W. Kip. "Promoting Smokers'
Welfare with Responsible Taxation."
National Tax Journal 47 (1994):
547-58.

H J 2240. N 315

General indexes:

> *Humanities Index* (1974–   ), formerly the *Social Sciences and Humanities Index* (1965–73) and the *International Index* (1907–65)
> *National Newspaper Index* (1979–   )
> *New York Times Index* (1913–   )
> *Newsbank* (1970–   ), microfiche compilation of articles from more than one hundred newspapers
> *Readers' Guide to Periodical Literature* (1900–   )
> *Social Sciences Index* (1974–   ), formerly the *Social Sciences and Humanities Index* (1965–73) and the *International Index* (1907–65)

Specialized indexes:

> *Applied Science and Technology Index* (1958–   )
> *Art Index* (1929–   )
> *Biography Index* (1946–   )
> *Biological and Agricultural Index* (1964–   )
> *Business Periodicals Index* (1958–   )
> *Central Index to Journals of Education* (1969–   )
> *Education Index* (1929–   )
> *General Science Index* (1978–   )
> *Index to Legal Periodicals* (1908–   )
> *MLA International Bibliography* [literature, language] (1921–   )
> *Music Index* (1949–   )
> *Public Affairs Information Service Bulletin* (1915–   )

See also the various abstracts, such as the following:

> *Abstracts of English Studies* (1958–   )
> *Biological Abstracts* (1927–   )
> *Chemical Abstracts* (1907–   )
> *Psychological Abstracts* (1927–   )

Reference books.   Also cited in the card catalog are the library's encyclopedias, dictionaries, atlases, and many other basic reference tools. Here are a few:

Special encyclopedias:

> *Encyclopedia of Education.* 10 vols.
> *Encyclopedia of Philosophy.* 8 vols.

Encyclopedia of World Art. 15 vols.
International Encyclopedia of the Social Sciences. 17 vols.
Langer, William L. *An Encyclopedia of World History*
McGraw-Hill Encyclopedia of Science and Technology. 15 vols.
The New Catholic Encyclopedia. 15 vols.
Van Nostrand's Scientific Encyclopedia

Other:

Britannica Book of the Year (1938–   )
Current Biography (1940–   )
Dictionary of American Biography. 10 vols.
Dictionary of National Biography. (British). 22 vols.
Facts on File (1941–   )
Statistical Abstract of the United States (1878–   )
The Times Atlas of the World
World Almanac and Book of Facts (1868–   )

Libraries also contain pamphlets, government documents, films, filmstrips, videos, tapes, records, and other nonprint sources.

The Internet.   Access to the Internet is available through most colleges and universities and through private-sector commercial services such as America OnLine, Compuserve, and Prodigy. The commercial services provide access to reliable, structured sources of information in many academic and general interest fields. If you look beyond the commercial services, you will find that the Internet offers many other forms of information, much of it transmitted by individuals and industry. Be cautious; no Internet "editor" exists to make sure that information is reliable or accurate.

73

73 Evaluate your sources of information.

Analyzing the material you find is always important. Not everything in print is reliable, and some sources carry more weight than others. A short article in a popular magazine will seldom be as authoritative as a book or journal article, but even a book may represent an extreme approach to a subject. Always be careful to distinguish between facts and opinions. As you examine any source, ask yourself these questions:

- Is the writer a recognized authority on the subject, one whose work is cited by other writers?
- Does the work seem to be biased? Does the author give sufficient attention to other points of view?
- Is the work recent enough to provide up-to-date information?

Aim for a balanced bibliography that reflects as many viewpoints as possible and that includes journal articles as well as books and magazine articles. In most cases, if half of your sources consist of articles from one periodical, search further. Scholarly journals provide more thoroughly documented material than do magazines, which might be general, exaggerated, or slanted to reflect a particular bias. For a paper on acid rain, for example, you would not consult a newspaper article but a journal such as *Nature* or *Science*. Interviews, if they provide information not easily found in published sources, can be useful as long as those interviewed are knowledgeable and objective. Corporations, museums, government agencies, specialized organizations (the Red Cross, for example), as well as your class notes can also provide information not found in libraries.

73

Primary and secondary sources. Primary sources are the actual texts of reports, novels, and documents, as well as interviews, questionnaires, recordings, and other original material. Secondary sources are the critical and historical accounts based on primary materials. For a documented essay on the space shuttle, for example, your primary sources might include reports from NASA as well as interviews with or letters from space officials. For a paper on educational television for children, reports of experiments in childhood learning as well as the programs themselves would be your primary sources.

Clearly, watching the programs would be essential to understanding the topic; you would not want to get most of your information secondhand. Whatever your topic, locate and use as many primary sources as possible.

Secondary sources may help you find additional primary sources, and they can point out ways of interpreting those sources. By examining a number of secondary sources, you can determine which ones offer the most convincing interpretation of the facts. Since you will probably not have time to read all the available secondary sources in their entirety, check their indexes and tables of contents and skim chapters that you think might help you. Also check each secondary source for a bibliography that might direct you to other sources.

74 Prepare a preliminary thesis statement and working outline.

As early as possible in your research, formulate a tentative statement of the main point you expect to make in your paper (see **6**). You will need to change this preliminary thesis statement if further research gives you a new perspective, but deciding on your thesis will help you concentrate your note taking on material that supports, contradicts, or in some other way bears directly on your main point.

74

Next, consider the subpoints you will need to support your thesis, and arrange these into a rough outline (see **7**). For example, if you are working on the future of the Olympic movement, your preliminary thesis and rough (working) outline might look like this:

THESIS: The Olympic Games will surrender to commercialism unless reforms are made.

  I. Most competitors are now professionals.

  II. Corporate sponsors are much too visible.

  III. Product merchandising should be curbed.

As you develop the topic further, you will find ways to develop each of the subtopics: When did the shift occur from amateur status to professional status? Why are corporate sponsors a problem? Is there a practical, equitable way to limit product merchandising? You may also find new subtopics or discover that you have to change some of the ones you have. You might also find that you need to sharpen your thesis statement. For example, you could specify how changes in the Olympics would solve the recent problems:

> The Olympics can regain some of its lost luster by emphasizing the importance of amateur athletics, curbing corporate sponsors, and limiting product merchandising.

Think of your working outline as a flexible guide in your search for pertinent information. If you code your note cards to the sections of your rough outline, you will be able to see if you are finding enough information for each section and if you are turning up new information that calls for changes in your outline.

---

 75 **Take thorough, accurate notes on your sources.**

75

Your aim in taking notes is to record accurately and concisely the important facts from your sources. A 4″ × 6″ note card will provide room for substantial notes as well as for a subject heading and a key to the corresponding bibliography card. Use one card for each idea so that you can later sort the cards as you refine your organization. Each card should contain the following information:

1. *Subject.* In a few words at the top of the card, identify the information that the card contains.
2. *Source.* List the author's name or an abbreviated title.
3. *Page number.* If a quotation runs from one page to the next, use a slash to indicate the page break. You may later want to use just part of the quotation.

The note itself may be a quotation, a paraphrase (rewording) of the original material, or a summary.

Quotation.   Although most note taking should not be word-for-word copying, quote your source directly whenever you think you might want to use the exact wording. When quoting, follow these guidelines:

1. On your note card, place quotation marks around all direct quotations to remind yourself that the wording is not yours. This distinction is essential.
2. Copy your source exactly, including punctuation marks. If an error appears in the original, put *[sic],* meaning *thus* or *so* ("this is the way I found it"), in your notes.
3. Use an ellipsis mark of three spaced periods (. . .) to indicate omitted material within a quoted sentence. Avoid using ellipses before quotations of only parts of sentences (see **40d** and the sample note card that follows).
4. Use square brackets for your own insertions in a quotation: "Last year [1993], Americans spent more than $3 billion on pet foods alone."

Paraphrase.   Direct quotation is not the only way to record the material you will use. You can reword passages from your sources, but be careful to capture the ideas of an author without copying his or her sentence structure or word choice. You do not have to change every word in your source; simply write in your own style, and note the exact location of the ideas you are rephrasing. When your source contains phrases that you think deserve direct quotation, you can combine paraphrase and quotation, but be sure to distinguish carefully between your words and those of your source.

Summary.   Instead of copying or carefully paraphrasing background information or other material that you do not plan on presenting in detail, write a brief summary. Record the important facts; skip unimportant details. Early in your note taking, you may want to take summary notes on sources that you expect to investigate more carefully later. Rough summary notes can include abbreviations and incomplete sentences. Such notes give a quick sketch of material you may use and will be more fluently worded in your paper.

The following examples illustrate each of these three note-taking methods. Be sure to include source information (author and page number) on all note cards.

NOTE CARD: ORIGINAL MATERIAL

Nazi loyalty

"The early foreign policy triumphs of the Nazis and the intensity of their own convictions made it possible for Germans to overlook the excesses and the brutalities of the regime. Long after the good days had passed and war had come and the shadow of defeat loomed before them, the majority of the people remained loyal to the regime and discountenanced disobedience or opposition.... Loyalty to Hitler persisted to the bitter end."

(Gordon Craig, "Facing up to the Nazis," The New York Review, February 2, 1989, p. 11.)

75

NOTE CARD: PARAPHRASE

Craig, p.11   Nazi loyalty

Most Germans during the Nazi era remained intensely loyal to Hitler and his regime even after defeat seemed inevitable. Recalling earlier government successes, people tended to ignore Nazi savagery and to feel ashamed of any disloyalty.

NOTE CARD: SUMMARY

Craig, p.11   Nazi loyalty

Source deals with loyalty to Hitler and his regime despite defeat. Reason: Early Nazi successes led most Germans to ignore brutal realities.

75

Careful note taking can help you avoid plagiarism (see p. 262) in your finished paper. It should also indicate your solid understanding of what you have read. For this reason, summaries and paraphrases are preferable to word-for-word copying. Some of the following examples are too close to the original wording to be effective paraphrases:

Original sentence: "*Gender* is a term that has psychological or cultural rather than biological connotations."

Poor paraphrase: *Gender* has psychological or cultural, not biological, implications.

Effective paraphrase: The word *gender* refers to behavior or culture, not biology.

Original sentence: "The ideal of strict objectivity is absurd."

Poor paraphrase: Complete objectivity is an absurd ideal.

Effective paraphrase: No one should strive to be completely objective.

Original quotation: "Words read from a screen or written onto a screen—words which appear and disappear, even if they can be retrieved and fixed into place with a keystroke—have a different status and affect us differently from words held immobile on the accessible space of a page. . . . Nearly weightless though it is, the word printed on a page is a thing. The configuration of impulses on a screen is not. . . . The former occupies a position in space—on a page, in a book—and is verifiably there. The latter, once dematerialized, digitalized back into storage, into memory, cannot be said to exist in quite the same way. It has potential, not actual locus."

—*From Sven Birkerts,* The Gutenberg Elegies *(Boston: Faber and Faber, Inc., 1994), 154–55.*

Compare this with the following student note cards:

75

NOTE CARD A (UNACCEPTABLE)

> Words on a screen have a status and effect different from those of words fixed on the space of a page. The word printed on a page is a thing, whereas the pattern of impulses on a screen is not (Birkerts 154). Thus, Birkerts concludes, electronic language does not exist in quite the same way as printed language (155).

This note is unacceptable because all three sentences closely follow the original wording. It will be difficult to determine later if these notes are quoted or paraphrased.

NOTE CARD B (ACCEPTABLE)

> Printed words and electronic words are essentially different, according to Sven Birkerts in _The Gutenberg Elegies_. Words on a page, he says, have a permanence that words on a screen do not have. Electronic writing is not "a thing" the way printed writing is and "cannot be said to exist in quite the same way" (155).

This note is acceptable because no plagiarism (see below) will result; the source is clearly introduced and acknowledged while the expert's key terms are assimilated into the student's own writing.

As you read and take notes, consider possible subtopics to complete the ideas in your rough outline (see **74**). These subtopics will help guide your reading and note taking, and your reading will then provide ideas for more subtopics. You will be organizing the paper as you prepare to write it. If you are investigating ways to restore the tarnished image of the Olympic Games, you might develop these subtopics:

> small countries with amateur athletes/large countries with professional athletes
> corporations as official providers of absurd or tangential services
> why souvenirs are valuable

The order of the subtopics, as well as the subtopics themselves, will doubtless change as you find material and as your ideas develop.

Plagiarism.   Plagiarism—presenting the words or ideas of others without giving proper credit—is both unethical and illegal. When you put your name on a piece of writing, the reader assumes that you are responsible for the information, wording, and organization and that you will acknowledge the source of any fact or idea that is not your own.

75

A writer cannot copy direct quotations without using quotation marks and without acknowledging the source. Paraphrasing material or using an original idea that is not properly introduced and documented is another common type of plagiarism. Sloppy note taking, in which the writer has not distinguished between his or her thoughts and those of the sources, is a frequent culprit. To avoid plagiarism, follow these guidelines:

1. Introduce every quotation and paraphrase by citing in the text of your paper the name of the source of the material used.

2. Place quotation marks around all directly quoted material.

3. Rewrite paraphrased material so that it is faithful to the original ideas; rearranging sentences is not enough.

4. Document all source material used.

5. Include on the Works Cited or References page every source referred to in your paper.

The penalties for plagiarism can be severe; it is a serious offense. A student who has been caught plagiarizing can expect, at the least, to receive no credit for the assignment, and at some schools, expulsion is the mandated result.

76   Organize, write, and revise the rough draft.

If you revise your outline as you collect information, you should be nearly ready to write your rough draft by the time you finish taking notes. But first review and refine the organization. Start with your thesis statement: Does it clearly express what you now see as the central, unifying idea of the paper? (See **6**.) If, for example, your initial thesis was "Library censorship is dangerous to our schools," your research might lead you to a more limited, precisely focused thesis: "Censorship in high school libraries denies students their constitutional right to the free exchange of ideas."

A *sentence outline* can be especially useful at this point. Write a sentence stating each of the main ideas supporting your thesis. Then complete the outline with sentences that represent the subdivisions of your main points. You will be able to see how well the parts of your paper fit together, and you may be able to use many of the sentences as topic sentences for your main subsections.

To help make the organization of your material clear and logical, follow these conventions when outlining:

1. Make sure that *all* the divisions and subdivisions are complete sentences; do not mix phrases with sentences.

2. Type your thesis statement at the head of the outline, followed by capitalized Roman numerals for the main headings; then A, B, etc., for main subheadings; then 1, 2, etc.; then a, b, etc.

3. Always use at least two subdivisions. If you have "I. A.," you must logically have "I. B." As a general rule, subdivisions stand for blocks of material in the essay, not for single sentences.

4. Make the subdivisions logically consistent. If your first main division is "I. Students in four-year colleges" and your first two subdivisions are "A. Freshmen" and "B. Sophomores," then you must continue with "C. Juniors" and "D. Seniors," not "C. History majors" or "D. Student athletes."

The following sentence outline was written for a research paper on year-round schools.

THESIS: The time for year-round schools has arrived, for they can solve many of the mounting problems, such as overcrowding and inefficiency, that our educational system faces.

I. Year-round schools are largely misunderstood.
  A. Parents' and students' misunderstandings are based on preconceived notions of how year-round schools operate.
  B. A wide variety of plans allows flexibility in implementing a year-round school system.

II. Year-round schools offer advantages to those directly involved in education as well as to the community at large.
  A. Parents' and students' apprehensions about year-round schools are often dispelled after they have experienced such a system.
    1. Year-round schools offer greater flexibility in vacation planning.

     2. Students often retain knowledge more easily in a year-round plan.

     3. Both marginal and gifted students benefit from a year-round school system.

  B. Year-round schools provide economic benefits to school systems.

     1. School facilities are used more efficiently.

     2. Year-round schools relieve overcrowding.

  C. Teachers also benefit from year-round plans.

     1. Smaller class sizes make for less stressful situations.

     2. Teachers have more time to plan curricula.

III. Although some teachers point out drawbacks to year-round school plans, students' experience is more positive.

IV. While year-round schools may not be the answer to every school system's problems, many communities are finding that the advantages of year-round schools far outweigh their disadvantages.

Handling source material. Identify your sources so that readers can make their own judgment about content and reliability. Make sure that material from your sources supports the points you wish to make and that your own voice is not drowned out by excessive quotations. If all the quoted and paraphrased passages were to be removed from the paper, it should still make sense. These guidelines will help you achieve that goal:

76

1. Write a topic sentence in your own words for each of your main paragraphs. Even if you later incorporate a quotation into a topic sentence or drop the topic sentence altogether, writing it in your own words will help you make sure that the paragraph expresses your thoughts. (See **16**.)

2. Use direct quotations only to emphasize significant points or to show your reader how your source expressed a key idea.

3. Avoid long paragraphs of quotations.

4. Make short quotations part of your own sentences:

> Frances FitzGerald says that history textbooks have changed so much that "many an adult would find them unrecognizable" (21).

5. Introduce quoted and paraphrased material so that your reader will know whose work you are citing:

> As B. F. Skinner said, "The goal of science is the destruction of mystery" (59).

6. After each paraphrase or quotation, place the page number in parentheses.

Revising the rough draft. You will probably need to revise your paper several times to make it read smoothly and say exactly what you want it to say. Check especially to see that your paragraphs are unified and sufficiently developed (see **17** and **19**) and that you have supplied transitions to guide your reader through the paper (see **18**).

Make sure that your final draft is free of errors (spelling, mechanics, grammar, punctuation) and that its sentences are logical and its diction clear. Compare the final draft with your outline to make sure that they are consistent. (If not, decide which needs to be changed.) Type from your bibliography cards a Works Cited page for those materials you have cited in the paper. Eliminate sources you have not used, but include each source that appears in your essay. Arrange the cards in alphabetical order by author (or title if there is no author), and type one continuous list according to the format outlined in **77b** and **78b**.

Choosing fonts. If your PC offers you a choice of fonts and type sizes, choose a roman, serif font between ten and twelve points. Never use italic, script, or all-capital letters for your text font. (Italic is used for emphasis, for foreign words, and for titles as appropriate—see **41**.) A serif font is easier to read than a sanserif font, since the characters are more distinctive:

Research is a worthy process. (Times Roman: serif)

Research is a worthy process. (Helvetica: sanserif)

If you would like to use a different font for heads (the title of your paper, *Works Cited,* or *References,* etc.), a sanserif font is a good choice.

Research paper formats

This chapter illustrates guidelines from two academic organizations: the Modern Language Association (MLA) and the American Psychological Association (APA). Their documentation formats are similar in that both use parenthetical notes rather than footnotes or endnotes. However, the two systems have substantial differences, so they are discussed separately. MLA guidelines tend to be used in English, foreign language, and humanities research papers, and APA guidelines are generally used in social sciences, education, and technical writing.

 Guidelines for MLA-style research paper   77

77a   Document sources accurately.

Documentation means including notes within your paper to tell readers where you located specific ideas and information and also including a list of your sources at the end of the paper. Documentation has two important functions: to give credit to the sources you have consulted and to enable your readers to look up the original material. Documenting also protects you against possible plagiarism (see p. 264): it distinguishes your thoughts and words from those of your sources.

According to MLA style, you document by using in-text citations of author and page, in parentheses, at the end of every sentence containing a quotation or paraphrase. For example:

```
American children need to learn traditional
information at an early age (Hirsch 31).
```

On your Works Cited page at the end of the paper, you will provide in an alphabetical list the complete information about each source; your in-text citation specifies the page from which the quotation or paraphrase is taken.

What must you document? Since you have read extensively to prepare your research paper, you may think at first that nearly every sentence in the paper will have to be documented. But readers are interested in what *you* have to say, in how you have used your reading. Information that is common knowledge, short dictionary definitions, and well-known quotations do not require documentation. But every sentence taken from a source requires a citation so that the reader knows who says what—and with a minimum of disruption. Whenever possible, introduce each quotation and paraphrase with the name of the authority.

You must document the following:

1. All directly quoted material:

```
Roger Rosenblatt writes that "Americans have
never hated big government as much as they
have loved its services" (33).
```

If you did not use the author's name to introduce the quotation, cite it along with the page:

```
(Rosenblatt 33).
```

If the source is a one-page article (common in popular magazines), citing the page number is optional—you may cite the author (or the title, if there is no author) without the page number.

2. All paraphrased and summarized material:

> The prestige of a college education, John W.
> Gardner says, has led many people to assume
> (falsely) that there is no other type of
> learning after high school (103).

or:

> According to John W. Gardner (103), the
> prestige of a college education has led many
> people to assume (falsely) that there is no
> other type of learning after high school.

3. Facts and data that are not common knowledge:

> The average American's life expectancy has
> increased from forty-seven years, when the
> twentieth century began, to seventy-four years
> today (Norman 36).

When two or more works by one author are listed in the Works Cited, provide a shortened version of the title to prevent confusion. Here the complete title—*The Presence of the Word*—is cited in shortened form at the end of the sentence:

> Speech as sound, Ong says, is "irrevocably
> committed to time" (<u>Presence</u> 40).

77

For repeated references to a primary source (such as a play or poem), simple citations (such as to act, scene, and line) will suffice once you have established the title of the work:

> Lear's dying words are "Look there, look there!" (5.3.316).

When several items are taken from the same source, such as four sentences in a paragraph giving statistics derived from a single book, use one citation at the end of the paragraph: doing so will indicate that all the data in the paragraph come from that book. In such cases, especially, introducing your sources is important. And strive for some variety in introducing quotations and paraphrases and in incorporating them into your sentences fluently. Some possibilities:

> In his famous study of the Third Reich, William L. Shirer describes the Nazi war machine (399).

> Others, like Koehl (360) and Bloch (36-37), present a different view.

> From 1939 on, Johnson says, Hitler became a militarist, ceasing "to play the politician, the orator, the demagogue" (356).

> As Bruce Pauley (102) has observed, . . .

> Yet, according to one scholar (Fussell 245), the issue in 1939 was . . .

> Other historians disagree with this interpretation (for example, O'Neill 52-59 and Binion 78-82).

Istvan Deak is surely right in agreeing with
Koehl that not even the SS in Nazi Germany was
totally committed (42).

Though you will most often use short quotations, occasionally you will need to use a longer quotation to present an
especially important point. If a quotation will take up more
than four lines in your paper, indent the quotation ten spaces
from the left margin and do not add quotation marks. Double-space the quotation. Introduce the quoted material, using
a colon to connect the introduction with the quotation, as in
this example:

Part of the reason for the Nazi party's
success was the German economy. In his 1983
survey of modern history, Paul Johnson
provides this summary evaluation:

>   Hitler's coming to power, therefore,
> provided German industry with
> precisely what it wanted to perform
> effectively: government stability,
> the end of politics and a sense of
> national purpose. It could do the
> rest for itself. Hitler was shrewd
> enough to realize this. While he
> allowed the party to invade every
> other sphere of government and
> public policy, he kept it out of
> industry and the army, both of which
> he needed to perform at maximum
> efficiency as quickly as possible.
> (295)

Note that in a long quotation, the parenthetical citation *follows* the period.

For subsequent citations to the same page in a source just cited, simply repeat the page. (*Ibid.* and other Latin abbreviations are no longer used.)

> Another writer argues that "it may turn out
> that apes do have a dim awareness of syntax"
> (Gardner 6). He also points out, however, that
> such a discovery may not be major (6).

Content endnotes. Certain types of information cannot appropriately be included in the body of your paper. Such items include comments on your research process or on the sources you used, or acknowledgment of assistance you received. This information should be placed on a separate page labeled "Notes," following the last page of your text and preceding the Works Cited. The accepted format for such notes is as follows:

> [1] On this point see also Kennedy (12) and
> Garrett (119).
> [2] All citations of Shakespeare are to the
> Bevington edition.
> [3] The data for this study were collected
> between 20 January 1996 and 7 August 1996 in
> Miami, Orlando, and Tampa, Florida.
> [4] This study has benefited from the research
> assistance of Brenda Gordon, graduate
> assistant, Department of English.

Include bibliographical information in the Works Cited, *not* in content endnotes. Place the consecutive note numbers in the text immediately following the relevant sentence. The note number is a superscript, as shown in this example:

> during the war.[2]

77b   Construct your list of Works Cited.

End the paper with an alphabetical list of the books, articles, and other sources you cite. This bibliography is titled "Works Cited." Although some instructors may require you to list all the works you consulted in preparing your research paper, the most common practice is to list only those sources you have used and cited. Copy on your bibliography cards the complete information for each such source, and keep the cards in alphabetical order by author's last name (or title if there is no author).

The following bibliography format is that of the Modern Language Association.*

1. Since the list is alphabetical, place authors' last names first. (If no author or editor is given, alphabetize by title, not taking into consideration *a, an,* or *the.*)
2. Then list the full title. Use italics (underlining) for titles of books and periodicals; use quotation marks for articles, poems, essays, and parts of books.
3. Separate the items within the entry with periods.
4. For books, cite the publisher's city and a shortened form of the publisher's name: New York: McGraw-Hill, 1996. Use only the first city printed on the title page and the most recent copyright date.
5. For journals, cite the volume, year, and full pages: 12 (1984): 122–49. For magazines, the date and full pages: *Esquire* Feb. 1991: 60–62. (If pages are not continuous, use 60+.)
6. Double-space the lines of each entry, and indent the second and following lines five spaces.
7. In listing two or more works by the same author, use three hyphens followed by a period instead of repeating the author's name. Alphabetize by title:

Schama, Simon. <u>The Embarrassment of Riches</u>. New
    York: Knopf, 1995.

*For full information, see Joseph Gibaldi, *MLA Handbook for Writers of Research Papers,* 4th ed. (New York: Modern Language Association, 1995).

---. <u>Landscape and Memory</u>. Berkeley: U of
      California P, 1988.

Works Cited format: Books

Single author:

Pemble, John. <u>Venice Rediscovered</u>. Oxford:
      Clarendon, 1995.

Two or three authors:

Marchetti, Victor, and John D. Marks. <u>The CIA
      and the Cult of Intelligence</u>. New York:
      Knopf, 1974.

Kagan, Jerome, Ernest Havemann, and Julius
      Segal. <u>Psychology: An Introduction</u>. 5th ed.
      San Diego: Harcourt, 1984.

More than three authors:

Baugh, Albert C., et al. <u>A Literary History of
      England</u>. 2nd ed. New York: Appleton,
      1967.

Translated and edited books:

Virgil. <u>The Aeneid</u>. Trans. Robert Fitzgerald.
      New York: Random, 1983.

Merton, Thomas. <u>The Hidden Ground of Love</u>. Ed.
      William H. Shannon. New York: Farrar, 1985.

Gong, Victor, and Norman Rudnick, eds. <u>AIDS:
      Facts and Issues</u>. New Brunswick: Rutgers
      UP, 1986.

A work in an anthology:

Rubinstein, Arye. "Children with AIDS and the
    Public Risk." AIDS: Facts and Issues. Ed.
    Victor Gong and Norman Rudnick. New
    Brunswick: Rutgers UP, 1986. 99-103.

Note: The full pages of the article or chapter are cited; if you
cite an article or essay in a collection of previously published
works, list the earlier publication data along with *Rpt. in*
(reprinted in):

Lewis, C. S. "Satan." A Preface to "Paradise
    Lost." London: Oxford UP, 1942. 92-100.
    Rpt. in Milton: Modern Essays in Criticism.
    Ed. Arthur E. Barker. New York: Oxford UP,
    1965. 196-204.

Encyclopedia entries:

"Melodeon." Encyclopedia Americana. 1984 ed.

Reprinted and revised editions:

Fitzgerald, F. Scott. The Great Gatsby. 1925.
    New York: Scribner's, 1953.

Here the date of the original edition is included after the title of a reprinted book. If an edition is other than the first,
cite *Rev. ed.* or *4th ed.* after the title.

Multivolume work:

If all volumes were used:

Parrington, Vernon L. Main Currents in American
    Thought. 3 vols. New York: Harcourt,
    1927-32.

If only one volume is used (with its own title):

```
Churchill, Winston S. The Age of Revolution.
     New York: Dodd, 1957. Vol. 3 of A History
     of the English-Speaking Peoples. 4 vols.
     1956-58.
```

Corporate author:

```
Committee on Telecommunications. Reports on
     Selected Topics in Telecommunications. New
     York: National Academy of Sciences,
     National Research Council, 1970.
```

Government publication:

```
United States. Dept. of Labor. Bureau of
     Statistics. Dictionary of Occupational
     Titles. 4th ed. Washington: GPO, 1977.
```

Works Cited format: Periodicals

Article in journal (paged by volume):

```
Weiss, Timothy. "Translation in a Borderless
     World." Technical Communication Quarterly 4
     (1995): 407-23.
```

Article in journal (paged by issue):

```
Hynes, Joseph. "Morality and Fiction: The
     Example of Henry James." South Atlantic
     Review 60.4 (1995): 27-34.
```

Article in monthly magazine:

```
Overbeck, Joy. "Sex Too Soon." Parents Sept.
     1994: 42-44.
```

Article in weekly magazine:

Bruck, Connie. "Jerry's Deal." The New
    Feb. 1996: 54+.

Note: Abbreviate all months except May, June, and July. When
the pages of an article are not continuous, list the first page followed by a plus sign. Otherwise, always list the inclusive pages.

Article in newspaper:

Halprin, Mark. "A Single Bullet." The Wall Street
    Journal 12 Jan. 1990, Eastern ed.: A12.

(Most daily newspapers have section indicators that precede
the page number.)

Book review:

Anderson, Jarvis. "Life with Father: Duke
    Ellington." Rev. of Duke Ellington in
    Person, by Mercer Ellington. New York Times
    Book Review 28 May 1978: 8.

Pamphlet:

Follow the format for books. If there is no date of publication, list *n.d.;* if there is no publisher, list *n.p.*

Interview or letter:

Willis, Dr. Susan L. Personal interview. 2 Feb.
    1995.

Fernandez, Luis. Telephone interview. 4 May 1996.

Film or TV program:

Pulp Fiction. Dir. Quentin Tarantino. Miramax
    Films, 1994.

<u>A Gathering of Men</u>. With Robert Bly and Bill
    Moyers. PBS. WNET, New York. 8 Jan.
    1990.

Works Cited format: Electronic media

CD-ROM:

Your entry on the Works Cited page should include as much
of the following material as possible:

1. Author (if given)
2. Title and date of print publication (if published)
3. If not published, title and date (in quotation marks)
4. Title of the database (underlined)
5. Publication medium *(CD-ROM)*
6. Name of vendor (company that distributes the CD-ROM—
   for example, *Wilson* or *Silverplatter*)
7. Electronic publication date (or dates, since many databases are updated regularly)

Strand, D. Rev. of <u>Behind the Tiananmen Square
    Massacre: Social, Political, and Economic
    Ferment in China</u>. <u>Political Science
    Quarterly</u> 106 (1991): 341-42. <u>Scholarly Book
    Reviews on CD-ROM</u>. CD-ROM. University
    Publications of America. Apr. 1995.

Eisenberg, Carol A., and David Bader. "QCE-6: A
    Clonal Cell Line with Cardialmyogenic and
    Endothelial Cell Potentials." <u>Developmental
    Biology</u> Feb. 1995: 469-81. <u>Wilson General
    Science Abstracts</u>. CD-ROM. Wilson. May
    1995.

Diskette:

Cite diskette publications as if they were
scription of the medium of publication:

Cookro, Theresa M. <u>Digital Data</u>
    <u>Geochemistry of Rocks from the Au~</u>
    <u>Mining District, Humboldt County, Nevada.</u>
    Diskette. Denver: U.S. Dept. of the
    Interior, U.S. Geological Survey, 1994.

For work in more than one publication medium, cite the product as you would a nonperiodical CD-ROM, specifying the
media that constitute the product.

Online database:

In citing online databases, include the following:

1. Author (if given)
2. Title of the material (in quotation marks) and date of material (if given). If there is a printed source, use the style
   for a book or article.
3. Title of the database (underlined)
4. Publication medium (*Online*)
5. Name of computer service (e.g., *Prodigy*) or computer network (e.g., *Internet*)
6. Date of access

77

Perlman, Judi. "Quayle Council Broke Law, Ethics
    Experts Suggest to House Panel." <u>Reuters</u>.
    Online. Lexis-Nexis. 20 June 1995.

If there is a printed version, cite the author, title of material
(in quotation marks), date of material (if given), title of database (underlined), publication medium *(Online),* name of computer service, and date of access.

in, Tom. "Technology Lets Remote Control
Finger Do the Shopping." <u>Orlando Sentinel
Tribune</u>. Online. Lexis-Nexis. 20 June 1995.

Electronic journal, newsletter, or conference:

In citing material from electronic journals, newsletters, and conferences, include the following:

1. Author (if given)
2. Title of article or document (in quotation marks)
3. Title of journal, newsletter, or conference (underlined)
4. Volume number, issue number, or other identifying number
5. Year or date of publication (in parentheses)
6. Number of pages or paragraphs (if given) or *n.pag.*
7. Publication medium *(Online)*
8. Name of computer network
9. Date of access

Hurst, J. A. "International Finance Questions."
<u>Business Library Discussion List</u> (10 Sept.
1992). Online. Internet. Nov. 1994.

Electronic mail:

Electronic mail (e-mail) citations should include the writer, description of the document and the recipient, and the date, as in this example:

Bayston, Tom. "Status Report." E-mail to Brook
Sizemore. 20 July 1995.

In all cases, if you cannot locate complete information, cite what is available.

77c   Research paper format

The following sample paper should answer most of your questions about the format of the research paper. It should be typed on white $8\frac{1}{2}'' \times 11''$ bond paper, double-spaced. Leave one-inch margins on all four sides of the page. Indent the first word of each paragraph five spaces from the left margin, and indent long quotations (more than four typed lines) ten spaces from the left margin. Such quotations, like the body and the list of works cited, are double-spaced.

Many instructors prefer a separate title page with an accompanying outline as a guide for the reader, but these are not required by MLA style. Instead, on the first page you can type your name, the instructor's name, the course number, and the date on separate lines, double-spaced, starting one inch from the top of the page and flush with the left margin; this first page may also be numbered. Note that the title is not underlined, fully capitalized, enclosed in quotation marks, or ended with a period. Capitalize the first and last words of the title and all other words except articles *(the, an)* and prepositions and conjunctions with fewer than five letters *(in)*. Double-space between the title and the first line of text.

Number your pages consecutively throughout the paper in the upper right-hand corner, one-half inch from the top. Type your last name, followed by the page number; this head is typed flush against the right margin. Double-space between this head and the text.

77

Mickelson 1

V. K. Mickelson

Dr. Pharr

ENC 1102

18 March 1996

The Need for Additional Cigarette Taxation

Gone are the days when actresses lounged in door frames, lighted cigarettes between their elegant fingers, emphasizing the sensuous lines of their silhouettes. No longer does the image of the "tough guy" include, of necessity, a cigarette dangling from the corner of his mouth. Once, the movie industry portrayed smoking as a "glamorous" and "sophisticated" mode of expression, but today that fascination has waned, and smoking now is viewed in a very different and increasingly negative light.

In those early days, the cigarette was ubiquitous, dominating restaurants, schools, airplanes, and even doctors' offices. Today, however, smokers have been sent outdoors, forced to stand by entranceways and in parking lots if they choose to indulge in their dubious pleasure. Only in bars, gambling

Mickelson 2

establishments, and parts of some restaurants is indoor smoking common. Medical science has proven what many had long suspected: cigarette smoking is lethal.

In addition to the obvious health risks facing smokers, cigarettes present a commonly overlooked danger known as secondhand smoke. Whereas the gases that make up cigarette smoke can cause a number of deadly diseases when inhaled directly, secondhand smoke also poses a significant threat of cancer to anyone in relatively close proximity to this exhalation, even if he or she has never smoked a cigarette in his or her life. The costs of treating people who are victims of cigarette smoke are enormous, totaling $22 billion per year in 1992 ("Wages of Sin" 26). Yet while pipe and cigar smoking have dwindled over the years, cigarettes have managed to retain considerable popularity, and now the question is clear: What must be done to cope with what is, in essence, a national nightmare? An additional tax on cigarettes is the most practical answer.

Mickelson 3

The federal government takes a peculiar, contradictory stand on this issue. Motivated by pressure from powerful, long-established senators from the tobacco-producing states, the government subsidizes farmers, controls the amount of tobacco they may grow, and generally helps to support the profitability of the industry.[1] However, the government also forces cigarette manufacturers to include warning labels. Meanwhile, although the number of American smokers drops appreciably every year, people in their fifties, sixties, and beyond still run up huge medical bills in trying to repair the damages caused by a lifetime of smoking.

Many people who face major smoking-related illnesses in middle age have health insurance. However, as Werner and Sharon Hoeger point out, "heavy smokers use the healthcare system, especially hospitals, twice as much as nonsmokers do" (243). Needless to say, the cost of this medical care is enormous, and since almost all health plans are capped, normally at about a million dollars,

Super-script alerts reader to endnote.

The page number suffices since the source (the Hoegers) is cited in the sentence.

Mickelson 4

eventually that cap is reached. For
instance, the cost of treating lung cancer
alone can easily exceed this figure, at
which point the "insured" find themselves
in the same position as those with no
insurance to start with: at the mercy of
hospitals and in some cases dependent on
Medicare or Medicaid. Three results issue
from the preceding scenario: everybody's
health insurance premiums go up to account
for smokers' medical expenditures;
hospitals pass along their costs for
providing what is supposedly free care for
the uninsured and/or indigent; and the
government--meaning the taxpayers--pay the
rest.

Thesis is restated, followed by block quotation that indicts the tobacco industry emphatically.

The situation is intolerable. As
Charles Scriven has asked,

> Can you name a respectable
> American industry that:
> - kills more than a third of its
>   long-time customers;
> - kills, every year, another
>   53,000 <u>involuntary</u> users of
>   its product;
> - paves the way to marijuana and
>   cocaine addiction;

Mickelson 5

- gets 90 percent of its new customers from the ranks of children;
- spends $500,000 an hour hawking its deadly merchandise?

The answer, by now well known, is the tobacco industry. (21)

Page reference follows end of block quotation.

Although Scriven's statement about "marijuana and cocaine addiction" is somewhat forced, the rest of his list reflects facts that the American public has grown weary of. During President Clinton's first year of office, various public-interest groups suggested adding a two-dollar-per-pack tax so that smokers could, in essence, pay as they use. Currently, as Scriven points out, "Among developed nations, U.S. cigarette taxes are, along with Spain's, the lowest of all" (21). The two dollars generated would be placed in a fund reserved for the payment of necessary medical care for smokers who persist in their habit. Although there are some problems with this idea, I believe that such an additional tax is the best solution to what has

Mickelson 6

become a national nightmare.

The American ideal is self-reliance, and a sense of responsibility is a major part of that ideal, if not the reality. Americans, on principle, dislike the idea that a person would choose a harmful lifestyle and then expect others to pay for the results. Even the occasional "libertarian," such as Daniel Seligman, does not dislike the idea (138). I believe that most Americans would be perfectly willing to put up with smokers (outdoors, of course) if smokers were forced to be financially responsible for their own behavior.

As mentioned above, there are a few legitimate objections to this proposal. One is a change in the way that convenience stores--and to a lesser extent, grocery stores and drugstores-- would do business. A two-dollar-per-pack tax increase would drive the cost of a carton of cigarettes to almost forty dollars, and in the case of convenience stores, a carton would become the most expensive item in the store. Given that most quick stops avoid keeping spare cash

To be impartial, the writer mentions objections to the proposal, then counters them.

Mickelson 7

in the register, it is easy to visualize thieves who steal not money but, say, twenty cartons of cigarettes, an easily transportable number. However, it is possible that convenience stores would either stop selling cigarettes altogether or, more likely, decrease the number and variety they carry. Perhaps specialty shops would emerge, similar to liquor stores, with greater security than the average quick stop. Then buying cigarettes would become more of a conscious choice, no longer just a last-minute, casual impulse.

Another objection is that smokers already pay enough, since many of them die in their mid-fifties. According to this view, it is entirely possible that all the contributions made by a smoker will remain the property of the federal government, never to be paid out (Huber 172). In effect, any worker (whether a smoker or not) is forced to gamble that he or she will live to receive Social Security payments, and in the case of smokers, the risks are obviously much greater that this will not happen, that the smoker will die

Para-
phrase
must be
docu-
mented.

Mickelson 8

at "a tax-efficient 60 or so" ("Wages of Sin" 27). Richard Aherne adds that, in 1979 dollars, the dead smoker misses out on benefits worth "a conservative $5000 per year per person" (qtd. in Troyer and Markle vi). However, tissue plasmogen activator, a new drug developed to prevent permanent damage after a heart attack, is already changing even this likelihood (Falla interview).

The source of the quotation is Troyer and Markle.

In any case, the proposal to tax cigarettes in proportion to the harm they cause has two goals: to convince people not to smoke and to create an ongoing fund to pay for the health care of those who persist. Cost may be a significant obstacle to many smokers, causing them to at least sharply curtail their intake if not actually quit. As Viscusi points out, "one can view taxes as a mechanism for selecting the optimum degree of discouragement of smoking" (547). A person who smokes one and one-half packs a day spends just over a thousand dollars per year. If that dollar figure were doubled, it is logical to assume that financial pressures would seriously affect most

Mickelson 9

smokers' perception of their habit. It would, at least, get their attention; Viscusi believes that smokers are short-sighted regarding their future and that additional costs would make them reconsider their choice to smoke (549). Also, the probability is that anyone willing to undergo such a large financial drain in order to obtain a deadly substance would be viewed as a pathetic addict, and this external perception could be a powerful motivator. Finally, Grossman, Sindelar, Mullahy, and Anderson stress the following:

> It is important to focus on teenagers and young adults, because cigarette smoking and alcohol abuse are addictive behaviors that generally begin early in life. Thus, policies to prevent their onset might be the most effective means to reduce them in all segments of the population. (215)

In terms of the second goal, large sums of money would flow into the federal coffers. The money could reasonably be

Note the use of the colon to introduce the long quotation.

Mickelson 10

expected to grow at an annual rate of ten percent. It seems doubtful that the money generated would pay for all the health care costs that would be applicable, but at least this funding would come from a focused, prepaid source, instead of from general revenues as it does today.

Canada has tried a proposal similar to the one described here, raising by way of taxation the average price of cigarettes to about $6.50 Canadian (Fennell, "Up in Smoke" 14). However, a significant problem soon developed: the smuggling of cigarettes from the United States through the vast, poorly patrolled border (Viscusi 555). Provincial governments and the national government obviously lose badly in such a situation: they receive no tax revenues at all, and in the case of Ontario's Cornwall, a popular tourist location, the battle between smugglers and police threatened the area's viability as an attraction (Fennell, "Up Smugglers' Alley" 46). But if the United States were to adopt the proposal concurrently with its northern neighbor, smuggling would be less of a

Mickelson 11

problem for Canada and little problem for U.S. interests. However, the smuggling issue that the United States would face would be contraband traveling north from Latin America. Nevertheless, in that circumstance it is illogical to believe that smuggling would test the much more stringent security of the southern United States when vastly superior profits can be made from the smuggling of narcotics.

What would happen to the tobacco companies? Obviously, their revenues would decline, but this has been true for years. American cigarette makers have been concentrating on markets in developing countries for some time now. Also, the current perception of tobacco companies in America makes it understandable that they should want to export their product instead of selling it domestically: they are starting to lose the product liability suits brought against them by individual consumers and, increasingly, by state governments tired of paying out health care benefits made necessary by the nicotine habit. Consequently, the perception of tobacco companies in the

The writer speculates on possible secondary effects of the proposal.

Mickelson 12

United States has begun to turn sour.

Many people criticize the federal government for inept and expensive social engineering, but the cigarette-tax proposal seems a clear improvement in terms of efficiency and general results. One condition, however, would have to be met in order for the program to succeed: the funds generated by the tax would have to be kept separate from other revenues. Americans have seen too much money flow down the maw of the General Fund to trust politicians' promises that tax dollars will be used as intended. If this condition is satisfied, an extremely valuable piece of social legislation could be put into effect, perhaps eventually enhancing the quality of life by decreasing the incidence of horrible, life-threatening illnesses caused by a habit unjustifiably considered acceptable for far too long.

The thesis is re-stated in the con-clusion.

Note

[1] The senators from North Carolina and Kentucky are, understandably, opposed to an increased cigarette tax. See Cohn and Hager (51) and "Wages of Sin" (27).

Mickelson 14

Works Cited

Cohn, Bob, and Mary Hager. "The Power of
    Sin." Newsweek 4 Oct. 1993: 51.

Falla, Colin. Personal interview. 5 Mar.
    1996.

Fennell, Tom. "Up in Smoke." Maclean's 6
    Dec. 1993: 14-16.

---. "Up Smugglers' Alley." Maclean's 4
    Oct. 1993: 46.

Grossman, Michael, et al. "Policy Watch:
    Alcohol and Cigarette Taxes." Journal
    of Economic Perspectives 7 (1993):
    211-22.

Hoeger, Werner W. K., and Sharon A.
    Hoeger. Principles & Labs for
    Physical Fitness and Wellness. 3rd
    ed. Englewood, CO: Morton, 1994.

Huber, Peter. "Health, Death, and
    Economics." Forbes 10 May 1993: 172.

Scriven, Charles. "A Tax We Can Live
    With." Christianity Today 8 Mar.
    1993: 21.

Seligman, Daniel. "Taxing Puffing."
    Fortune 14 June 1993: 138.

Troyer, Ronald J., and Gerald E. Markle.
    Cigarettes: The Battle Over Smoking.
    New Brunswick, NJ: Rutgers UP, 1983.

Viscusi, W. Kip. "Promoting Smokers'
    Welfare with Responsible Taxation."
    National Tax Journal 47 (1994): 547-
    58.

"The Wages of Sin." Economist 20 Mar.
    1993: 26-27.

Guidelines for APA-style research paper

78a Document sources accurately.

Documentation means including notes within your paper to tell readers where you located specific ideas and information and also including a list of your sources at the end of the paper. Documentation has two important functions: to give credit to the sources you have consulted and to enable your readers to look up the original material. Documenting also protects you against possible plagiarism (see p. 264): it distinguishes your thoughts and words from those of your sources.

According to APA style, you document by using in-text citations of author, year, and page, in parentheses, at the end of every sentence containing a quotation or paraphrase. For example:

```
The EPA's GIS system will provide various
benefits (Copeland, 1994, p. 44).
```

On your References page at the end of the paper, you will provide in an alphabetical list the complete information about each source; your in-text citation specifies the page from which the quotation or paraphrase is taken.

What must you document? Since you have read extensively to prepare your research paper, you may think at first that nearly every sentence in the paper will have to be documented. But readers are interested in what *you* have to say, in how you have used your reading. Information that is common knowledge and quotations that are well-known do not require documentation. But every sentence taken from a source requires a citation so that the reader knows who says what— and with a minimum of disruption. Whenever possible, introduce each quotation and paraphrase with the name of the authority.

78

You must document the following:

1. All directly quoted material:

   > Aaron Shearer points out that the midrange of
   > a finger joint is "approximately the middle
   > two-quarters of the range between the
   > comfortable limits of flexion and extension"
   > (1990, p. 31).

   If you did not use the author's name to introduce the quotation, cite it along with the page:

   > (Shearer, 1990, p. 31).

2. All paraphrased and summarized material:

   > Nikola Tesla's realization about alternating
   > current, Stephen Hall explains, came when
   > Tesla was walking with a friend in Budapest
   > (1986, p. 125).

   or:

   > According to Stephen Hall (1986, p. 125),
   > Nikola Tesla's realization about alternating
   > current came when Tesla was walking with a
   > friend in Budapest.

3. Facts and data that are not common knowledge:

   > Flextime scheduling includes a fixed, base
   > period and a flexible period in the morning
   > and/or afternoon (Thomas, 1986, p. 43).

When you cite two or more works by one author in the same year, add *a, b, c,* and so on to the year to prevent confusion:

```
Walkerson points out that "age and
intelligence quotient can be correlated"
(1989a, p. 457).
```

When a work has been written by two authors, document
it as follows:

```
Baldanza and Mackinnon point out that Alan
Shepard's bout with Ménière's disease was
probably the reason that Shepard became the
oldest astronaut to fly in the Apollo program
(1989, p. 4).
```

or:

```
Alan Shepard's bout with Ménière's disease was
probably the reason that Shepard became the
oldest astronaut to fly in the Apollo program
(Baldanza & Mackinnon, 1989, p. 4).
```

Note the use of the ampersand (&) when the authors' names
are listed parenthetically.

If a source has three to five authors, list all of them in your
first citation of the source. In following citations, use only the
first author's name followed by *et al.*:

78

First citation: ```Brown, Walker, Stein, and Litrola (1994)```
    ```or: (Brown, Walker, Stein, & Litrola, 1994)```

Further citations: ```Brown et al. (1994)```
    ```or: (Brown et al., 1994)```

If a source has six or more authors, use *et al.* after the first
author's name in each citation, including the first one.

When several items are taken from the same source, such as four sentences in a paragraph giving statistics derived from a single book, use one citation at the end of the paragraph: doing so will indicate that all the data in the paragraph come from that book. In such cases, especially, introducing your sources is important.

Though you will most often use short quotations, occasionally you will use a longer quotation to present an especially important point. If a quotation has more than forty words, indent the quotation five spaces from the left margin and do not add quotation marks. Double-space the quotation. Introduce the quoted material, using a colon to connect the introduction with the quotation, as in this example:

> Part of the reason for the Nazi party's success was the German economy. In his survey of modern history, Paul Johnson (1983) provides this summary evaluation:
>
> > Hitler's coming to power, therefore, provided German industry with precisely what it wanted to perform effectively: government stability, the end of politics and a sense of national purpose. It could do the rest for itself. Hitler was shrewd enough to realize this. While he allowed the party to invade every other sphere of government and public policy, he kept it out of industry and the army, both of which he needed to perform at maximum efficiency as quickly as possible. (p. 295)

Note that in a long quotation, the parenthetical citation *follows* the period.

Content footnotes.   Certain types of information cannot appropriately be included in the body of your paper. Such items include comments on your research process or on the sources you used, or acknowledgment of assistance you received. This information should be placed in footnotes. The accepted format for such notes is as follows:

[1] On this point see also Kennedy (1994, pp. 216—238).
[2] This study has benefited from the research assistance of Brenda Gordon, graduate assistant, Department of English.

Include bibliographical information on the References page, *not* in footnotes. Place the consecutive note numbers in the text immediately following the relevant sentence, raised slightly above the line, as in this example:

during the war.[2]

78b   Construct your list of References.

End the paper with an alphabetical list of the books, articles, and other sources you cite. This bibliography is titled "References." Although some instructors may require you to list all the works you consulted in preparing your research paper, the most common practice is to list only those sources you have used and cited. Copy on your bibliography cards the complete information for each such source, and keep the cards in alphabetical order by author's last name (or title if there is no author).

The following bibliography format is that of the American Psychological Association.*

78

*For full information, see *Publication Manual of the American Psychological Association,* 4th ed. (Washington, DC: American Psychological Association, 1994).

1. Since the list is alphabetical, place authors' last names first. (If no author or editor is given, alphabetize by title.)

2. Then list the date, in parentheses, and the full title. Use italics for titles of books and periodicals. For periodicals, use normal capitalization; for all other titles, capitalize only the first word of a title or subtitle and proper nouns.

3. Separate the items within the entry with periods.

4. For books, cite the publisher's city and a shortened form of the publisher's name: New York: McGraw-Hill. Use only the first city printed on the title page and the most recent copyright date.

5. For articles in journals and magazines, cite the volume, year, and full range of pages.

6. Double-space the lines of each entry, and indent the first line five spaces.

7. In listing two or more works by the same author, place the earliest work first.

```
        Ong, W. J. (1962). The barbarian within.
New York: Macmillan.

        Ong. W. J. (1967). The presence of the
word. New Haven: Yale University Press.
```

If two (or more) works were published in the same year, add *a, b, c* as needed to the year and alphabetize by the first important word of each title (see the Menzel entries on the Reference page of the sample essay, p. 325).

Reference format: Books

Single author:

```
        Pemble, J. (1995). Venice rediscovered.
Oxford: Clarendon.
```

Two authors:

Marchetti, V., & Marks, J. D. (1974). The CIA and the cult of intelligence. New York: Knopf.

Three or more authors:

Kagan, J., Havemann, E., & Segal, J. (1984). Psychology: An introduction (5th ed.). San Diego: Harcourt.

Translated and edited books:

Virgil. (1983). The Aeneid. (R. Fitzgerald, Trans.). New York: Random.

Merton, T. (1985). The hidden ground of love. (William H. Shannon, Ed.). New York: Farrar.

Gong, V., & Rudnick, N. (Eds.). (1986). AIDS: Facts and issues. New Brunswick, NJ: Rutgers University Press.

A work in an anthology:

Rubinstein, A. (1986). Children with AIDS and the public risk. In V. Gong and N. Rudnick (Eds.), AIDS: Facts and issues (pp. 99–103). New Brunswick, NJ: Rutgers University Press.

Note: The full pages of the article or chapter are cited. If you cite an article or essay in a collection of previously published works, list the earlier publication data:

Lewis, C. S. (1965). Satan. In A. E. Barker (Ed.), <u>Milton: Modern essays in criticism</u> (pp. 196–204). New York: Oxford University Press. (Reprinted from <u>A preface to "Paradise Lost,"</u> pp. 92–100, by C. S. Lewis, 1942, London: Oxford University Press)

Encyclopedia entries:

Melodeon. (1984). In <u>Encyclopedia Americana</u> (Vol. 18, p. 669). Danbury, CT: Grolier.

Reprinted and revised editions:

Fitzgerald, F. S. (1953). <u>The great Gatsby</u>. New York: Scribner's. (Original work published in 1925)

Here the book has been reprinted, and the date of the original edition is included after the title. If an edition is other than the first, cite *Rev. ed.* or *4th ed.* in parentheses after the title.

Multivolume work:

If all volumes were used:

Parrington, V. L. (1927-32). <u>Main currents in American thought</u> (Vols. 1-3). New York: Harcourt.

If only one volume is used (with its own title):

Churchill, W. S. (1957). <u>A history of the English-speaking peoples: Vol. 3. The age of revolution</u>. New York: Dodd.

Corporate author:

Committee on Telecommunications. (1970). <u>Reports on selected topics in telecommunications</u>. New York: National Academy of Sciences, National Research Council.

Government publication:

United States Department of Labor, Bureau of Statistics. (1977). <u>Dictionary of occupational titles</u> (4th ed.). Washington, DC: GPO.

Reference format: Periodicals

Article in journal (paged by volume):

Weiss, T. (1995). Translation in a borderless world. <u>Technical Communication Quarterly, 4</u>, 407-423.

Article in journal (paged by issue):

Hynes, J. (1995). Morality and fiction: The example of Henry James. <u>South Atlantic Review, 60</u> (4), 27-34.

Article in monthly magazine:

Moffett, M. W. (1990, January). Dance of the electronic bee. <u>National Geographic, 177</u>, 134-140.

78

Article in weekly magazine:

Bruck, C. (1996, February 19). Jerry's deal. The New Yorker, 72, 54-59, 61-66, 68-69.

Note: The pages for the Bruck article are discontinuous. The commas show where the article "jumps."

Article in newspaper:

Halprin, M. (1990, January 12). A single bullet. The Wall Street Journal, p. A12.

(Most daily newspapers have section indicators that precede the page number.)

Book review:

Anderson, J. (1978, May 28). Life with Father: Duke Ellington. [Review of the book Duke Ellington in person]. New York Times Book Review, p. 8.

Pamphlet:

78

Follow the format for books. If there is no date of publication, list *n.d.* in parentheses after the title.

Interview, letter, or telephone conversation:

Personal communication is cited in text only—for example, S. L. Willis (personal communication, February 2, 1991).

Film or TV program:

Bender, L. (Producer), & Tarantino, Q. (Director). (1994). Pulp fiction [Film].

Bullock, H. (1962). Jailbreak. (B. Sweeney, Director). In A. Ruben (Producer), The Andy Griffith show. Los Angeles: CBS.

Reference format: Electronic media

Standards are still evolving for the documentation of electronic media. The following guidelines will help you provide thorough information about an electronic source.

CD-ROM:

Strand, D. (1995). Review of Behind the Tiananmen Square massacre: Social, political, and economic ferment in China [CD-ROM]. Political Science Quarterly, 106, 341-342. University Publications of America.

Eisenberg, C. A., & Bader, D. (1995). QCE-6: A clonal cell line with cardialmyogenic and endothelial cell potentials [CD-ROM]. Developmental Biology, 167, 469-481. Abstract from: Wilson General Science Abstracts.

List the retrieval number (if available) immediately after the supplier, preceded by a colon.

Diskette:

Cookro, T. M. (1994). Digital data for quantitative geochemistry of rocks from the Adelaide Mining District, Humboldt County, Nevada [Diskette]. Denver: U.S. Department of the Interior, U.S. Geological Survey.

78

On-line database:

Perlman, J. (1995). Quayle council broke law, ethics experts suggest to House panel. <u>Reuters</u> [On-line]. Available: www.reuters.com

On-line journal:

Hurst, J. A. (1992, September 10). International finance questions. <u>Business Library Discussion List</u> [On-line serial]. Available: buslib-L@idbsu.idbsu.edu

In all cases, if you cannot locate full information, cite what is available.

78c   Research paper format

Requirements vary for student papers using the APA style. However, the following format is derived from the APA guidelines for manuscript preparation. The essay should be typed on white $8\frac{1}{2}'' \times 11''$ bond paper, double-spaced. Leave one-inch margins on all four sides of the page. Indent the first word of each paragraph five spaces from the left margin, and indent long quotations (more than forty words) five spaces from the left margin. Such quotations, like the body and the list of works cited, are double-spaced.

On the title page, type your name, the instructor's name, the course number, and the date on separate lines, double-spaced and centered on the page. Note that the title is not underlined, fully capitalized, enclosed in quotation marks, or ended with a period. Capitalize the first and last words of the title and all other words except articles *(the, an)* and prepositions and conjunctions with fewer than four letters *(in)*.

Number your pages consecutively throughout the paper in the upper right-hand corner, one-half inch from the top. Type a shortened version of your essay title, then a five-space gap followed by the page number, which should be flush against the right margin. Double-space between this head and the text.

Fingerprinting Techniques   1

An Analysis of
Fingerprinting Techniques
Jyll Holzworth
Dr. Pharr
ENC 3241
7 December 1995

Fingerprinting Techniques   2

Abstract

Since the beginning of the century, fingerprints have been used in criminal investigations to identify someone as having been at the scene of a crime. The reason is that no two people have exactly the same fingerprint pattern. Thus, if a person's fingerprint is found at the scene of a crime, then this person was definitely there at some point in time.

Because fingerprints are so important in solving crimes, it is necessary that they be discovered at the scene. Since fingerprints are almost always invisible to the naked eye because they are composed of very little material, many techniques are used by police officers to make the latent, or hidden, fingerprint visible. The type of technique used depends on a variety of factors, such as how old the print is and what type of surface it is on. Some techniques are more successful than others in certain situations.

Although there are many different techniques to choose from, the four most popular techniques are dusting, Super Glue fuming, ninhydrin, and lasers.

Abstract is provided as brief summary of paper.

Fingerprinting Techniques   3

An Analysis of Fingerprinting Techniques

Title is repeated on first text page.

Whenever a crime is committed, the police officers called to the scene of the crime almost always check for latent, or hidden, fingerprints. Why? Because fingerprints are the surest way of proving that someone was at the scene of a crime. No two people have the exact same pattern of ridges on their fingers. In other words, everyone has a unique fingerprint pattern.

Introductory paragraphs provide context for paper.

Over the years, different techniques have been used to find latent fingerprints. Although there are many techniques available, not all techniques are successful in every situation. The technique used depends on various factors, such as what type of material the fingerprint was left on and how long it has been since the fingerprint was left. There are some situations in which one technique may be unsuccessful while another technique is successful. Again, it depends on the situation. While there are many techniques, the four most commonly used ones are dusting, Super Glue fuming, ninhydrin, and lasers. An analysis of

Fingerprinting Techniques   4

these four techniques shows that they have advantages and disadvantages based on their effectiveness, cost, and possible health hazards.

Fingerprint Residue

To begin with, it is important to understand exactly what a fingerprint is. When someone touches something, a slight residue from the person's finger is left behind. This residue is composed of approximately .0001 grams of material. Approximately 98% to 99% of this material is just water, which evaporates quickly, leaving only .000001 grams of material on the surface that was touched. About one-half of this material is inorganic while the other half is an "organic mixture of amino acids, lipids, vitamins, and other matter" (Menzel, 1989b, p. 89).

Using this knowledge about fingerprint residue, police officers are able to locate the latent fingerprint through a variety of techniques. The technique used will be determined by factors such as the type of material the print was left on and the length of time

Subheads are under lined per APA style

Fingerprinting Techniques   5

that has elapsed since the print was left
(Olsen, 1978, p. 6).

Dusting

The technique most commonly used by
police officers is dusting (Wingate, 1992,
p. 75). Dusting involves taking a small
brush, dipping it into a powder, which is
usually black, and then lightly brushing
the surface where a latent fingerprint is
thought to be (Moenssens, 1969, p. 24). If
the procedure is done correctly, the
latent fingerprint will become visible.

Whereas dusting is the preferred
method because it is safe, inexpensive,
and easy to use, it does have some
disadvantages. First, it can be used only
while the latent print still contains
water, since that is what the powder
adheres to. Since the water content of a
print evaporates within a couple of days,
dusting would be unsuccessful on older
prints (Hartsock, 1982, p. G2). Second,
dusting works well only on smooth,
nonporous surfaces, such as metal or glass
(Hartsock, 1982, p. G2). It is
unsuccessful on porous surfaces such as
vinyl and leather because the powders tend

Fingerprinting Techniques   6

to "paint such surfaces" (Olsen, 1978, p. 223). As a result, the ridge details of any latent print will be hard to see because the powder covers both the print and the surface that the print is on. Dusting also does not work well on plastic bags since brushing may rub off any latent print residue (p. 223). In addition, dusting is not a good technique for uncovering latent fingerprints on paper because "brushing disturbs the fibers of the paper to the extent that ridge detail may be destroyed in the developed image" (Olsen, 1978, p. 220).

Super Glue Fuming

    Other techniques have successfully been used to bring out latent fingerprints on the surfaces where dusting does not work. On vinyl, leather, and plastic bags, for example, a technique called Super Glue fuming is the preferred method for finding latent fingerprints. As the name implies, this technique relies on the use of Super Glue, which costs less than three dollars a bottle (Hartsock, 1982, p. G2). This technique works by putting the item containing the print onto a hard,

Introductory sentence links new section to the preceding one.

Fingerprinting Techniques   7

nonflammable surface. The glue is then poured next to the item. Both are put into a container, which is then sealed shut. The fumes from the Super Glue will bring out any latent prints on the item. The main ingredient in the Super Glue that works to bring out the latent prints is cyanoacrylate ester. When the prints develop, in about two days, they will be white (Wingate, 1992, p. 82).

Super Glue fuming is a cheap and effective method of bringing out latent prints on surfaces where dusting does not work. It is, however, somewhat unsafe because it produces highly toxic fumes, which can be harmful if inhaled (Wingate, 1992, p. 82). Therefore, it is very important that the person opening the container holding the glue not have his or her face right above it when it is opened, or the person will certainly inhale the noxious fumes.

<u>Ninhydrin</u>

While Super Glue fuming may work well on porous surfaces such as vinyl and leather, it is not successful on paper. Since dusting does not work well on paper

Introductory sentence links new section to the preceding one.

Fingerprinting Techniques   8

either, police officers needed something that would show latent prints on paper. A chemical known as ninhydrin was discovered to be very successful in bringing out latent prints on not only paper but also cardboard, wood, and wallboard (Menzel, 1989a, p. 557A).

Unlike the dusting procedure, ninhydrin can develop prints that have lost their water content. Thus, prints several years old can be developed with the use of ninhydrin (Hartsock, 1982, p. G2). Ninhydrin works by reacting with the amino acids in the fingerprint residue to form a bluish-purple product called Ruhemann's Purple (Menzel, 1989a, p. 557A).

Ninhydrin in powder form is white. To be used correctly, it must be dissolved in a suitable solvent. The item to be treated is then either sprayed with or dipped into the ninhydrin solution (Moenssens, 1969, p. 25). The solvent to be used depends on whether the ink on the document must be protected and on the possible health risks (Olsen, 1978, p. 282).

Fingerprinting Techniques 9

The two most common solvents used today are acetone and amyl acetate. While both are quite effective in uncovering latent prints on paper, both also have some disadvantages. The use of acetone will cause most inks to run. Also, too much exposure to acetone fumes can "irritate the mucous membranes and cause headaches, fainting, and general poisoning" (Olsen, 1978, p. 285). Amyl acetate, on the other hand, does not cause inks to run, but it is just as likely to cause severe headaches (Wingate, 1992, p. 80). Thus, while ninhydrin is inexpensive, it may damage documents and may cause health problems.

Laser

Today, there is a new technique that can be used by itself or in conjunction with the previously mentioned techniques. This technique involves the use of lasers. It was discovered that the organic matter in fingerprint residue is inherently fluorescent (Menzel, 1989b, p. 89). When the appropriate light from a laser beam is shone onto a latent fingerprint, the print

Fingerprinting Techniques   10

will "glow like a firefly in the dark" (Hotz, 1986, p. G5).

Since the fluorescent components in fingerprint residue absorb light in the blue-green range, the Argon laser has become the accepted laser to use for fingerprint detection (Menzel, 1989b, pp. 89—90). The Argon laser is used both in crime labs and at crime scenes, although portable lasers offer less sensitivity because they have less power (Menzel, 1989b, p. 90).

Using lasers to bring out the fluorescence inherent in fingerprint residue is a very simple procedure. The area to be studied is placed in a dark room. Then the laser travels through a fiber optic cable for "convenient illumination of the fingerprint area" (Menzel, 1989b, p. 90). Due to the danger in working with lasers, goggles must be worn to reflect the laser light but allow the fluorescent fingerprint to be seen (p. 90).

Using lasers to detect the fluorescence inherent in fingerprint residue is successful only on smooth or

Fingerprinting Techniques   11

porous surfaces and only if there is almost no background fluorescence. This is necessary because inherent fluorescence is not very strong. Thus, if the background fluorescence is as strong or stronger than the inherent fluorescence, the print will not be seen (Menzel, 1989a, p. 558A). Since many surfaces fluoresce strongly, the use of lasers was at first restricted to specific surfaces (Menzel, 1989b, p. 90).

In order to be able to increase the use of lasers, fingerprints began to be first treated with something that would make them fluoresce more strongly than the background (Menzel, 1989b, p. 90). These treatments make use of the previously mentioned fingerprint techniques. One such treatment is to dust with fluorescent powders. Another is to stain with a fluorescent dye, such as Rhodamine 6G, after Super Glue fuming. The cyanoacrylate ester in the Super Glue combines with the ridges of the fingerprint residue to form a white product. This white product is stable and will not wash away after it is treated with a fluorescent dye. Without

Fingerprinting Techniques   12

Super Glue fuming first, the dye would wash away the latent print (Menzel, 1989a, p. 558A). Still another method involves ninhydrin. A document treated with ninhydrin does not fluoresce, but add the right amount of zinc chloride, and a highly fluorescent orange coordination compound is produced (Menzel, 1989a, p. 559A).

There are more than a hundred police departments that use lasers to detect latent fingerprints. Although laser equipment is very expensive, these departments feel that the "laser is already paying for itself in guilty pleas" (Hotz, 1986, p. G5). Lasers are dangerous to work with, but they are extremely accurate and can be used to check for prints from as far back as forty years ago (p. G5).

Evaluative paragraph states social benefits of laser detection of fingerprints.

Certain rates of crime appear to be declining. In a comparison of homicide rates from 1994 to 1995 among nine major cities in the United States, only Dallas and Phoenix saw an increase in their homicide rate. The other seven cities all had a lower homicide rate

Fingerprinting Techniques   13

than the levels of 1994 (Steckner, 1995, p. C10). Laser technology may be one of the reasons for the decline. The use of lasers could have resulted in more fingerprints being discovered at crime scenes, which would have resulted in more guilty verdicts. If this is so, then there may be many more police departments that are willing to stretch their budget in order to make room for laser technology.

Distribution

Finding a latent fingerprint is only half the battle. Once a print is found, it must be digitally photographed and then entered into a computer system known as the Automated Fingerprint Identification System, or AFIS. This system narrows the number of suspects from hundreds to about eight or ten in a short period of time. Police officers used to have to do this task manually by comparing the print to hundreds of other prints on file, but with this new computer system, much time is saved, and police officers can spend more time solving other crimes as well.

Final paragraphs emphasize social benefits of using modern technology to retrieve fingerprints to help solve crimes.

Fingerprinting Techniques   14

Thus, by using the right technique to uncover a latent fingerprint, and then putting the print into AFIS, police officers can solve more crimes. This is technology working together to make the world a safer place to live.

Fingerprinting Techniques   15

References

Hartsock, J. (1982, October 27). Glue clue. Annapolis Evening Capital, p. G2.

Hotz, R. L. (1986, April 1). Laser method to detect fingerprints enlightening police on crime cases. Atlanta Journal, p. G5.

Menzel, E. R. (1989a). Detection of latent fingerprints by laser-excited luminescence. Analytical Chemistry, 61, 557A-561A.

Menzel, E. R. (1989b, November). Ion-laser detection of fingerprints grows more powerful. Laser Focus World, pp. 89–92.

Moenssens, A. A. (1969). Fingerprints and the law. Philadelphia: Thomas Nelson.

Olsen, R. D. (1978). Scott's fingerprint mechanics. Springfield: Charles C. Thomas.

Steckner, S. (1995, July). Phoenix homicide rate fastest rising in the nation. Phoenix Gazette, p. C10.

Wingate, A. (1992). Scene of the crime: A writer's guide to crime-scene investigations. Cincinnati: Writer's Digest Books.

Other Types of Writing

The writing techniques discussed in this book apply to many writing situations outside the composition class, including the four special applications treated in this chapter: the literary analysis, the business letter, the memorandum, and the résumé.

 Writing literary analyses

Responding to what you read and putting your responses into words is a basic part of most college courses, which often require you to summarize, analyze, or discuss various texts. Analyzing literature is an excellent way to develop these writing skills and to learn about your own experiences as a reader.

Most college essays that require writing about other writing are analytical: you explain the reasons for an economic downturn, the effects of a disease, or the meaning of a poem. That is, you explain relationships and what they mean. Rather than merely summarizing a work or event, you will most often comment on and interpret it, pointing out why a work or

327

event means what it does. Explaining the reasons for your opinions about a piece of literature requires critical reading and thinking, skills that will be of value in many real-world tasks. All serious thinking is analytical: it is only by mentally taking a subject apart and then reconstructing it that a person can understand how it functions, why it occurred, or what it is.

79a   Analysis requires interpretation.

In explaining the reasons for your opinions about a novel, short story, poem, or play (as well as essay, film, song, or advertisement), you learn about yourself, your values, the values of your society, and the values of the author. You read such texts not merely for information but for pleasure and insight. Writing a good analysis adds to your original pleasure and deepens your first insights by bringing you closer to the work and to your own thoughts and feelings about it. You analyze a text to explain what it means to you and why it affected you as it did.

Your assignment might be to write a *response statement* that indicates your personal reactions to a work. Or you might be asked to write a *review*. Sometimes you will write a *summary* of the action or plot. But most often you will be expected to write an *analytical essay* that explains how the elements of the work (plot, character, setting, and point of view, among others) add up to some overall meaning or theme. To develop a convincing analysis, you will provide evidence from the text to back up your *interpretation,* your explanation of a meaning that is not readily apparent. You may discover that a work reveals meanings other than what the author intended, that there is no single "right" interpretation. However, an interpretation is not merely a subjective reaction; it is a reasoned evaluation that is supported by examples and quotations from the text. As long as you can support your interpretation and prove your solid understanding of the work, your readers will be satisfied that your opinions are worth considering.

79b   Read the work carefully.

Unlike newspapers, which are read quickly for facts, literary texts are meant to be read slowly and carefully, not just for information but for understanding. The first reading serves mainly to help you discover what the work is about. In your second reading, make sure that you have a pencil handy to mark passages that strike you as important, interesting, or revealing. Check your dictionary for the definitions of any unfamiliar words. With each reading, you will be conscious of your reactions to different aspects of a work and to the cultural background; the text's meanings will gradually become clear to you.

79c   Choose a limited topic.

As you reread a work, consider possible topics that interest you. Although you will be considering the significance of the whole work, you must choose a limited topic. To write an essay about everything in a novel or even a short story would result in general, superficial comments. A limited topic—on a symbolic color, unusual title, or revealing characterization, for example—will not be trivial or dull; in fact, if developed properly, this kind of topic can shed light on the whole work, helping you and your reader understand it from a specific point of view. (See 5.)

Literary analysis has one advantage over many other types of writing. A literary text is filled with human experiences; it provides many subjects for you to analyze and contains the evidence needed to develop the essay. You can always return to the text for ideas, and many more topics than you can use will occur to you as you read. Selecting the most interesting and appropriate topics, those that mean the most to you and to your readers, may be the most challenging task.

79

79d   Formulate a thesis statement.

Once you have your topic, take an attitude toward it. This attitude or stance should be expressed in the introduction to give your writing a unifying purpose. If the subject of a poem is death, try to determine what the poet's attitude toward death is—and how it reflects your attitude or differs from it. Be sure to formulate your own thesis so that you will develop *your* views and not rely on those of others. If you are assigned a topic, consider the importance of this topic in relation to the work as a whole. If, for example, your topic is "The Importance of the Town in William Faulkner's 'A Rose for Emily,'" your thesis statement might be as follows: "The town in Faulkner's 'A Rose for Emily' is one of the principal characters." Once you have your thesis, read the text again, this time with the eye of a private investigator eager to make a good case. Look for evidence— examples, descriptive details, quotations—that proves the importance of the town as a "character" in Faulkner's story. (See **6**.)

79e   Assume that your reader has read the work.

Unlike the readers of a book report or a review, readers of a literary analysis are familiar with the work and do not require summaries or long quotations. (In explicating a poem, however, you may want to supply the text of the poem for the readers' convenience.) Summarize only those events of the plot necessary to make your observations clear. In the following two paragraphs, you can see the difference between retelling what happens in a work and analyzing it:

79

A.   Paul Morel in D. H. Lawrence's *Sons and Lovers* is a sensitive, tormented character. As a very young man, he begins a long relationship with the spiritual Miriam that is never fulfilling. Later, he has a more mature, physical relationship with Clara, but this, too, is unsuccessful. Throughout his life, his strong, possessive mother is a dominating presence. It is not until her death that Paul is able to free himself.

B.   Paul Morel in D. H. Lawrence's *Sons and Lovers* is a sensitive, tormented character whose failure is linked to his mother's strong presence. He has a relationship with Miriam, whose reserved, spiritual character is an extension of his mother's.

Therefore, Paul never sees Miriam as a woman but as an entity who wants to possess him. In his more mature relationship with Clara, Paul finds no genuine satisfaction because he sees in her the physical aspects of his mother, to whom he is forever tied. By failing to relate to either Miriam or Clara, Paul is unable to find himself or the freedom he needs to break away from his mother's domination, which ends only with her death.

Whereas the first paragraph relies on plot summary, the second paragraph develops the *reasons* for its opening sentence by exploring the relationship between the women in Paul's life and his lack of freedom and fulfillment. Literary analysis, then, presents ideas, reflections, and judgments about the work rather than merely facts; it explains *why,* not just *what.*

79f Write an interesting introduction.

Your opening paragraph should capture the reader's interest and clearly state your main point (see **8**). Also, identify the full title and author of the work.

79g Develop the body of the essay with evidence.

Rather than follow the structure of the work you are analyzing, arrange your body paragraphs according to major ideas. Each paragraph should support one aspect of your thesis statement (see **7**) and should contain examples or quotations from the work. If, for example, your introduction mentions that two characters in a play have some similarities despite their many differences, you could devote one paragraph to their differences and two paragraphs to their similarities. Or you could have a thesis statement such as the following: "Through his references to darkness, robbing, and animals, Iago establishes the pervasive atmosphere of evil in *Othello.*" You could structure such an essay in terms of the three types of references.

79

An essay will be convincing to the extent that it contains evidence from the text in support of your main point. The sample paper (p. 333) shows how you can combine your comments with supporting quotations. Note that an essay about literature must be written in the present tense: the work is ongoing. Use the past perfect (*had lived,* etc.) for events occurring before the time frame you are discussing.

Include only your final opinions about the work, and eliminate any sentences that do not advance your thesis. Your purpose is not to congratulate the author, not to discuss his or her life, not to preach to the readers about your philosophy, not to find fault, as a reviewer might, but to express your understanding of the ideas and artistry of the work.

79h   Use quotations correctly.

In developing the body of the essay with selected quotations, be sure to copy each quotation exactly from the original. Include the page number (or line numbers, in the case of poetry) from the original in parentheses at the end of the sentence:

> Connie "knew she was pretty and that was everything" (212).

A brief literary analysis usually does not require a bibliographical citation of the primary source, but any secondary (critical) sources should be acknowledged (see **77a**). For repeated references to your primary source, simple citations are acceptable once you have identified the work in your essay. In the following example from a play, the act, scene, and line are cited:

> Othello speaks of himself as one "that lov'd not wisely but too well" (5.2.344).

When writing about a short story, you will sometimes need to use a long quotation (defined as more than four of your typed lines). Indent a long quotation (set it off ten spaces from

79

the left margin), and do not add quotation marks. Incorporate all other quotations into your own sentences. Short passages of poetry (one or two lines) should be included in your text:

> Butler speaks of "a leering company / Of unholy ghosts" (lines 10–11).

But longer quotations of poetry (three or more lines) are set off (indented ten spaces from the left margin), written line for line, and have no added quotation marks. Note that in a long quotation involving either prose or poetry, the parenthetical citation is placed after the end punctuation (see **40a**).

79i Develop an effective conclusion.

Conclude your analytical essay by summarizing your main points and by assessing the significance and impact of the work. Do not introduce new ideas, cite critics' views, or provide quotations; instead, emphasize what your analysis has discovered.

Here is a sample student analysis of a poem by Sylvia Plath titled "Daddy."

Sylvia Plath: Resolving Paternal Conflict
in "Daddy"
by Karen Crew

To Sylvia Plath, poetry is a method of controlling the emotionally disturbing events of her life. Although her work is not exclusively autobiographical, Plath uses elements from her own experiences as foundations for the thematic elaborations presented in her poems. Through these elaborations, she attempts to put the disturbing events of her life into perspective. One of Plath's later poems, "Daddy," shows a great effort to organize and control the pain resulting from personal experience. The poem exemplifies Plath's attempt to release herself from the conflicts resulting from rage, guilt, and grief. As a basis for the tone of despair and anger in "Daddy," Plath uses personal allusions to the loss of her father, to her failed marriage with Ted Hughes, and to her own suicide attempt. In addition, Plath draws on historical allusions, on the theory of the Electra complex, and on her own archetypal ideas of death and rebirth to extend the initial theme of loss and grief even further. As she extends the theme presented in "Daddy" into a greater, internal conflict, Plath develops and reiterates the meaning through the literary devices of allusion, allegory, diction, and symbolic enactment.

Plath draws on personal experience to develop the speaker (a woman who cannot escape the memory of her father) and the initial conflict (between the woman and her oppressive father) of "Daddy." Explicit allusions to the death of her father, to her suicide attempt (at age twenty), and to her seven-year marriage with Ted Hughes serve as a foundation for the grief-stricken theme of loss and pain

in the poem. Plath also relies on many
external allusions to elaborate the theme.
The first stanza establishes a childlike tone
with an allusion to the nursery rhyme of
"the little old lady who lived in a shoe" as
she compares the constraining memory of her
father to a "black shoe / In which I have
lived like a foot" (2-3). Historical
allusions to the Holocaust serve to heighten
the conflict, for the speaker calls her
father "panzer-man" (45) and she thinks she
"may well be a Jew" (35). Finally, allusions
to the Electra complex are found throughout
the poem; for example, the speaker declares
that "Every woman adores a Fascist" (48),
and she marries a man who is "a model" (64)
of her father. This allusion to the
Electra complex serves to internalize the
conflict for the speaker; she realizes how
she has projected her love (and hate) for
her father into her marriage and into her
life.

   As Plath uses allusions to develop the
speaker and the conflict, she employs
allegories to characterize the father and to
dramatize the speaker's rebellion against him.
At the time of her father's death, the speaker
idealizes him as "God" (8), but as she grows
older, she begins to resent him for deserting
her. This resentment dominates her imagination

as his memory becomes a "Ghastly statue" (9), an effigy that she wishes to destroy. Through allegory, she equates her father with a Nazi, a devil, and a vampire--all of which characterize him as an oppressive, destructive force. Throughout the poem, the speaker attempts to do away with the idealized father, but the allegories demonstrate how difficult that task has become: "Daddy" keeps returning in different guises.

Plath's precise use of diction develops the conflicts of the poem and reveals the tone. Throughout the poem, the speaker characterizes the images of her father as black: "black shoe" (2), "a swastika / So black" (46-47), "black man" (55), and "your fat black heart" (76). These ominous images contrast with the image of the speaker as "poor and white" (4) and show how her father's memory corrupted her as he "bit [her] pretty red heart in two" (56). The repetition of "wars, wars, wars" (18) serves to intensify the external and internal conflicts that result in a suicide attempt as the speaker tries to "get back, back, back" (59) to her father. As the poem progresses, the words become angrier as the innocent tone of an emotionally abused child is sacrificed. The speaker destroys her love for her father and replaces it with hatred as she drives "a stake in [his] fat black heart" (76) and declares, "Daddy, daddy, you bastard, I'm through" (80).

Finally, Plath develops and reiterates the meaning of "Daddy" with a symbolic enactment of the Electra complex and of her own archetypal ideas of death and rebirth. The speaker idealizes her father and is equally oppressed by him, so she must act out the complex before she is free of it. Therefore, she marries a man with "a love of the rack and screw" (66), endures her torture as her mother endured "The boot in the face" (49), and finally drives a stake through the heart of "the vampire" (72) husband. By symbolically killing her husband, the speaker kills her Electra complex. Neither can oppress her anymore: "The voices just can't worm through" (70), and she is "finally through" (68).

The speaker also attempts to release herself from the pain of her father's death (thus extending the theme of loss and grief) by acting out Plath's own archetypal ideas of death and rebirth. Due to the overwhelming sense of loss in her life, Plath believed that death would cleanse her of the grief and pain associated with life; in this sense, she would undergo the purification of "rebirth." Although she hated the death of others because it destroyed her love and left her in a world of "Ghastly statue[s]" (9), she idealized her own death because it enclosed her in a protective, womb-like world. The speaker of "Daddy" realizes that the world of her father is closed to her while she is alive, so she "tried to die" (58) in order to "get back" (59) to him and continue loving him. After she is rescued, she realizes that he is still "alive" in her memory, so she puts him to rest by killing him: "Daddy, you can lie back now. / There's a stake in your fat black heart" (75-76). The speaker realizes that she can bury her love for her father, but the pain of loss will follow her to the grave. This realization is apparent through the anger of the last line: "you bastard, I'm through" (80). The speaker is through with loving her father, her husband, and maybe even life, for she has resigned herself to a life devoid of love.

Through allusion, allegory, and diction, Plath develops the external and internal conflicts and the theme of loss in "Daddy." By allowing the speaker symbolically to enact the Electra complex and her own archetypal ideas of death, Plath reinforces the meaning of loss and adds her own methods of dealing with that loss. Plath uses personal experience as a foundation for the conflict of the poem, elaborates the conflict through literary devices and Freudian theory, and uses personal theories to resolve that conflict.

79

80 **Use conventionally accepted style and form for business letters.**

No other type of writing today is as stylized as the business letter. Although conventional practices concerning letter form and tone vary somewhat, you must follow some standards if you want your reader to accept and respect your letters. The suggestions below reflect current conventions.

80a Arrange the parts of your letter according to standard form.

The eight parts listed below are required in all business letters. Arrange them as shown in the sample. Use a conventional font (not one that calls attention to itself), and use at least 10-point type. Never use italic or script as your text font. Single-space within each part, but double-space between parts and between paragraphs. Use at least one-inch margins at the sides and one and one-half inches at the top and bottom. However, vertically center a short letter.

Letterhead or return address. If no printed letterhead is available, type your return address starting at the left margin.

Date. Type the correct date two lines below the letterhead. If you are using a return address instead, type the date immediately below the last line of the address.

Inside address. Two spaces below the dateline, enter the name, title, and mailing address of the person to whom you are writing. The inside address may require several lines, each starting at the left margin.

Salutation. Write the salutation flush with the left margin, two spaces below the inside address. If the letter is addressed to an individual, use *Dear Ms. X, Dear Mrs. X,* or *Dear Miss X*

80

for women and *Dear Mr. X* for men. (If you do not know how a female addressee prefers to be called, use *Ms.*) When appropriate, use a title such as *Dr.* or *Professor.* If the letter is addressed to a job title without a specific person's name (such as *Director of Personnel*), use *Dear Sir or Madam.* If the letter is addressed to a group, such as a company or department, use *Gentlemen or Ladies.* Put a colon (:) at the end of the salutation.

Body. Begin the body two lines below the salutation. Start the first line of each paragraph at the left margin. Double-space between paragraphs.

Complimentary close. Put the complimentary close two lines below the end of the letter, flush left. Use only standard closings such as *Sincerely yours, Sincerely,* or *Cordially.* Capitalize the first word, and put a comma after the last word.

Signature. Type your name four spaces directly below the complimentary close.

Written signature. Sign your name in the space between the complimentary close and the typed signature.

In addition to these eight required elements, certain others are sometimes needed:

Identification line. When typing someone else's letter, list that person's initials before your own in the following manner:

```
DEF: lf
```

Start the identification line at the left margin, two lines below the typed signature.

Enclosure notation. If you enclose anything with the letter, place an enclosure notation two spaces below the identification line or typed signature. Use one of the following forms:

```
Encl.    or    Encl. 2
```

Copy notation. If anyone other than you and the addressee is to receive a copy of the letter, note this fact on the left margin two spaces below the previous notation. Use the following form:

```
cc: Mr. Anthony Canteras
```

Second-page heading. If a letter requires more than one page, use plain paper instead of letterhead for the second and subsequent pages. Leave a one-inch margin at the top, type a second-page heading as shown below, skip three spaces, and then continue the letter.

```
Mr. Bushee 2
```

Envelopes. Placement of the address is important so that the address can be read by the postal service's optical scanners. The last line should be no more than three inches and no less than one-half inch from the bottom of the envelope. Leave at least one inch from the end of the longest line to the right-hand edge.

80b Use the all-purpose letter pattern.

Nearly any letter that you will have to write can be developed by using a three-phase pattern. Begin by getting to the point in a brief introduction, stating the basic purpose of your letter much as you would the thesis of an essay. Then develop your point by adding specific details and examples as needed in the body of your text. Be concise, and use short paragraphs so that your reader can refer quickly to each specific point you make. Finally, write a brief one- or two-sentence paragraph to close the letter smoothly. Note how the sample letter on page 343 follows this pattern.

80

Adapt your tone to your reader and the situation, and be cordial but businesslike. Avoid the jargon often associated with business letters: *in reference to, pursuant to, yours of the 12th received,* and so on. You can communicate more clearly and effectively without such phrases (see **69**).

80

5100 Fair Oaks Blvd.
Winter Park, FL 32790
September 25, 1996

Ms. Elena J. Rogers
Advanced Colortech, Inc.
18 Orange Trail
Orlando, FL 32802

Dear Ms. Rogers:

I am writing to apply for the position of Vice
President, Graphic Division as advertised in
the Orlando Sentinel on September 20. With a
B.A. and three years' experience in the field,
I believe that I am qualified for the
position.

As indicated in the enclosed résumé, I
received my B.A. in 1993. While in school, I
was responsible for the design and production
of three serial documents, including
Crosscurrents, the student literary magazine
recognized in statewide competition during my
senior year as the winning design/conception
among twenty-four entries. After graduation,
I accepted a position at Clovis Magazine

Group as a graphic artist. Within a year, I was assigned my own production group and given the responsibility of designing and producing art for Clovis's new four-color fashion magazine, _Else_. During the two years that I have been art director for _Else_, I have had a wide range of duties, from maintaining high-end computers to liaising with printers and separators to attending our weekly executive planning sessions. I am experienced from the bottom to the top of graphic design, and now I would like to move to the next level.

Ms. Rogers, I have known of and admired your organization since I was an undergraduate, and I believe that my background and experience meet your requirements. I am available for an interview at your convenience.

Sincerely,

Anne Walker

Anne Walker

Encl.

80

▼ 81 Writing memorandums

A memorandum is used to communicate within an organization. Memos are frequently short and are always direct, highlighting essential information in clear, easy-to-read form.

Heading

The heading of a memo, clearly separated by white space from the text, is divided into four sections:

TO:	List the name and job title (if applicable) of your recipient.
FROM:	List your name, and list your job title (if you did so in the **TO:** line). Always initial memos to certify that you are the writer.
DATE:	Include either the date that you wrote the memo or the date on which you want it distributed.
SUBJECT:	Write a brief phrase indicating your memo's topic. Be specific; many readers, backlogged by paperwork, will decide at this point whether to continue.

The message that follows the heading is separated by enough white space to clearly distinguish between the heading and the body, which is single-spaced. At the end of the message there is no complimentary close or signature.

Content

Most memos inform readers about a course of action, recommend policies, or announce decisions. Because it is circulated inside an organization, a memo takes for granted a general knowledge concerning the products, practices, or personnel of the organization. Therefore, background information and formal documentation are frequently omitted.

81

In your first sentence, come directly to the point: "This memo summarizes . . . ," "The practice of ninety-minute lunch breaks violates company policy and must cease immediately," etc. If your memo is very brief, one paragraph will normally suffice. In a longer memo, however, move from a short introduction to the body of your text. Here, be objective, thorough, and clear. In your conclusion, which may well consist of a single sentence, ask your reader for a response or volunteer to answer any questions that might arise.

Style

Since you are writing to people with whom you work, an informal style is appropriate. Avoid long sentences. Abbreviations, contractions, in-house jargon, and technical terms (provided that everyone knows them) are acceptable.

81

MEMO

TO: Dave O'Reilly, Manager of Building Services *MS*

FROM: Mikhail Savinsky, Professor of Sociology

DATE: November 10, 1996

SUBJECT: Heating/cooling in Office 9-147

The temperature in my office has ranged from 51° to 83° during the last three weeks. Despite my repeated requests by phone, your technicians can't seem to fix the problem.

I realize that the weather has been quite unpredictable lately, but my office (and myself) would seem to be suffering more than should be expected. On Monday and Tuesday of last week, for example, my office was boiling. After my phone call, a technician came by and then said that he had fixed the problem. Indeed, on Tuesday afternoon the office was more comfortable. When the cold front moved through on Tuesday evening, however, my office got colder and colder, aided by the fact that the vent blew cold air--nonstop--for the rest of the week.

Is it possible to reach a "happy medium" here? Please call me at 2298 if you have any questions. Thank you.

81

82 Prepare a clear, concise résumé to emphasize your strengths.

Few things you ever write will be as important to you as the résumé you submit to prospective employers. The facts about your education and work experience do not speak for themselves; a well-prepared résumé will always help you in a job search.

82a Include the appropriate information in your résumé.

When preparing a résumé, select facts about your background that will present you as positively as possible. Never lie or concoct fictitious credentials, but select those that present the best impression.

Position desired. Many applicants name the actual position being sought; others list a broader "objective." Use either if you wish, but your accompanying letter of application should state the position you are seeking; stating that position in your résumé may prevent your being considered for other openings.

Personal data. By law, you do not have to furnish personal data to prospective employers, but many people include such information on their résumés. You might choose to include your date of birth, marital status, and number of children (if any). However, consider whether this information will help you. If you are very young (or very old) relative to the other applicants against whom you logically expect to compete, don't include your date of birth. Also, if the position for which you are applying is one that will require you to travel extensively or move every year or so, your being single would be an asset. However, a company that wants its employees to be a part of the community and prefers "settled" people would see a spouse as a good sign. Since personal information can be used against you, make sure that you consider the issue carefully, and note that many résumés avoid this category.

Educational background.   Begin with the college you are currently attending and work backward. Give dates of attendance or degrees, names of degrees or majors and minors, memberships in organizations and honor societies, and grade point average (if it is impressive).

Work experience.   Begin with your present or most recent job and work back to your high school graduation date; include significant part-time work. Give your past employers' names and addresses, dates of employment, and job descriptions.

Professional skills.   If you have relevant experience or training, develop a special section summarizing your skills. The exact skills will vary with your field, but the following suggestions should help: equipment, procedures, or special techniques used; supervisory positions held; unusual promotions or awards; certifications or registrations.

Related skills or activities.   If you have acquired through elective courses, hobbies, or other means any skills that might be useful in the desired position, include them. You may also mention community activities. Use anything that might give you a slight edge over other candidates. Do not bother listing interests or hobbies merely to give the reader a notion of what you are like.

References.   Including references is usually unnecessary, but references can be used to fill out an otherwise very short résumé. If you do include references, give the names, titles, and business addresses of three or four people (except for relatives and clergy members) who know you well and who can be trusted to speak favorably about you. Try to get variety, selecting people who know you in various ways.

82

82b   Carefully prepare your résumé in an effective form.

The following checklist will help you prepare an effective résumé:

1. Put your name, address, and telephone number at the top.

2. Use correct grammar. You may use fragments instead of complete sentences, but be sure you are consistent.
3. Use common abbreviations to save space.
4. Single-space within sections; double-space between sections.
5. State everything as positively as possible.
6. Make the final copy clean and neat.

Hermann G. Eichner
13869 Country Place Drive
Orlando, FL 32826
407/273-0474

OBJECTIVE   To continue my professional
career in accounting.

EDUCATION   **University of Central Florida,**
Orlando, FL
Master of Science in
Accounting. Degree expected:
12/97. GPA: 3.9.
Bachelor of Science in
Accounting, May 1993. GPA:
3.3/3.9 (in major).
Valencia Community College,
Orlando, FL
Associate of Arts in General
Studies, April 1988. GPA: 3.7.
**United States Air Force
Academy,** Colorado Springs, CO

	June 1982-May 1983. Completed freshman year of the engineering core.
EXPERIENCE	**Distributed Processing Technology,** Maitland, FL
Oct. '95-Present	<u>Assistant Controller</u>

- Negotiate and administer all general business and disability insurance policies.
- Supervise the cost accounting department.
- Implement job cost program as team leader.
- Perform analyses of profitability by product line.
- Retain all responsibilities below.

June '93-Oct. '95 <u>Cost Accounting Manager</u>

- Maintained all inventory, sales, CoGS, reserve and manufacturing variance accounts.
- Performed actual to standard cost variance analyses.
- Compiled and produced company sales reports.
- Planned and conducted physical inventories.
- Prepared all audit leads for inventory, profit and

82

loss, and reserve and field auditor questions.
- Wrote operating procedures for the receiving, order entry, and shipping functions.

Oct. '91–
June '93

Martin Marietta, Orlando, FL
Cost Accountant
- Employed through UCF's work-study program.
- Prepared departmental financial and labor budgets.

Mar. '89–
Aug. '91

Frontier Electronics, Winter Park, FL
Operations Manager
- Responsible for all procurement and inventory control activities.
- Instituted the computerization of the inventory control system.

Sept. '84–
Mar. '89

Martin Marietta, Orlando, FL
Energy Management System Technician
- Responsible for program-ming, troubleshooting, and daily operation of the facility's energy management system.

<u>Engineering Material Acquisi-</u>
<u>tion and Control Specialist</u>
- Administered the procurement
  of electronic components and
  hardware.

<u>Research and Development</u>
<u>Technician</u>
- Supervised stockroom.
- Developed and wrote an
  inventory control program.

PROFESSIONAL ACTIVITIES   Member of the Institute of
Management Accountants;
member of the Institute of
Internal Auditors; Junior
Achievement Volunteer;
participant in the IRS's
Volunteer Income Tax
Assistance Program.

ADDITIONAL INFORMATION   Passed Certified Internal Auditor examination on first
attempt. Extensive knowledge
of computer applications in
DOS and Windows environments,
including MFG/PRO, Progress
Results, Lotus, Microsoft
Word, and WordPerfect.

REFERENCES   Available upon request.

82

Grammatical Definitions and ESL Concerns

ps

83 **Know the parts of speech and their uses.**

The parts of speech are the classifications of English words according to their forms and their uses in sentences: verbs, nouns, pronouns, adjectives, adverbs, prepositions, conjunctions, and interjections. Many words can serve as more than one part of speech. For example, *round* can be a noun ("We won the *round*"), a verb ("They *rounded* the corner"), or an adjective ("I have a *round* table"). Being able to recognize parts of speech will help you analyze and discuss the sentences that you write.

83a Verbs show action, process, or existence.

The **verb** is an essential part of every sentence. Most verbs show some kind of action or process:

Barry *resigned.*   The lady *screamed.*   The water *boiled.*

Other verbs, known as **linking verbs,** express a state or condition. They link the subject with the noun, pronoun, or adjective that describes or identifies it. (The word linked to the subject is the **subject complement.**) Linking verbs include *be (am, is, are, was, were, being, been)* and *become, remain, grow, seem, appear, look, sound, feel, taste,* and *smell:*

Rosa *is* a brilliant attorney.   The meat *smelled* rancid.

Tense.   Tense refers to the time indicated in the sentence. The form of the verb indicates the time of the action or statement:

Sam *writes.* Sam *wrote.* Sam *will write.* (see **55**)

Voice.   If the subject of the sentence does the action, its verb is in the active voice. If the subject receives the action, the verb is in the passive voice (see **23e**, **57**):

Active voice: The reviewer condemned the film's violence. (*Subject* [reviewer] *acts.*)

Passive voice: The film's violence was condemned by the reviewer. (*Subject* [violence] *receives action.*)

Forms.   The English verb has a limited number of forms. Verbs may be regular *(walk, walked, walked)* or irregular *(see, saw, seen).*

Infinitive:	to walk; to see
Present:	walk, walks; see, sees
Past:	walked; saw
Past participle:	walked; seen
Present participle:	walking; seeing

83

The infinitive, the past tense, and the past participle are known as the **principal parts** of a verb. Most verbs are regular: they just add *-ed* to form the past and past participle. Irregular verbs may change spelling: *go, went, gone; see, saw, seen.* The present participle always ends in *-ing.* For the addition of *-s* in the present tense, see **55**.

Predicates. The main verb in a sentence is called the **simple predicate.** The main verb with all the words that belong to it or qualify it is called the **complete predicate** because it completes the subject (see **84c**).

Verb phrases. A **verb phrase** is made up of a **main verb** preceded by one or more **auxiliary verbs:** "I *will have left* by Friday." The most commonly used auxiliaries are *have (has, had), be (am, is, are, was, were, been), do (does, did), will, would, shall, should, can, could, may, might, must,* and *ought.*

The first word in a verb phrase shows tense and agrees with the subject: she *has* gone, she *had* gone; they *have* gone, they *had* gone. In identifying verb phrases, note that other words may come between the first auxiliary verb and the rest of the phrase:

His writing *has* never *made* sense to me.

Most children *have,* at least once in their lives, *dreamed* of riding on a spaceship.

Verbals. Forms of the verb may function as nouns, adjectives, or adverbs. When they do, they are called **verbals,** and they may combine with other words in **verbal phrases:**

Waiting for the train every day is not my idea of happiness.

Gerunds are verbals ending in *-ing* that are used as nouns: "*Jogging* is popular." Sometimes a gerund has an object and/or modifiers:

Paying bills promptly is not easy. (The gerund phrase—*paying bills promptly*—also functions as a noun.)

Laughing is good for one's health. (gerund as subject)

I would enjoy *laughing all the way to the bank.* (gerund phrase as direct object)

83

Present participles have the same form as gerunds but are used as adjectives, not as nouns:

The man *laughing* too loudly annoyed us. (*Laughing* is a present participle modifying *man.*)

83b   Nouns name things.

Nouns are the names given to things real or imagined, tangible or intangible:

trees   endurance   Colorado   woman   physics

In sentences, nouns can be used as subjects, objects of active verbs, complements of linking verbs, and appositives:

Subject	Appositive	Object of preposition	
John Nolan,	*assistant* to the	*mayor,*	gave

Indirect object		Direct object
reporters	a written	*statement.*

Nouns can also function as modifiers: *stone* wall, *television* news.
   Almost all nouns take an *-s* or *-es* ending or change spelling to form plurals (see **47**). They also take an apostrophe and *s* or apostrophe alone to show possession: *women's* rights, *prospectors'* expeditions (see **42**).

83c   Pronouns take the place of nouns.

The noun that a pronoun refers to is called the *antecedent:*

The men rushed in. *They* were angry. (The antecedent of *they* is *men.*)

83

There are six different kinds of pronouns:

Personal pronouns (*I, he, she, it, they, we,* etc.) take different forms according to their function in a sentence. See **51**.

Relative pronouns (*who, whom, whose, which, that*) join a dependent clause to a noun. See **83h**.

Interrogative pronouns *(who, whom, whose, which, what)* are used in questions.

Demonstrative pronouns *(this, that, these, those)* point to nouns: "*This* is better than *that*." (When used with nouns, they are called demonstrative adjectives: "*This* VCR is cheaper than *that* VCR.")

Indefinite pronouns refer to indefinite persons or things. Examples are *someone, everyone, anything, another.* For verb agreement with indefinite pronouns as subjects, see **50**.

Reflexive pronouns are used when the antecedent takes action toward itself: "The tomcat bathed *himself* after eating the bowl of food."

83d   Adjectives and adverbs are modifiers.

To modify is to describe, qualify, or limit the meaning of a word. **Adjectives** modify nouns and pronouns; **adverbs** modify verbs, adjectives, and other adverbs:

> The saleswoman approached the *reluctant* customer. (adjective *reluctant* modifying noun *customer*)

> The program progressed *quite rapidly.* (adverb *quite* modifying adverb *rapidly,* which modifies verb *progressed*)

> We faced *extremely* serious problems. (adverb *extremely* modifying adjective *serious*)

Most adjectives and adverbs can be arranged in order of intensity: *happy, happier, happiest; angrily, more angrily, most angrily.* See **54**.

Conjunctive adverbs are words that can introduce independent clauses and join independent clauses to form compound sentences (see **36**, **49**):

> *Therefore,* I move that we vote on the bill today.

> Rain is forecast; *however,* let's go ahead and start the game.

83

The conjunctive adverb, which indicates transition, can also appear within or at the end of an independent clause:

> He felt, *moreover,* that the job didn't pay enough to warrant moving to another state.

> All things are not equal, *however.*

Conjunctive Adverbs

accordingly	finally	likewise	similarly
also	furthermore	meanwhile	specifically
anyway	hence	moreover	still
besides	however	nevertheless	subsequently
certainly	incidentally	next	then*
consequently	indeed	nonetheless	therefore
conversely	instead	otherwise	thus

*Then is the only conjunctive adverb that is not usually followed by a comma.

Note that **transitional phrases** have the same function as conjunctive adverbs and require the same punctuation:

> Nina did not like the car; *as a matter of fact,* she hated it. *For example,* she especially disliked the exterior color, the cramped interior, and the diesel engine.

Transitional Phrases

after all	even so	in fact
as a matter of fact	for example	in other words
as a result	for instance	in the first place
at any rate	in addition	on the contrary
at the same time	in conclusion	on the other hand

83

83e Prepositions and conjunctions are structural words that work with the major parts of speech.

Verbs, nouns, adjectives, and adverbs express most of the information in sentences, but the meaning of a whole sentence also depends on structural words that show relationships among those major words. Two main groups of structural words are prepositions and conjunctions.

Prepositions relate and link one word with another; examples are *of, in, on, into, at, to, for, after, with, with regard to,* and *aside from.* They are followed by nouns and pronouns that form the **object of a preposition.**

> *After the long wait,* we enjoyed the concert.
> ↑   ↑
> **Preposition   Object of preposition**

A preposition and its object together are called a **prepositional phrase:**

> The old tree *in the center of town* stood *near the condemned building.*

Prepositional phrases can function as adjectives or as adverbs. See **83g.**

Conjunctions connect words or word groups. The **coordinating conjunctions** *and, but, or, nor,* and *yet* join words, phrases, or clauses of the same grammatical type:

> The *camera* and the *lens* must be purchased separately. (*And* joins two nouns.)
>
> He *lied* and *stole.* (*And* joins two verbs.)
>
> The hunter was *old* yet *strong.* (*Yet* joins two adjectives.)
>
> Neither *on land* nor *on sea* did they meet any resistance. (*Nor* joins two prepositional phrases.)

83

The coordinating conjunctions *for* and *so* are used only between word groups that express complete thoughts:

> He used the wrong film, *so* the pictures did not turn out.

Subordinating conjunctions introduce word groups and make them subordinate, or dependent: they need other word groups for their completion (see **20**).

> ***Since*** *Jamie moved to Dallas* [subordinate], she has matured.

> I feel weak ***because*** *I have not eaten* [subordinate].

Subordinating Conjunctions

after	if	unless
although	in order that	until
as	rather than	when
as if	since	where
because	so that	whereas
before	that	whether
even though	though	while

83f Interjections express emotion.

Interjections such as *oh* and *ah* show emotion. They may be punctuated as sentences *(Oh!)* or included in sentences *(Oh, I wish you would say something),* but they are not grammatically related to other words in the sentence.

83g A phrase is a group of related words without a complete subject and verb.

The function of a single word can be filled by a group of words. Such a group of words that work together, but lack a subject and verb, is called a **phrase:**

Noun:	I enjoy *art.*
Phrase as noun:	I enjoy *visiting museums.*
Verb:	He *went.*
Verb phrase:	He *should have been going.*
Adjective:	The *tall* man is my uncle.

83

Phrase as adjective: The man *towering over the others* is my uncle.

Adverb: She tried *hard*.

Phrase as adverb: She tried *with all her strength*.

There are four other common types of phrases:

Prepositional phrase:

Adjective: The clock *on the mantel* belonged to my grandfather.

Adverb: He drove the truck *around the block*.

Infinitive phrase:

Noun: He wants *to fight with everyone*.

Adjective: There must be another way *to settle this problem*.

Adverb: The plumber came *to fix the sink*.

Gerund phrase:

Noun: *Playing on a winning team* adds to the fun of baseball.

Participial phrase:

Adjective: The smoke *rising from the house* alerted the neighbors.

A house *built on a rock* will endure.

83

83h   A clause is a group of words with a subject and verb that is used as part of a sentence.

If a clause expresses a complete thought and can stand alone as a sentence, it is called an **independent clause** (or *main* clause). If it does not express a complete thought, it is called a **dependent clause** (or *subordinate clause*) and cannot stand alone as a sentence.

> The mayor spoke last night. (independent clause properly punctuated as a sentence)

> When the mayor spoke last night. (dependent clause improperly punctuated as a sentence)

Dependent clauses are introduced and made dependent or subordinate by subordinating conjunctions (such as *because, when, after, although*—see the list on p. 362). Such clauses cannot stand alone; they modify the main part of the sentence.

> *When the mayor spoke last night,* reporters were strangely absent.
>
> ↑   ↑
>
> **Dependent/subordinate**   **Independent/main**
> **clause**   **clause**

A subordinate clause functions as a noun, adjective, or adverb:

Noun: They do not know *who wrote the threatening letter.*
(clause as object of *know*)

Adjective: People *who exercise* live longer than people *who do not.*

Adverb: I ate the cake *because I was hungry.*

---

84 Know the elements of a sentence.

84a Subject

When a noun, pronoun, or verbal is doing something or is being described by a verb in a sentence, it is a **subject**.

> *I* [subject] saw the game Tuesday night.

Joan's *portrait* [subject] was painted.

Walking [subject] is excellent exercise.

84b   Compound subject

When a subject consists of more than one noun, pronoun, or verbal, it is a **compound subject:**

Bushes and shrubs obscure our rusty old back door.

84c   Predicate

The main verb in a sentence is called the **predicate.** It can be one word: "I *saw* the game Tuesday night." More often, the predicate will consist of several words that make up the complete verb:

He never *wants to leave.*

She *has* always *been able to learn* languages easily.

84d   Compound predicate

When a predicate has more than one main verb, it is a **compound predicate:**

Every fall, we *prune and fertilize* our azalea bushes.

The complete verb or predicate includes all the words related to the predicate; likewise, the complete subject includes all the words related to the subject.

The first person who comes to the party [complete subject] *never wants to leave* [complete predicate].

84

84e   Objects

A noun, pronoun, or verbal that directly receives the action of a verb is called a **direct object.**

Jennifer despises *housekeeping.* (*Housekeeping* is the direct object of *despises:* What does Jennifer despise?)

The library discarded forty-eight *books.* (*Books* is the direct object of *discarded:* What did the library discard?)

A noun, pronoun, or verbal that is related to the action but that is not the direct receiver of the action is called an **indirect object.** It states to whom (or to what) or for whom (or for what) something is done:

Mystery writers usually give *readers* a few clues.

Writers give clues (direct object) to readers (indirect object).

The teacher told *Jay* some sad news about his grades.

Teacher told news (direct object) to Jay (indirect object).

84f   Complements

Whereas action verbs may have direct objects, linking verbs—forms of the verb *be* such as *is, are, was, were, been*—as well as those verbs that describe a condition or position—such as *feel, look, seem, become, taste, smell*—take a **complement.** Subject complements complete the meaning of a subject:

Cocoa, in its natural state, is *bitter.* (*Bitter* describes *cocoa,* the subject.)

Object complements complete the meaning of verbs such as *call, elect, find, make, name;* they identify or qualify the direct object:

84g   Compound sentences

When two independent clauses are joined by a coordinating conjunction *(and, but, or, nor, for, so, yet)* or by a semicolon, the result is a **compound sentence:**

84

Word processors have much to offer a student writer; they greatly simplify revising and editing.

Working while being a full-time student is difficult, **yet** many students manage to do both.

84h   Complex sentences

When a dependent clause is joined to an independent clause, the result is a **complex sentence:**

When the snow stopped, the ground was white.

Dependent   **Independent**

84i   Compound-complex sentences

When one or more dependent clauses are joined to two or more independent clauses, the result is a **compound-complex sentence:**

Because the machine parts were defective [dependent clause], the manager made an angry phone call to the supplier [independent clause]; in fact, she threatened to sue [independent clause].

ESL concerns

English has a number of features that can cause difficulty for international students. The following guidelines will help to clarify these issues.

84

85   **Use plurals and possessives carefully.**

As in most languages, English nouns usually change spelling when they move from singular to plural:

Singular	*Plural*
boy	boys
chair	chairs
cactus	cactuses
woman	women

However, unlike most languages, English nouns show possession by using the apostrophe and *s* (for singular and some plurals) and the apostrophe only (for most plurals):

boy's (regular singular possessive)

boys' (regular plural possessive)

chair's (regular singular possessive)

chairs' (regular plural possessive)

cactus's (regular singular possessive)

cactuses' (regular plural possessive)

woman's (regular singular possessive)

women's (irregular plural possessive)

Make sure that you know whether the word you are spelling is singular or plural and if it is possessive. A possessive is a shortened form:

the car of John = John's car

the issues of women = women's issues

85

Using this distinction can help you when you are dealing with a troublesome word such as *company* (in the sense of a business or firm). There are four possible spellings of this word, according to the singular/plural/possessive context:

company (singular, not possessive)

company's (singular possessive = of the company)

companies (plural—more than one—not possessive)

companies' (plural possessive = of the companies)

See also **47** for spelling plurals and **42** on apostrophe usage.

86 Make sure that your sentence has a subject.

Some languages use understood subjects, with sentences frequently starting with a verb. However, in English, subjects must be stated in all sentences except imperatives (commands), in which the subject *(you)* is understood:

Start the car.

Close your books before beginning the exam.

Wake up and smell the coffee.

The subjects of all other English sentences must be present:

Incorrect: Is a very effective computer analyst.

Correct: She is a very effective computer analyst.

English sometimes uses *there* and *it* as expletives, words that postpone the subject. Do not omit these:

Incorrect: Is a very nice day.

Correct: It is a very nice day.

86

Incorrect: Is a troubleshooting manual in my desk.

Correct: There is a troubleshooting manual in my desk.

87   **Distinguish between count and noncount nouns for correct article use.**

87a   **The indefinite articles (*a* and *an*) should be used with nouns that refer to persons, places, things, or ideas that can be counted.**

a woman	four women
an estate	seven estates
a computer monitor	three computer monitors
a theory	several theories

Some nouns refer to quantities, collections, or abstractions and are called "noncount":

sugar	wisdom
rice	information
furniture	advice

Do not use an article with a noncount noun. These words are either not modified or are preceded by words such as *some, any,* or *more:*

Incorrect: Can I have a rice, please?

Correct: Can I have some rice, please?

Incorrect: Is there a sugar left?

Correct: Is there any sugar left?

Incorrect: Ralph bought a new furniture yesterday.

Correct: Ralph bought some new furniture yesterday.

Also correct: Ralph bought new furniture yesterday.

Also correct: Ralph bought a new piece of furniture yesterday.

Incorrect: Can I get an information from you?

Correct: Can I get some information from you?

Some English nouns are both count and noncount. Frequently, this situation reflects the noun both as a thing and as a concept:

> His writings about world currency gained him the Nobel Prize in Economics. (Here, *currency*—money—is used as a concept and is noncount.)

> Some of the currencies of that region are extremely colorful. (Here, the reference is to actual pieces of money: things that can be counted.)

87b   The definite article *(the)* can be used with most singular nouns.

When introducing a new noun, use an indefinite article:

> *A car* broke down in the passing lane of the interstate this morning.

In a subsequent reference to the same noun, switch to the definite article, *the*:

> *The car* blocked traffic for almost an hour.

Similarly, when a noun's context is fixed, *the* should be used:

Incorrect	Correct
a ground beneath my feet	*the* ground beneath my feet
a nose on her face	*the* nose on her face
a moon circling the earth	*the* moon circling the earth

87

Sometimes elements in the sentence define the context of the noun:

The cat *in the window* is the one that I want.

The problem *on page 428 of my algebra textbook* is very difficult.

Do not use *the* with nouns in the following situations:

Noncount nouns reflecting unmodified abstractions:

Incorrect: The wisdom is a very good thing to attain.

Correct: Wisdom is a very good thing to attain.

But: The wisdom of the ages is a very good thing to attain. (Here, the abstract noun *wisdom* is followed by a modifier.)

Noncount nouns reflecting quantity:

Incorrect: The sugar is a good thing to add to coffee.

Correct: Sugar is a good thing to add to coffee.

But: The sugar *grown in South Florida* has a curious history.

Proper nouns:

Incorrect: I went to the Atlanta for the 1996 Summer Olympics.

Correct: I went to Atlanta for the 1996 Summer Olympics.

Incorrect: I asked the Robert if he had a spare pencil.

Correct: I asked Robert if he had a spare pencil.

87

There are numerous exceptions to this rule, most of them involving large geographical areas or features:

the Great Lakes	The Atlantic Ocean
the Great Plains	The Hague
the Adirondack Mountains	the West Coast
the Appalachians	the Bahamas

Use cumulative adjectives in a commonly accepted order.

Cumulative adjectives are those in which one adjective modifies the rest of the expression (see **29d**):

a wonderful old house

English requires that these adjectives be ordered according to their type. The normal order is as follows:

Determiner: a, an, the, this, those, my, our, many, two
Evaluation: wonderful, excruciating, interesting, awful
Size: big, small, minute
Shape: round, oblong, trapezoidal
Age: old, new, young, antique
Color: green, teal, brown
National or Geographic Origin: Irish, Scandinavian, Middle Eastern
Religion: Catholic, Methodist, Jewish
Material: wood, iron, paper

Correct: a wonderful little antique French saucer

Correct: a dreadful old brown cotton dress

 Be careful with complex verb structures.

89a   With modal verbs and forms of *do*, use the base (infinitive) form.

89

Incorrect: The letter carrier *will brings* us good news, I hope.

Correct: The letter carrier *will bring* us good news, I hope.

Incorrect: I *can plays* a violin very well.

Correct: I *can play* a violin very well.

Incorrect:	*Do* you *wants* to go to a movie?
Correct:	*Do* you *want* to go to a movie?

89b   Use infinitives or gerunds after verbs according to convention.

Some verbs are followed by infinitives ("I choose *to write*"), some by gerunds ("I enjoy *writing*"), and some by either ("I like *to write*; I like *writing*").

Verbs That Must Be Followed by Infinitives

agree	decide	mean	refuse
ask	expect	need	venture
beg	fail	offer	wait
bother	have	plan	want
choose	hope	pretend	wish
claim	manage	promise	

Incorrect:	I need *telling* you something.
Correct:	I need *to tell* you something.

Incorrect:	I promise *taking* good care of your dog.
Correct:	I promise *to take* good care of your dog.

In some instances, a noun or pronoun follows the verb and precedes an infinitive:

She *convinced Tony to change* his mind.

His sleepless night *caused him to fail* the exam.

Have, let, and *make* are special cases that are followed by the verb (but without *to*):

My uncle *let me drive* his car.

My wife *made me change* my shirt before dinner.

The customs officer *had her complete* a new set of forms.

89

Verbs That Must Be Followed by Gerunds

admit	deny	imagine	recall
appreciate	discuss	keep	resist
avoid	dislike	miss	risk
consider	enjoy	postpone	suggest
delay	finish	practice	tolerate

Incorrect: He recalled *to meet* with me last week.

Correct: He recalled *meeting* with me last week.

Incorrect: I avoided *to take* the class.

Correct: I avoided *taking* the class.

Verbs That Can Be Followed by Either Infinitives or Gerunds

begin	like
continue	love
hate	start

Correct: I began *to sing.*

Correct: I began *singing.*

Correct: Eduardo hates *talking* to Melissa.

Correct: Eduardo hates *to talk* to Melissa.

Note that the meaning is the same in each pair of sentences. With *forget, remember, stop,* and *try,* however, the choice of infinitive or gerund will radically alter the sentence's meaning:

The old man *stopped to take* his medicine.

The old man *stopped taking* his medicine.

For a discussion of other problems involving complex verb structures, see **55**, **56**.

89

89c   Use phrasal verbs according to convention.

Phrasal verbs are sometimes called "two-word verbs." Although they can seem redundant *(sit down, stand up),* phrasal verbs in English often have figurative, idiomatic usages:

> Jim *stood* me *up* on our last date. (Jim didn't arrive for the date.)

> The boss *sat* Mario *down* and explained what he would have to do to succeed in his new job. (The boss may or may not have asked Mario to be seated.)

The two examples are of **separable phrasal verbs**—an object comes between them. In an **inseparable phrasal verb**, however, the two words stay together.

> The car *broke down* sixty miles from the nearest mechanic.

> I *got up* at 5:00 this morning.

> Linda's secretary will *look into* the situation.

Note that phrasal verbs can contain three words, the last being a preposition:

> I have *put up with* his insults for too long.

> You don't expect to *get away with* that plan, I hope.

> Maria was *looking forward to* the end of the semester.

absolute construction A phrase that qualifies a sentence but is not grammatically related to it: *This being true,* she left.

abstract A brief summary of the key ideas in a work.

active voice See *voice.*

adjective A word that describes or limits a noun or pronoun: the *rude* remark.

adverb A word modifying a verb (ran *quickly*), an adjective (*very* grateful), or another adverb (*quite* smoothly).

analogy The use of a comparison to note a resemblance between two otherwise very different things. Analogies often explain complex things by showing how they resemble simpler things.

analysis A type of writing in which you explain a subject by examining the parts that constitute it.

antecedent A noun to which a pronoun refers: The *men* are coming; here they are. (*They* refers to, or stands for, *men,* the antecedent of *they.*)

appositive A noun, noun phrase, or pronoun placed next to a noun to explain it: Sam, *the teller,* was wrong.

argumentation Writing that uses logic and persuasion to prove a point and convince the reader.

auxiliary verb A form of *be, can, could, do, get, have, may, might, must, ought, shall, should, will,* or *would* used in a verb phrase (*had* seen, *will be* going).

GL

case   The grammatical category of a noun or pronoun that indicates its relationship to other elements in a sentence. The nominative case is used for subjects of verbs (*he* is); the objective case is used for objects of verbs and prepositions (I hit *him*); and the possessive case indicates ownership (*his* arm).

clause   A group of words containing a subject and a verb that is used as part of a sentence. An independent clause can stand alone as a sentence; a dependent or subordinate clause cannot stand alone: *Although he ran his fastest race.* When a sentence contains both a dependent and an independent clause (*Although he ran his fastest race, he lost to Juan),* the independent clause may also be called the main clause.

coherence   The logical flow from point to point in an essay or paragraph.

collective noun   A word that names a group of persons or things, for example, *class* or *committee;* it may take a singular or plural verb.

comparison and contrast   Explaining by showing similarities (comparison) and differences (contrast) between two or more things.

complement   A word or phrase that completes the verb. A subject or nominative complement is a word or phrase that follows a linking verb and belongs to the subject: Her paper is a *masterpiece.* An objective complement completes the action of the verb and follows its object: The jury found the defendant *innocent.*

conclusion   The end of an essay, summing up the main points and restating the thesis; it does not introduce new ideas.

conjunction   A word used to connect parts of a sentence or to relate sentences. Coordinating conjunctions (*and, but, or, nor, for, yet, so)* link equal elements; subordinate conjunctions (such as *because, although, if*) link a dependent clause with an independent clause.

conjunctive adverb   A word such as *thus, moreover,* or *however* that connects one independent clause to another.

coordinating conjunction   See *conjunction.*

GL

count noun A noun that refers to an individual entity or thing and can thus be counted: *a woman, the cars, an elephant.* See *noncount noun.*

cumulative adjectives A group of adjectives modifying a noun in such a way that each adjective modifies the rest of the expression: *a wonderful old Ford truck.*

deduction The type of reasoning that moves from a general proposition to a specific conclusion.

dependent clause A clause that functions as an adjective, adverb, or noun and that cannot stand alone as a sentence.

description Developing a topic by using sensory experience to show the reader what a person, place, or object is like.

draft The text of an essay in progress, from its first to its final version.

editing Making corrections and final additions or deletions to the final draft of a paper.

elliptical construction A phrase or clause in which clearly understood words are omitted: He is taller than you [are tall].

evidence Facts, examples, statistics, etc., needed to support an argument and to make it convincing.

exposition Writing that explains a topic.

figurative language The use of metaphor, simile, personification, and other imaginative devices to express a meaning beyond the literal.

freewriting A form of prewriting in which you jot down whatever thoughts you have about a subject as they occur to you.

future tense See *tense.*

gerund The *-ing* form of a verb used as a noun: *Making money* [gerund phrase] is his only concern.

idiom An expression that cannot be logically explained but is commonly understood.

independent clause A clause that can stand alone as a sentence; see *clause.*

indirect object See *object.*

induction The type of reasoning that proceeds from specific evidence to a general conclusion or hypothesis.

infinitive   The form of a verb usually preceded by *to*; it sometimes functions as a noun: Sally decided not ◉ *smoke* [infinitive as direct object]. Sometimes the infinitive can appear without *to*: He does nothing but *complain*.

interjection   A word used as an exclamation: *No!*

intransitive verb   See *verb.*

introduction   The opening of an essay that expresses the writer's purpose, thesis, and tone and that captures the reader's attention.

irregular verb   See *verb.*

linking verb   Any form of the verb *be* as well as such words as *seem, feel, become,* and *look* that link the complement with the subject: Jack *is* a hunter.

modifier   A word that describes or limits another word or word group.

mood   The form of a verb that indicates whether the action or condition it expresses is a factual question or statement (indicative mood), a command or request (imperative mood), or a wish or condition contrary to fact (subjunctive mood).

narration   A type of writing that tells a story.

nominative   See *case.*

noncount noun   A noun such as *furniture* and *rice* that cannot be counted and is never preceded by an indefinite article *(a, an).* See *count noun.*

nonrestrictive   A modifying phrase or clause that gives nonessential information about a noun; it is set off by commas. A restrictive modifier gives essential information about the noun it modifies and is not set off by commas.

noun   A word that names something: *lady, squirrel, patience, writing* (common nouns); proper nouns, for specific names and places, are capitalized: *Michael, Nevada, Exxon.*

number   A grammatical term used to establish the singular or plural status of nouns and verbs: *colleges* is plural in number.

object   A noun or pronoun that receives the action of a verb. The object may be direct (Susan hit *the ball*) or indirect (She gave *him* a kiss). Participles, gerunds, infinitives, and prepositions take objects to complete their meaning (turning the *corner*).

objective   See *case.*

outline   A diagram of an essay's organization in which the main points are listed as major items in a column, with subordinate points indented under the main points to which they belong.

paragraph   A group of related sentences that develop one subject.

participle   A verbal that may be in either one of two tenses. The present participle, which always ends in *-ing,* is used with forms of *be* in verb phrases (is *sinking*) or as a modifier (*sinking* ship). The past participle, which ends in *-ed* for regular verbs, is used as part of a verb phrase (has *used*) or as a modifier (*used* car). See also *verbal.*

parts of speech   The classification of words according to their function in a sentence: nouns, pronouns, adjectives, adverbs, verbs, prepositions, conjunctions, and interjections.

passive voice   See *voice.*

past tense   See *tense.*

person   A grammatical term used to distinguish the person speaking (first person) from the person spoken to (second person) and from anyone or anything else (third person). Nouns, except those in direct address (*John,* please leave), are always considered third person.

persuasion   A type of writing that aims to convince the reader to do or believe something.

phrasal verb   Sometimes called a "two-word" verb, a phrasal verb consists of a verb plus one or two accompanying words that form an idiomatic construction (*break down, put up with*).

phrase   A group of words that can function as a noun, verb, or modifier and that does not contain a subject-verb combination.

plagiarism   Using the words or ideas of another without giving credit to the source.

possessive   See *case.*

predicate   The verb by itself (simple predicate) or the verb with all its modifiers, complements, and objects (complete predicate).

G

preposition   A word that relates a noun or pronoun to another word in the sentence: *after, before, by, for, from, in, of, on, to, up,* and *with* are some commonly used prepositions.

present tense   See *tense.*

prewriting   Any device you use to get started before beginning the first draft of an essay.

principal parts   The three basic forms of a verb: infinitive *(to eat),* past tense *(ate),* and past participle *(eaten).*

pronoun   A part of speech that stands for or refers to a noun.

proper noun   See *noun.*

purpose   Your reason for writing; your answer to the question "Why am I writing?"

regular verb   See *verb.*

relative pronoun   A pronoun that can introduce a subordinate clause: *who, whom, whose, that, which, what, whoever, whomever, whichever, whatever.*

report   An essay in which a writer summarizes the content of another person's work.

restrictive   See *nonrestrictive.*

review   An evaluation in which a writer assesses the strengths and weaknesses of another's work by using supportive evidence.

revising   The part of the writing process that enables you to alter and clarify what you have written by rethinking, rereading, and rewriting.

sentence   A word group that expresses a complete thought, consisting of a subject and a predicate. A simple sentence contains one independent clause; a compound sentence has two or more independent clauses. A complex sentence contains one independent clause and at least one dependent clause. A compound-complex sentence contains two or more independent clauses and at least one dependent clause. Sentences also differ in purpose: declarative (statement), imperative (command), interrogative (question), and exclamatory (strong feeling).

subject   The word or word group about which the predicate says (or asks) something in a sentence.

subjunctive   See *mood.*

GL

subordinate conjunction   See *conjunction*.

tense   The form of a verb that expresses time: present, past, future. Perfect tenses express completed action: present perfect (I *have run*), past perfect (I *had run*), future perfect (I *will have run*). The progressive tense expresses continuing action (I *am running*).

thesis   A sentence that states your main point, usually placed in the introduction of an essay.

topic   A specific aspect of a broad subject.

topic sentence   A sentence that states the main idea of a paragraph, guiding and unifying it much as a thesis statement guides the development of the essay.

transition   A word, phrase, or sentence that guides the reader from one point to another by linking sentences or paragraphs.

transitive verb   See *verb*.

verb   A word or word group expressing action, process, or being. Regular verbs form the past and past participle by adding *-d* or *-ed* to the infinitive: *walk, walked, have walked.* Irregular verbs *(drink, drank, have drunk)* do not follow this rule. A transitive verb requires an object to complete its meaning: He *wrote* [verb] a *letter* [object]; an intransitive verb does not require an object: He *sings* well. See also *linking verb, mood, tense,* and *voice*.

verbal   A word formed from a verb and used as an adjective, adverb, or noun: the *laughing* hyena. Gerunds, participles, and infinitives are verbals.

voice   A verb is in the active voice when the subject names the doer of the action: Joan *read* the book. A verb is in the passive voice when the subject names the receiver of the action: The book *was read* by Joan.

GLOSSARY OF USAGE

This glossary discusses words that are commonly confused and usages that appear frequently, especially in speech, but are disapproved of by many dictionaries and books on style. Look over the entries, noting any usages with which you are unfamiliar, and refer to this glossary or to a good college dictionary whenever you are unsure of the way you are using a particular word. For a discussion of the varieties of writing referred to in this glossary, see **59.**

a, an   Use *a* before a consonant sound, *an* before a vowel sound: *a* university, *a* horror; *an* uncle, *an* hour.

absolutely   Often meaningless intensifier (*absolutely* the finest cook) that is redundant with such words as *complete* and *perfect*.

accept, except   See *except, accept*.

adapted, adopted   *Adapted* means "changed"; *adopted* means "accepted":

> After the mayor *adopted* the housing rule, it was *adapted* to suit local needs.

administrate   Use *administer*.

adverse, averse   *Adverse* means "opposite" or "unfavorable": *adverse* criticism, *adverse* winds. *Averse* means "reluctant" or "disliking": He is *averse* to manual labor.

affect, effect   *Affect* (to influence) is usually a verb; *effect* (result) is usually a noun. As a noun, *affect* is psychological jargon meaning "personal magnetism or impact." As a verb, *effect* means "bring about":

> His injury did not *affect* his performance.
>
> The protest had little *effect*.
>
> The new chair *effected* several changes.
>
> The schizophrenic exhibited very little *affect*.

afflict, inflict   *Afflict* typically takes *with* and an animate object: He was *afflicted with* measles. *Inflict* takes an inanimate object: The judge *inflicted* the maximum penalty.

again, back   Unnecessary after words meaning "again" or "back," such as *refer, revert,* and *resume:*

> In reaching its decision, the court *referred* [not *referred back*] to a 1948 Supreme Court ruling.

ahold   Use *hold:* Dan tried to get *hold* [not *ahold*] of himself.

ain't   Most writers avoid this colloquial contraction.

all ready, already   *All ready* means "fully prepared" or that everyone or everything is ready: The letters were *all ready* to be signed. *Already* is an adverb meaning "at or before this time": The book has *already* sold a million copies.

all right   Use this spelling. *Alright* is not a standard spelling.

all the farther   Use *as far as:* This is *as far as* we can go.

allude   A verb meaning "mention indirectly": He often *alludes* to Shakespeare. Do not confuse it with *refer,* "to mention directly." Also do not confuse the noun *allusion* with *illusion,* a false perception or impression.

a lot   Two words; do not spell as one.

alternate(ly), alternative(ly)   As an adjective, *alternate* means "by turns, first one and then the other": *alternately* hot and cold weather. *Alternative* means "another choice," such as an *alternative* course of action.

altogether, all together   *Altogether* is an adverb meaning "completely"; *all together* is an adjective phrase meaning "in a group":

> The hikers were *all together* at the campsite.

> They were *altogether* unprepared for the storm.

alumnus, alumna, alumni   A male graduate is an *alumnus,* and a female graduate is an *alumna; alumni* is the plural for both sexes (although *alumnae* is sometimes still used for female graduates). Note that this distinction could be seen as sexist and that you might be safer using *alumnus* to refer to a graduate of either sex.

among, between   Use *among* with more than two, *between* with two.

amoral, immoral   *Amoral* means without moral principles; *immoral* means contrary to such principles.

amount, number   Use *number* for things that can be counted, *amount* for quantities of things that cannot be counted:

> A large *number* of books have been stolen.

> The old furnace wasted a large *amount* of fuel.

analyzation   Use *analysis*.

and etc.   See *etc.*

anyone, any one   *Anyone* means "any person"; *any one* refers to a single person or thing from a group:

> *Anyone* can learn to spell better.

> Choose *any one* point of view and stick with it.

anyway, any way   Use *anyway* to mean "in any case" or "nevertheless," *any way* to mean "any course" or "any direction." To mean "in any manner," use either one.

We played well but lost *anyway.*

The traffic will be heavy *any way* you go at that hour.

Do it *any way* [or *anyway*] you choose.

Anyways is nonstandard.

appraise, apprise   *Appraise* means to set a value, as on real estate: The house was *appraised* at $95,000. *Apprise* means to notify, tell, or inform: The attorney was *apprised* of the facts of the case.

apprehend, comprehend   *Apprehend* means to catch the meaning of something, whereas *comprehend* means to understand it fully.

as   Often ambiguous when used to mean *since, when,* or *because:* She forgot her lines *because* [not *as*] she was nervous. *As* is often unnecessary: He was voted [not *voted as*] the most likely to succeed. Do not use *as* to mean "whether" or "that": I can't say *that* [not *as*] I understand. See also *like, as.*

as regards   Wordy—use *concerning.*

awhile, a while   *Awhile* is an adverb; *a while* is a noun: wait *awhile;* wait for *a while.*

bad, badly   Use *bad* as an adjective, *badly* as an adverb:

I wanted a drink of water so *badly* that I was ready to do almost anything.

It was *bad.* I feel *bad.* He looks *bad.*

basically   Like *essentially* and *ultimately, basically* is overused and often adds little emphasis: *[Basically,]* the problem is serious.

being   Often a weak connective in sentences: He writes well, *being* the son of a novelist. Instead of *being that* or *being as,* use *because* or *since:* He writes well *because* [not *being that*] he is the son of a novelist.

beside, besides   *Beside* means "at the side of"; *besides* means "in addition to"; either may be used to mean "except":

The map lay *beside* the lamp.

Besides her regular job, she plays bass in a blues band.

No one *beside* [or *besides*] you had a key.

better   Avoid as a synonym for *more:* More [not *Better*] than half of the workers were present.

between   See *among, between.*

both   Redundant with words such as *agree* or *together:* We agreed [not *both agreed*] to stop bickering.

but   Avoid redundant combinations such as *but however* or *but nevertheless.* Use *that* rather than *but that* or *but what* in sentences such as: I do not doubt *that* [not *but that*] he will succeed.

can, may   In strict usage, *can* expresses ability; *may* expresses permission:

May I go fishing?

Yes, if you *can* find your rod.

cannot   Spell as one word unless you wish to place especially heavy emphasis on the *not.*

can't hardly, can't scarcely   Avoid these double negatives; use *can hardly* or *can scarcely.*

case, line   Both are often deadwood:

In [the case of] English, single adjectives usually precede nouns.

I would like to buy [something in the line of] a mystery.

center around   *Center on* is more exact, but either phrase is usually roundabout and imprecise:

The story *concerns* [not *centers around*] a jewel thief.

cf.   The abbreviation of the Latin *confer* ("compare"). Except in endnotes or footnotes, *compare* is preferable.

climactic, climatic   *Climactic* refers to climax (as in a story), *climatic* to climate (weather).

close to   Not a substitute for *nearly* or *almost:* Nearly [not *close to*] fifty guests are coming.

complement, compliment *Complement* means "to complete"; *compliment* means "to praise."

considerable, considerably Avoid using the adjective *considerable* as an adverb:

> The injury to the first-string center hurt the team *considerably* [not *considerable*].

consist in, consist of *Consist in* means "to reside in" or "inhere": Virtue *consists in* doing good. *Consist of* means "to be composed of": The book *consists of* seven chapters.

continual, continuous *Continual* means "frequently repeated" and is not the same as *continuous,* "uninterrupted":

> Robbery is a *continual* problem in our neighborhood.

> Chicago suffered forty-three days of *continuous* subfreezing weather.

convince Use *convince* when someone changes his or her opinion; use *persuade* when someone is moved to take action:

> The dean *persuaded* (not *convinced*) us to cancel the meeting.

could of An error for *could have.* See *of.*

council, counsel, consul A *council* is a governing body; *counsel* is advice or the act of giving advice; a *consul* is a government official in a foreign country:

> The town *council* met last night.

> Mr. Adamson *counseled* me to choose a career other than medicine.

> The *consul* was expelled from the country.

G

couple *Couple* takes a plural verb when it refers to people, as does *pair:* The couple *are* [not *is*] in Bermuda.

credible, credulous, creditable All have to do with belief, but they are not interchangeable. *Credible* means "believable"; *credulous* means "naive"; *creditable* means "deserving praise."

data   Plural for the rarely used singular *datum*. *Data* is best used as a plural.

different   *Different from* is standard usage: Frye's approach to the poem is *different from* [not *than*] Ellman's approach. Watch for needless use of *different*: I read three [*different*] novels last winter. Use *various* to indicate diversity unless you wish to stress unlikeness. *Differ from* indicates dissimilarity (Boys *differ from* girls); *differ with* indicates disagreement (She *differed with* his view of the film).

disinterested, uninterested   *Disinterested* means "impartial"; *uninterested* means "not interested."

done   Nonstandard as a substitute for *did:* They *did* [not *done*] the work already.

due to the fact that   Use *because.*

each and every   Use one word or the other.

economic, economical   *Economic* usually concerns economics (*economic* policy), whereas *economical* always means "thrifty."

effect   See *affect, effect.*

e.g.   The abbreviation for the Latin *exempli gratia* ("for example"). Use *for example.*

elicit, illicit   *Elicit* is a verb meaning "draw forth": The article *elicited* an angry response. *Illicit* is an adjective meaning "unlawful": The police cracked down on *illicit* gambling.

emigrate, immigrate   *Emigrate* means to move out of a country; *immigrate* means to move in. An American who emigrates to England is, from the English standpoint, immigrating.

eminent, imminent   *Eminent* means "prominent" or "famous"; *imminent* means "upcoming, about to happen":

An *eminent* economist predicted *imminent* disaster.

enthuse   A colloquial substitute for "be enthusiastic" or "show enthusiasm."

equally as   *As* alone is sufficient: The film was *as equally* [not *equally as*] good as the book.

etc. An abbreviation of the Latin *et cetera* ("and other things"). It is often a lazy or evasive substitute for specifics: Work was delayed by rain, *etc.* Do not use *and etc.,* in which *and* is redundant.

everyone, every one See *anyone, any one.*

except, accept *Except,* meaning "other than," is not a substitute for *but.* Also, do not confuse *except* with *accept,* "to receive" or "to agree."

> The British might have scored a decisive victory, *but* [not *except*] they did not pursue the retreating American army.

> Everyone *except* Aunt Agatha *accepted* the invitation.

expect Informal when used to mean "suppose" or "think": I *expect* it will rain." *Suppose, assume, think,* and *believe* are preferable.

explicit, implicit *Explicit,* meaning "expressed directly," is the opposite of *implicit,* meaning "suggested" or "expressed indirectly."

factor A factor helps to produce a given result, so *contributing factor* is redundant. *Factor* is often misused to mean "item" or "point": There are several *points* [not *factors*] in favor of the new proposal.

farther, further *Farther* usually refers to physical distance, *further* to additional time or degree:

> We managed to drive *farther* than we expected during the first three days.

> The economists decided to wait for *further* developments before making a decision.

feature As a verb, *feature* should not be used to mean "contain" (The magazine *contained* [not *featured*] many recipes) but to mean "give prominence to" (The magazine *featured* an article by John Updike).

few, little; fewer, less *Few* and *fewer* refer to things that can be counted, *little* and *less* to things that cannot be

GL

counted: *few* apartments, *little* space; *fewer* calories, *less* food.

finalize   Jargon for *complete*.

former, first; latter, last   Use *former* and *latter* when you refer to one of two items; with three or more items, use *first* and *last*.

goes   Not acceptable as an equivalent for *says:* Then he *says* [not *goes*], "I didn't mean it."

good, well   *Good* is an adjective: The air smells *good*. *Well* is usually an adverb: The choir sings *well*. *Well* is also used as an adjective referring to health: I have stayed *well* since I started the new diet.

half   Use *half a* (can) or *a half* (can), not *a half a* (can).

hardly   See *can't hardly*.

hisself   Nonstandard for *himself*.

hopefully   Colloquial substitute for "I hope" or "it is hoped."

idea, ideal   *Idea* (thought or notion) can be confused with *ideal* (a conception of something in its most perfect state):

> He did not have a clear *idea* of the ancient Greek *ideal* of heroic virtue.

i.e.   The abbreviation for the Latin *id est* ("that is"). Use *that is.*

if and when   Like *when and if,* a wordy and trite phrase. Use one word or the other.

imminent   See *eminent, imminent*.

implicit   See *explicit, implicit*.

imply, infer   *Imply* means "to suggest"; *infer* means "to conclude." Writers imply; readers infer.

> The reporter *implied* that the President would fire the Attorney General.

> From the reporter's remarks, I *inferred* that the President would fire the Attorney General.

inflict, afflict   See *afflict, inflict*.

in regards to   The standard forms are *in regard to* or *as regards*. But *concerning* is usually preferable to either phrase.

inside of   Use just *inside* or *within*.

irregardless   Nonstandard for *regardless.*

its, it's   *Its* is the possessive (belonging to *it*): The company issued *its* report. (Compare *his, hers.*) It's is the contraction for *it is* or *it has.* There is no such word as *its'.*

kind of, sort of   Colloquial: The lecture was [*kind of*] interesting.

kind of a   Drop the *a:* That kind of [a] story always amuses young readers.

latter   See *former, first; latter, last.* Do not confuse *latter* with *later.*

lay, lie   See *lie, lay.*

learn, teach   Students learn; instructors teach:

> My grandfather *taught* me how to cast a fly.

> I *learned* to cast a fly before I was six years old.

leave, let   *Leave* means "to depart or go away from"; *let* means "to permit." Do not use *leave* for *let.*

less   See *few, little; fewer, less.*

let's us   Since *let's* is the contraction for *let us,* do not add a second *us.*

liable   See *likely, liable.*

lie, lay   *Lie* means "to rest" or "to recline"; *lay* means "to put or place (something) down." The past of *lie* is *lay;* the past of *lay* is *laid:* She *laid* the book on the table and *lay* down to rest.

like, as   In making comparisons, use *like* as a preposition; use *as, as if,* or *as though* as a conjunction introducing a dependent clause:

> *Like* Hamlet, he is indecisive.

> The lab researcher will examine the slides *as* she always has— slowly and carefully.

> After the race, all of the runners looked *as though* they might faint.

GL

Some writers mistakenly go out of their way to avoid using *like:* This hotel looks similar to [preferably like] the one in Johnstown.

likely, liable   *Likely* expresses probability; *liable* expresses obligation but is sometimes used loosely to mean *likely:* She is *likely* [not *liable*] to receive an award.

line   See *case, line.*

loose, loosen, lose   A *loose* screw (adjective); *loosen* a tie (verb); *lose* a bet (verb).

may, can   See *can, may.*

media   The plural of *medium.* Compare *criterion, criteria; phenomenon, phenomena.*

The *media are* [not *is*] often accused of bias.

might of   An error for *might have;* see *of.*

most   Informal as a substitute for *almost:* He comes here *almost* [not *most*] every evening.

myself   *Myself* can be used as a direct object referring to the subject of the sentence (I hurt *myself*) or as an intensive (I will do the job *myself*). Do not use it as a substitute for *I:* Two of us finished the puzzle: John and *I* [not *myself*].

nohow, nowheres   Nonstandard forms. Use *in no way, not at all, nowhere.*

not too, not that   Colloquial substitutes for *not very:* I'm *not very* [not *not that*] concerned with politics.

nowhere near   Colloquial for *not nearly:* Sam's pizzas are *not nearly* [not *nowhere near*] as good as Tony's.

number, amount   See *amount, number.*

of   Do not use *of* for *have* in verb phrases such as *could have, would have, might have, must have:* I should *have* [not *of*] attended the meeting.

off of   Use just *off:* He would not get *off [of]* the subject.

oftentimes   Use just *often.*

on account of   Use this phrase as a preposition (*on account of* the rain), not as a conjunction (*on account of* it rained). *Because* or *because of* is preferable: *because of* the rain; *because* it rained.

opinionated   An *opinionated* essay (as opposed to an essay of opinion) is one that unreasonably or obstinately maintains the writer's own opinions.

orientate   *Orient* is simpler and preferable.

ought   Do not use with auxiliaries such as *had* and *did:* Eve wondered if she *ought* [not *hadn't ought*] to leave.

outside of   Use just *outside.*

party   Except in law, *party* is a poor substitute for *person:* Would the *person* [not *party*] who requested a change in seating please come to the counter?

per   Jargon for *according to:* Use the insecticide *according to* [not *per*] the instructions.

percent, percentage   Use *percent* with numbers (ten *percent*), *percentage* without numbers: A high *percentage* [not *percent*] of those responding rated inflation as the chief problem. Do not use *percentage* loosely for *part:* A large *part* [not *percentage*] of the work was done before we arrived.

persuade   See *convince.*

plenty   Informal as an adverb meaning "very": She must be *very* [not *plenty*] rich.

plus   *Plus* is technically a preposition meaning "with the addition of," not a conjunction:

> After the game, Bill was tired *and* [not *plus*] his leg hurt.

> The principal *plus* the interest comes to $368.55.

practical, practicable   Something *practical* works well in practice; something *practicable* can be put into practice but has not yet been shown to work:

> Conversion to solar energy is *practicable* in many parts of the country, but few systems have so far proved *practical.*

precede, proceed   See *proceed, precede.*

predominant, predominate   *Predominant* is the adjective (the *predominant* opinion); *predominate* is the verb: For twenty years, conservative opinion *predominated* in the court.

presently   Use *now.*

previous to, prior to   Use *before.*

GL

principal, principle   *Principal* can be an adjective or a noun: the *principal* cause; the *principal* of our school; the *principal* plus the interest charged by the bank. *Principle* is always a noun meaning "basic rule or truth": Although customs vary, the *principles* of good behavior are the same in both countries.

proceed, precede   *Proceed* means "to go forward," "to continue"; *precede* means "to go before." *Proceed* is not a good choice if the meaning is simply "go."

quite, rather   See *rather, quite.*

quotation, quote   *Quote* is the verb, *quotation* the noun: an apt *quotation* [not *quote*].

raise, rise   *Raise* takes a direct object (*raise* something); *rise* does not:

> They *raise* the flag every day.

> Farmers *rise* early.

rather, quite   Both can weaken the force of a strong modifier: a *[quite]* huge fireplace. *Rather* often adds no meaning and produces ambiguity: Does *rather clear* mean "very clear" or "a little clear"?

real, really   *Real* is the adjective, *really* the adverb: a *real* distinction; *really* late. But *really* is often just an empty word: They *[really]* worked hard.

reason is . . . because   Redundant. Use *that:* The reason is *that* [not *because*] he is shy.

refer back   See *again, back.*

relevant   If you call something *relevant* or *irrelevant,* be sure to say *to what* it is relevant or irrelevant.

respectfully, respectively   *Respectfully* means "with respect"; *respectively* means "singly in the order given":

> They treated the ambassador *respectfully.*

> Her three children weighed *respectively* eight, nine, and ten pounds at birth.

rise, raise   See *raise, rise.*

GL

sensual, sensuous *Sensual* refers to bodily (usually sexual) pleasures; *sensuous* refers more generally to sensory appeal.

set, sit *Set* takes a direct object (*set* something down); *sit* does not (*sit* down).

shall, will The distinction between these words has largely broken down.

should of An error for *should have.* See *of.*

so Not a substitute for *very* (It was *so* cold); as an adverb, *so* requires some further explanation: It was *so* cold that the pipes froze.

some In writing, avoid the colloquial use of *some* for *somewhat:* I feel *somewhat* [not *some*] better today.

somewheres Nonstandard for *somewhere.*

stationary, stationery *Stationary* means "fixed in course or position"; *stationery* refers to writing materials.

supposed to, used to Be careful not to drop the *-d* from the end of *supposed* or *used* before *to.*

sure, surely *Sure* as an adverb is colloquial; in writing, use *surely:* We *surely* [not *sure*] enjoyed the concert.

teach, learn See *learn, teach.*

than, then *Than* is a conjunction used in comparisons; *then* is an adverb indicating time:

> The balloon rose faster *than* they expected.

> *Then* it drifted out over the lake.

their, there, they're Watch for misspellings: *Their* books are here (possessive adjective); *there are* my glasses (adverb); *they're* coming tonight (contraction of *they are*).

theirselves Nonstandard for *themselves.*

thusly Error for *thus.*

till, until Both are acceptable; *til* and *'til* are not.

to, too, two Spelling errors with these words are common but unnecessary. *To* is a preposition (*to* the fair) or the sign of an infinitive (*to* run). *Too* means either "also" or "excessively." *Two* is a number.

GL

John, *too,* found the path *to* the top *too* steep.

It takes *two to* argue.

try and   *Try to* is preferred by most stylists, although *try and* is common.

-type   This suffix should usually be omitted in phrases: a temperamental*[-type]* person.

unique   *Unique* means "single" or "without equal" and therefore does not need qualification: not *very unique* or *quite unique* but just *unique.*

used to   See *supposed to, used to.*

utilize   Often bureaucratic jargon for *use,* especially with reference to people.

wait on   Use *wait on* to mean "serve" but not as a substitute for *wait for:*

The army stopped to *wait for* [not *on*] reinforcements.

She feigned illness and persuaded everyone to *wait on* her.

ways   Use *way* for distance: a long *way* [not *ways*] to go.

where   Avoid using *where* as a substitute for *that:* I read in the paper *that . . .* [not *where . . .*].

whose, who's   Be careful not to confuse the possessive *whose* (*Whose* notes are these?) with *who's,* the contraction for *who is.*

-wise   Avoid this suffix, a common type of jargon: *garden-wise, profitwise.*

your, you're   *Your* is the possessive (*your* copy), and *you're* is the contraction for *you are.*

ACKNOWLEDGMENTS

SVEN BIRKERTS, excerpt from *The Gutenberg Elegies.* Copyright © 1994. Reprinted by permission of Faber & Faber, Inc.

RACHEL L. CARSON, excerpt from *The Sea Around Us*, Rev. Ed., by Rachel L. Carson. Copyright 1950, 1951, 1961 by Rachel L. Carson; renewed 1979 by Roger Christie. Reprinted by permission of Oxford University Press, Inc.

MALCOLM COWLEY, excerpt from *The View from 80* by Malcolm Cowley. Copyright © 1976, 1978, 1980 by Malcolm Cowley. Reprinted by permission of Viking Penguin, a division of Penguin Books USA Inc.

GORDON CRAIG, excerpt from "Facing Up to the Nazis," *The New York Review of Books*, February 2, 1989. Excerpt from "Above the Abyss," *The New York Review of Books,* copyright © 1992 Nyrev, Inc. Reprinted by permission of the publisher.

NANCY GIBBS, excerpt from "When Is It Rape?" *Time*, 6/3/91, © 1991 Time Inc. Reprinted by permission.

PAUL JOHNSON, excerpt from *Modern Times.* Copyright © 1983, reprinted by permission of HarperCollins Publishers, Inc.

JOHN MCPHEE, excerpt from "The Woods from Hog Wallow." From *The Pine Barrens* by John McPhee. Copyright © 1967, 1968 by John McPhee. Reprinted by permission of Farrar, Straus & Giroux, Inc.

RIGOBERTA MENCHÚ, for excerpt from "Birth Ceremonies" in *I, Rigoberta Menchú: An Indian Woman in Guatemala.* Copyright © 1985. Reprinted by permission of Verso Publishers, New York.

399

OCTAVIO PAZ, excerpt from *Convergences: Essays on Art and Literature* by Octavio Paz, English translation copyright © 1987 by Harcourt Brace & Company, reprinted by permission of the publisher.

WALKER PERCY, excerpt from *Southern Comfort.* Copyright © 1979 by Walker Percy, reprinted by permission of McIntosh & Otis, Inc.

WEBSTER'S NEW WORLD DICTIONARY, Second College Edition, for synonyms for "rare." Reprinted with permission of Macmillan Reference USA, a Division of Simon & Schuster, from *Webster's New World Dictionary,* Second College Edition. Copyright © 1970, 1972, 1974, 1976, 1978, 1979, 1980, 1982, 1984, 1986 by Simon & Schuster Inc.

DONALD J. WILCOX, excerpt from *In Search of God and Self: Renaissance and Reformation of Thought.* Copyright © 1975 by Houghton Mifflin. Adapted with permission.

W. B. YEATS, from "Easter 1916." Reprinted with permission of Simon & Schuster from *The Poems of W. B. Yeats: A New Edition,* edited by Richard J. Finneran. Copyright © 1924 by Macmillan Publishing Company, renewed 1952 by Bertha Georgie Yeats.

IND

IND

IND

IND

IND

IND